Complete
Junior
Praise

THE BESTSELLING SONGBOOK
FOR CHILDREN AND YOUNG PEOPLE

Compiled by

Peter Horrobin and Greg Leavers

WORDS EDITION

Collins

Electronic words, sheet music and MIDI files are available from
www.missionpraise.com

Collins, a division of HarperCollinsPublishers
77–85 Fulham Palace Road, London W6 8JB
www.collins.co.uk

First published in Great Britain in 2008 by HarperCollins*Publishers*

4

Compilation Copyright © Peter Horrobin and Greg Leavers
The compilers assert the moral right to be identified as the compilers of this work.

A catalogue record for this book is available from the British Library.

ISBN–13   978 0 00 7259786
Complete Music Edition   ISBN   978 0 00 7259779

Text set by Barnes Music Engraving Ltd, East Sussex, England
Printed and bound in Great Britain by Clays Ltd, St Ives plc

1

1 **A boy gave to Jesus
five loaves and two fish,**
not much, you might say, for a crowd;
but Jesus, He took them
and smiled at the lad,
gave thanks to His Father
and blessed them out loud.

2 The boy then saw Jesus
take loaves and the fish,
not much for the folk on that day;
but Jesus, He broke them
and smiled at the lad,
gave bits to disciples to then give away.

3 Then all worshipped Jesus
as enough loaves and fish
were given to everyone there.
But Jesus just watched them,
and smiled at the lad
who'd given his lunch-box
for Jesus to share.

2

Abba Father, let me be
Yours and Yours alone.
May my will for ever be
evermore Your own.
Never let my heart grow cold,
never let me go,
Abba Father, let me be
Yours and Yours alone.

3

*Alleluia, alleluia,
give thanks to the risen Lord;
alleluia, alleluia,
give praise to His name.*

1 Jesus is Lord of all the earth,
He is the King of creation.
Alleluia, alleluia . . .

2 Spread the good news
through all the earth,
Jesus has died and has risen.
Alleluia, alleluia . . .

3 We have been crucified with Christ;
now we shall live for ever.
Alleluia, alleluia . . .

4 God has proclaimed the just reward,
life for all men, alleluia.
Alleluia, alleluia . . .

5 Come let us praise the living God,
joyfully sing to our Saviour:
Alleluia, alleluia . . .

4

1 **All people that on earth do dwell,**
sing to the Lord with cheerful voice:
serve Him with joy, His praises tell,
come now before Him and rejoice!
Know that the Lord is God indeed,
He formed us all without our aid;
we are the flock He loves to feed,
the sheep who by His hand are made.

2 O enter then His gates with praise,
and in His courts His love proclaim;
give thanks and bless Him all your days:
let every tongue confess His name.
The Lord our mighty God is good,
His mercy is for ever sure;
His truth at all times firmly stood,
and shall from age to age endure.

3 All people that on earth do dwell
sing to the Lord with cheerful voice:
serve Him with joy, His praises tell,
come now before Him and rejoice!
Praise God the Father, God the Son,
and God the Spirit evermore;
all praise to God, the Three-in-One,
let heaven rejoice and earth adore!

5 Roy Turner
© 1984 Thankyou Music

1 **All over the world the Spirit is moving,**
all over the world
    as the prophet said it would be;
all over the world
    there's a mighty revelation
of the glory of the Lord,
    as the waters cover the sea.

2 All over His Church
    God's Spirit is moving,
all over His Church
    as the prophet said it would be;
all over His Church
    there's a mighty revelation
of the glory of the Lord,
    as the waters cover the sea.

3 Right here in this place
    the Spirit is moving,
right here in this place
    as the prophet said it would be;
right here in this place
    there's a mighty revelation
of the glory of the Lord,
    as the waters cover the sea.

6 Cecil Frances Alexander (1818–95)

All things bright and beautiful,
all creatures great and small,
all things wise and wonderful,
the Lord God made them all.

1 Each little flower that opens,
each little bird that sings,
He made their glowing colours,
He made their tiny wings.
    All things bright . . .

2 The purple-headed mountain,
the river running by,
the sunset, and the morning
that brightens up the sky;
    All things bright . . .

3 The cold wind in the winter,
the pleasant summer sun,
the ripe fruits in the garden,
He made them every one.
    All things bright . . .

4 He gave us eyes to see them,
and lips that we might tell
how great is God almighty,
who has made all things well.
    All things bright . . .

7 © 1986 Greg Leavers

All around me, Lord, I see Your goodness,
all creation sings Your praises,
all the world cries, 'God is love!'

8 John Newton (1725–1807)

1 **Amazing grace –**
    how sweet the sound –
that saved a wretch like me!
I once was lost, but now am found,
was blind, but now I see.

2 'Twas grace that taught my heart to fear,
and grace my fears relieved;
how precious did that grace appear
the hour I first believed.

3 Through many dangers, toils and snares,
I have already come;
'tis grace has brought me safe thus far,
and grace will lead me home.

4 When we've been there
    ten thousand years
bright shining as the sun,
we've no less days to sing God's praise
than when we've first begun.

9 William Chatterton Dix (1837–98)
altered © 1986 Horrobin/Leavers

1 **As with gladness men of old**
   did the guiding star behold;
   as with joy they hailed its light,
   leading onward, beaming bright,
   so, most gracious God, may we
   led by You for ever be.

2 As with joyful steps they sped,
   Saviour, to Your lowly bed,
   there to bend the knee before
   You whom heaven and earth adore,
   so may we with one accord,
   seek forgiveness from our Lord.

3 As they offered gifts most rare,
   gold and frankincense and myrrh,
   so may we, cleansed from our sin,
   lives of service now begin,
   and in love our treasures bring,
   Christ, to You our heavenly King.

4 Holy Jesus, every day
   keep us in the narrow way;
   and when earthly things are past,
   bring our ransomed souls at last
   where they need no star to guide,
   where no clouds Your glory hide.

5 In the heavenly country bright
   need they no created light;
   You its light, its joy, its crown,
   You its sun which goes not down.
   There for ever may we sing
   hallelujahs to our King.

10 James Montgomery (1771–1854)
© in this version The Jubilate Group

1 **Angels from the realms of glory,**
   wing your flight through all the earth;
   heralds of creation's story
   now proclaim Messiah's birth!
     Come and worship
     Christ, the new-born King;
     come and worship,
     worship Christ the new-born King.

2 Shepherds in the fields abiding,
   watching by your flocks at night,
   God with man is now residing:
   see, there shines the infant light!
     Come and worship . . .

3 Wise men, leave your contemplations!
   brighter visions shine afar;
   seek in Him the hope of nations,
   you have seen His rising star:
     Come and worship . . .

4 Though an infant now we view Him,
   He will share His Father's throne,
   gather all the nations to Him;
   every knee shall then bow down:
     Come and worship . . .

11 Anon
Copyright control

Ask! Ask! Ask! and it shall be given you;
Seek! Seek! Seek! and you shall find;
Knock! Knock! Knock!
       it shall be opened unto you,
your heavenly Father is so kind.
He knows what is best for His children
in body, soul and mind;
So ask! Ask! Ask! Knock! Knock! Knock!
Seek and you shall find.

12 verses 1 and 2: Anon
verse 3: J T McFarland (c1906)

1 **Away in a manger, no crib for a bed,**
   the little Lord Jesus
       laid down His sweet head;
   the stars in the bright sky
       looked down where He lay;
   the little Lord Jesus asleep in the hay.

2 The cattle are lowing, the baby awakes,
   but little Lord Jesus, no crying He makes:
   I love You, Lord Jesus!
       look down from the sky
   and stay by my side until morning is nigh.

3 Be near me, Lord Jesus; I ask You to stay
close by me for ever and love me, I pray;
bless all the dear children
    in Your tender care,
and fit us for heaven to live with You there.

5 Brothers, this Lord Jesus
shall return again,
with His Father's glory,
with His angel-train;
for all wreaths of empire
meet upon His brow,
and our hearts confess Him
King of glory now.

13 Caroline Maria Noel (1817–77)
altered © 1986 Horrobin/Leavers

1 **At the name of Jesus**
every knee shall bow,
every tongue confess Him
King of glory now.
'Tis the Father's pleasure
we should call Him Lord,
who from the beginning
was the mighty Word.

2 Humbled for a season,
to receive a name
from the lips of sinners
unto whom He came,
faithfully He lived here
spotless to the last,
raised was He victorious,
when from death He passed.

3 Lifted high, triumphant,
far above the world,
into heaven's glory,
our ascended Lord;
to the throne of Godhead,
at the Father's side,
there He reigns resplendent
who for man had died.

4 In your hearts enthrone Him;
there let Him subdue
all that is not holy,
all that is not true;
crown Him as your captain
in temptation's hour,
let His will enfold you
in its light and power.

14 Morris Chapman
© 1983 Word Music, LLC / CopyCare

Be bold, be strong,
for the Lord your God is with you;
be bold, be strong,
for the Lord your God is with you!
    I am not afraid, (No! No! No!)
    I am not dismayed, (Not me!)
for I'm walking in faith and victory:
come on and walk in faith and victory,
for the Lord your God is with you.

15 Patricia van Tine
© 1978 Maranatha! Music / CCCM Music /
CopyCare

**Behold, what manner of love
        the Father has given unto us,**
Behold, what manner of love
        the Father has given unto us,
that we should be called the sons of God,
that we should be called the sons of God.

16 Graham Kendrick
© 1986 Thankyou Music

1 **Big man standing by the blue
            waterside,**
mending nets by the blue sea.
Along came Jesus, He said,
'Simon Peter, won't you leave your nets
        and come, follow me.'
    *You don't need anything,
        I've got everything,
    but, Peter, it's going to be a hard way.
    You don't have to worry now,
        come on and hurry now,
    I'll walk beside you every day.*

2 Life wasn't easy for the big fisherman,
but still he followed till his dying day.
Along came Jesus, He said,
'Simon Peter, there's a place in heaven
    where you can stay.'
You don't need anything . . .

3 But Jesus some folk hated,
they called, 'Put Him away!'
when Pilate made them choose the one
to free, that fatal day.

4 So Jesus, though a good man,
was killed on Calvary,
but three days on, He rose again
to live eternally.

17 Bob Gillman
© 1977 Thankyou Music

Bind us together, Lord,
bind us together
with cords that cannot be broken;
bind us together, Lord,
bind us together,
O bind us together with love.

1 There is only one God,
there is only one King,
there is only one body –
that is why we sing:
    Bind us together . . .

2 Made for the glory of God,
purchased by His precious Son.
Born with the right to be clean,
for Jesus the victory has won.
    Bind us together . . .

3 You are the family of God,
You are the promise divine,
You are God's chosen desire,
You are the glorious new wine.
    Bind us together . . .

18 © 1986 Peter Horrobin

1 **Barabbas was a bad man,**
condemned to die was he,
he'd done so many awful things,
was bad as bad could be.

2 But Jesus was a good man,
God's only Son was He.
He did so many lovely things –
the blind He made to see.

19 From Psalm 103
Copyright control

Bless the Lord, O my soul,
bless the Lord, O my soul,
and all that is within me
bless His holy name.
Bless the Lord, O my soul,
bless the Lord, O my soul,
and all that is within me
bless His holy name.

King of kings (for ever and ever),
Lord of lords (for ever and ever),
King of kings (for ever and ever),
King of kings and Lord of lords!

Bless the Lord, O my soul . . .

20 Fanny J Crosby (1820–1915)

1 **Blessèd assurance, Jesus is mine:**
O what a foretaste of glory divine!
Heir of salvation, purchase of God;
born of His Spirit, washed in His blood.
    This is my story, this is my song,
    praising my Saviour all the day long;
    this is my story, this is my song,
    praising my Saviour all the day long.

2 Perfect submission, perfect delight,
visions of rapture burst on my sight;
angels descending, bring from above
echoes of mercy, whispers of love.
    This is my story . . .

3 Perfect submission, all is at rest,
  I in my Saviour am happy and blest;
  watching and waiting, looking above,
  filled with His goodness, lost in His love.
    This is my story . . .

21 Roger Jones
© 1981 Christian Music Ministries /
Sovereign Music UK

1 **Brothers and sisters**
  in Jesus our Lord,
  brothers and sisters,
  believing His word!
  Now we're united,
  made one in His love,
  we're brothers and sisters
  in Jesus our Lord!

2 Jesus has saved us,
  from sin set us free.
  Always His people
  together we'll be!
  This is the story
  we're telling the world,
  we're brothers and sisters
  in Jesus our Lord!

3 Jesus has told us
  to be of good cheer,
  for He is with us,
  His Spirit is here!
  He gives us power
  His message to share.
  We're brothers and sisters
  in Jesus our Lord!

22 Anon
Copyright control

1 **Be still and know that I am God.**
  Be still and know that I am God.
  Be still and know that I am God.

2 I am the Lord that healeth thee.
  I am the Lord that healeth thee.
  I am the Lord that healeth thee.

3 In Thee, O Lord, I put my trust.
  In Thee, O Lord, I put my trust.
  In Thee, O Lord, I put my trust.

23 E H Swinstead (d1976)
Copyright control

By blue Galilee Jesus walked of old,
by blue Galilee wondrous things He told.
Saviour, still my teacher be,
showing wondrous things to me
as of old by Galilee, blue Galilee.

24 John Henley (1800–42)
altered © 1986 Horrobin/Leavers

1 **Children of Jerusalem**
  sang the praise of Jesus' name;
  children, too, of modern days,
  join to sing the Saviour's praise:
    Hark, hark, hark!
      while children's voices sing,
    hark, hark, hark!
      while children's voices sing
    loud hosannas, loud hosannas,
    loud hosannas to our King.

2 We are taught to love the Lord,
  we are taught to read His word,
  we are taught the way to heaven;
  praise for all to God be given:
    Hark, hark, hark . . .

3 Parents, teachers, old and young,
  all unite to swell the song;
  higher let God's praises rise,
  as hosannas fill the skies:
    Hark, hark, hark . . .

25 © Michael Saward / The Jubilate Group

1 **Christ triumphant, ever reigning,**
  Saviour, Master, King,
  Lord of heaven, our lives sustaining,
  hear us as we sing:
    Yours the glory and the crown,
    the high renown, the eternal name.

2 Word incarnate, truth revealing,
  Son of Man on earth!
  power and majesty concealing
  by your humble birth:
    Yours the glory . . .

3 Suffering servant, scorned, ill-treated,
   victim crucified!
   death is through the cross defeated,
   sinners justified:
      Yours the glory . . .

4 Priestly King, enthroned for ever
   high in heaven above!
   sin and death and hell shall never
   stifle hymns of love:
      Yours the glory . . .

5 So, our hearts and voices raising
   through the ages long,
   ceaselessly upon You gazing,
   this shall be our song:
      Yours the glory . . .

26 Jimmy Owens
        ©1972 Bud John Songs / Alliance Media Ltd /
        CopyCare

Clap your hands, all you people,
shout unto God with a voice of triumph,
clap your hands, all you people,
shout unto God with a voice of praise!
Hosanna, hosanna,
shout unto God with a voice of triumph,
praise Him, praise Him,
shout unto God with a voice of praise!

27 R Hudson Pope (1879–1967)
        © Scripture Gift Mission

Cleanse me from my sin, Lord,
put Your power within, Lord,
take me as I am, Lord,
and make me all Your own.
Keep me day by day, Lord,
in Your perfect way, Lord,
make my heart Your palace,
and Your royal throne.

28 Sue McClellan, John Paculabo, Keith Ryecroft
        © 1974 Thankyou Music

1 **Colours of day dawn into the mind,**
   the sun has come up, the night is behind.
   Go down in the city, into the street,
   and let's give the message
         to the people we meet.
      So light up the fire
         and let the flame burn,
      open the door, let Jesus return.
      Take seeds of His Spirit,
         let the fruit grow,
      tell the people of Jesus,
         let His love show.

2 Go through the park, on into the town;
   the sun still shines on,
         it never goes down.
   The Light of the world is risen again,
   the people of darkness
         are needing our friend.
      So light up the fire . . .

3 Open your eyes, look into the sky,
   the darkness has come,
         the sun came to die,
   the evening draws on,
         the sun disappears,
   but Jesus is living, His Spirit is near.
      So light up the fire . . .

29 Robert Walmsley (1831–1905)
        altered © 1986 Horrobin/Leavers

1 **Come, let us sing of a wonderful love,**
   faithful and true;
   out of the heart of the Father above,
   streaming to me and to you:
   wonderful love
   dwells in the heart of the Father above.

2 Jesus, the Saviour, this gospel to tell,
   joyfully came;
   came with the helpless
         and hopeless to dwell,
   sharing their sorrow and shame;
   seeking the lost,
   saving, redeeming at measureless cost.

3 Jesus is seeking all lost people yet;
why can't they see?
Turning to Him, He forgives and forgets,
longing to set their hearts free.
Wonderful love
dwells in the heart of the Father above.

4 Come fill my heart
with Your wonderful love,
come and abide,
lifting my life till it rises above
envy and falsehood and pride;
seeking to live
life that is humble,
with strength that You give.

30 Anon
Copyright control

Come, listen to my tale
of Jonah and the whale,
way down in the middle of the ocean.
Well, how did he get there?
Whatever did he wear?
Way down in the middle of the ocean.
A-preaching he should be
at Nineveh, you see –
to disobey's a very foolish notion.
But God forgave his sin,
salvation entered in,
way down in the middle of the
way down in the middle of the
way down in the middle of the ocean.

31 Graham Kendrick
© 1986 Thankyou Music

Come on, let's get up and go,
let everyone know.
We've got a reason to shout and to sing
'cause Jesus loves us
and that's a wonderful thing.

Go! go! go! go! get up and go,
don't be sleepy or slow!
You, you, you, you know what to do,
give your life to Him.

Come on, let's get up and go . . .

32 Henry Alford (1810–71)
© in this version The Jubilate Group

1 **Come, you thankful people, come,**
raise the song of harvest home!
Fruit and crops are gathered in
safe before the storms begin:
God our maker will provide
for our needs to be supplied;
come, with all His people, come,
raise the song of harvest home!

2 All the world is God's own field,
harvests for His praise to yield;
wheat and weeds together sown
here for joy or sorrow grown:
first the blade and then the ear,
then the full corn shall appear –
Lord of harvest, grant that we
wholesome grain and pure may be.

3 For the Lord our God shall come
and shall bring His harvest home;
He Himself on that great day,
worthless things shall take away,
give His angels charge at last
in the fire the weeds to cast,
but the fruitful ears to store
in His care for evermore.

4 Even so, Lord, quickly come –
bring Your final harvest home!
Gather all Your people in
free from sorrow, free from sin,
there together purified,
ever thankful at Your side –
come, with all Your angels, come,
bring that glorious harvest home!

33 © 1986 Peter Horrobin

'Come to Jesus, He's amazing!'
people cried out when they saw
people walking who were crippled,
blind eyes seeing, healed once more.

34 Traditional, adpt.
© Geoffrey Marshall-Taylor / Lindsay Music

Come and praise the Lord our King,
hallelujah,
come and praise the Lord our King,
hallelujah.

1 Christ was born in Bethlehem, hallelujah,
Son of God and Son of Man, hallelujah.
Come and praise . . .

2 From Him love and wisdom came,
hallelujah,
all His life was free from blame, hallelujah.
Come and praise . . .

3 Jesus died at Calvary, hallelujah,
rose again triumphantly, hallelujah.
Come and praise . . .

4 He will cleanse us from our sin, hallelujah,
if we live by faith in Him, hallelujah.
Come and praise . . .

5 He will be with us today, hallelujah,
and for ever with us stay, hallelujah.
Come and praise . . .

6 We will live with Him one day, hallelujah,
and for ever with Him stay, hallelujah.
Come and praise . . .

35 Sidney E Cox
© Brentwood Benson Catalogue

Deep and wide, deep and wide,
there's a fountain flowing deep and wide;
deep and wide, deep and wide,
there's a fountain flowing deep and wide.

36 Anon
Copyright control

Daniel was a man of prayer,
daily he prayed three times.
Till one day they had him cast
into a den of lions.
In the den, in the den,
fear could not alarm him.
God just shut the lions' mouths
so they could not harm him.

37 John Greenleaf Whittier (1807–82)
© in this version The Jubilate Group

1 **Dear Lord and Father of mankind,**
forgive our foolish ways;
re-clothe us in our rightful mind;
in purer lives Your service find,
in deeper reverence, praise.

2 In simple trust like theirs who heard,
beside the Syrian sea,
the gracious calling of the Lord,
let us, like them, obey His word:
'Rise up and follow Me!'

3 O Sabbath rest by Galilee!
O calm of hills above,
where Jesus shared on bended knee
the silence of eternity,
interpreted by love!

4 With that deep hush subduing all
our words and works that drown
the tender whisper of Your call,
as noiseless let Your blessing fall,
as fell Your manna down.

5 Drop Your still dews of quietness,
till all our strivings cease;
take from our souls the strain and stress,
and let our ordered lives confess
the beauty of Your peace.

6 Breathe through the heats of our desire
Your coolness and Your balm;
let sense be dumb, let flesh retire;
speak through the earthquake,
wind, and fire,
O still small voice of calm!

38 George Ratcliffe Woodward (1848–1934)
Copyright control

1 **Ding dong! Merrily on high**
in heaven the bells are ringing.
Ding dong! Verily the sky
is riven with angels singing:
Gloria, hosanna in excelsis;
gloria, hosanna in excelsis!

2 E'en so, here below, below,
   let steeple bells be swungen,
   and i-o, i-o, i-o,
   by priest and people sungen!
      Gloria . . .

3 Pray you, dutifully prime
   your matin chime, ye ringers;
   may you beautifully rime
   your eve-time song, ye singers:
      Gloria . . .

39 Karen Lafferty
© 1981 Maranatha! Praise Inc. / CopyCare

Don't build your house on the sandy land,
don't build it too near the shore.
Well, it might look kind of nice,
but you'll have to build it twice,
oh, you'll have to build your house
   once more.

You'd better build your house upon a rock,
make a good foundation on a solid spot.
Oh, the storms may come and go,
but the peace of God you will know.

Rock of ages, cleft for me,
let me hide myself in Thee.

40 E H Swinstead (d1976)
Copyright control

Do you want a pilot?
Signal then to Jesus;
do you want a pilot?
Bid Him come on board.
For He will safely guide
across the ocean wide,
until you reach at last
the heavenly harbour.

41 Love Maria Willis (1824–1908)

1 **Father, hear the prayer we offer:**
   not for ease that prayer shall be,
   but for strength, that we may ever
   live our lives courageously.

2 Not for ever in green pastures
   do we ask our way to be;
   but the steep and rugged pathway
   may we tread rejoicingly.

3 Not for ever by still waters
   would we idly rest and stay;
   but would smite the living fountains
   from the rocks along our way.

4 Be our strength in hours of weakness,
   in our wanderings be our guide;
   through endeavour, failure, danger,
   Father, always at our side.

42 Jenny Hewer
© 1975 Thankyou Music

1 **Father, I place into Your hands**
   the things that I can't do.
   Father, I place into Your hands
   the times that I've been through.
   Father, I place into Your hands
   the way that I should go,
   for I know I always can trust You.

2 Father, I place into Your hands
   my friends and family.
   Father, I place into Your hands
   the things that trouble me.
   Father, I place into Your hands
   the person I would be,
   for I know I always can trust You.

3 Father, we love to seek Your face,
   we love to hear Your voice.
   Father, we love to sing Your praise,
   and in Your name rejoice.
   Father, we love to walk with You
   and in Your presence rest,
   for we know we always can trust You.

4 Father, I want to be with You
   and do the things You do.
   Father, I want to speak the words
   that You are speaking too.
   Father, I want to love the ones
   that You will draw to You,
   for I know that I am one with You.

43 J P Hopps (1834–1912)
altered © 1986 Horrobin/Leavers

1 **Father, lead me day by day**
   ever in your own good way;
   teach me to be pure and true –
   show me what I ought to do.

2 When in danger, make me brave;
   make me know that You can save.
   Keep me safe by Your dear side;
   let me in Your love abide.

3 When I'm tempted to do wrong,
   make me steadfast, wise and strong;
   and when all alone I stand,
   shield me with Your mighty hand.

4 When my work seems hard and dry,
   may I never cease to try;
   help me patiently to bear
   pain and hardship, toil and care.

5 May I do the good I know,
   be Your loving child below,
   then at last in heaven share
   life with You that's free from care.

44 Terrye Coelho
© 1972 Maranatha! Music / CCCM Music /
CopyCare

1 **Father, we adore You,**
   lay our lives before You:
   how we love You!

2 Jesus, we adore You,
   lay our lives before You:
   how we love You!

3 Spirit, we adore You,
   lay our lives before You:
   how we love You!

45 Donna Adkins
© 1976, 1981 Maranatha! Music / CCCM Music /
CopyCare

1 **Father, we love You,**
   we worship and adore You:
   glorify Your name
   in all the earth.
   Glorify Your name,
   glorify Your name,
   glorify Your name
   in all the earth.

2 Jesus, we love You,
   we worship and adore You:
   glorify Your name
   in all the earth.
   Glorify Your name,
   glorify Your name,
   glorify Your name
   in all the earth.

3 Spirit, we love You,
   we worship and adore You:
   glorify Your name
   in all the earth.
   Glorify Your name,
   glorify Your name,
   glorify Your name
   in all the earth.

46 © 1986 Greg Leavers

'Follow Me,' says Jesus,
'I can keep you safe.
I am the good shepherd,
so why not be My sheep?
If you're lost and lonely
I can keep you safe.
I gave My life to save you,
so come, just follow Me.'

47
Dave Richards
© 1977 Thankyou Music

For I'm building a people of power
and I'm making a people of praise,
that will move through this land
        by My Spirit,
and will glorify My precious name.
Build Your Church, Lord,
make us strong, Lord,
join our hearts, Lord, through Your Son;
make us one, Lord, in Your body,
in the kingdom of Your Son.

48
Folliott Pierpoint (1835–1917)
altered © 1986 Horrobin/Leavers

1   **For the beauty of the earth,**
    for the beauty of the skies,
    for the love which from our birth
    over and around us lies;
    Father, unto You we raise
    this our sacrifice of praise.

2   For the beauty of each hour
    of the day and of the night,
    hill and vale, and tree and flower,
    sun and moon, and stars of light;
    Father, unto You we raise
    this our sacrifice of praise.

3   For the joy of love from God,
    that we share on earth below;
    for our friends and family,
    and the love that they can show;
    Father, unto You we raise
    this our sacrifice of praise.

4   For each perfect gift divine
    to our race so freely given,
    thank You, Lord, that they are mine,
    here on earth as gifts from heaven;
    Father, unto You we raise
    this our sacrifice of praise.

49
From Psalm 113, Paul S Deming
Integrity's Hosanna! Music /
Integrity Praise! / Sovereign Music UK

From the rising of the sun
to the going down of the same,
the Lord's name is to be praised.
From the rising of the sun
to the going down of the same,
the Lord's name is to be praised.
Praise ye the Lord,
praise Him, O ye servants of the Lord,
praise the name of the Lord;
blessèd be the name of the Lord
from this time forth,
and for evermore.

50
A Sevison
Copyright control

1   **Give me oil in my lamp,**
        keep me burning,
    give me oil in my lamp, I pray;
    give me oil in my lamp, keep me burning,
    keep me burning till the break of day.
        Sing hosanna, sing hosanna,
        sing hosanna to the King of kings!
        Sing hosanna, sing hosanna,
        sing hosanna to the King!

2   Give me joy in my heart,
        keep me singing,
    give me joy in my heart, I pray;
    give me joy in my heart, keep me singing,
    keep me singing till the break of day.
        Sing hosanna . . .

3   Give me love in my heart,
        keep me serving,
    give me love in my heart, I pray;
    give me love in my heart,
        keep me serving,
    keep me serving till the break of day.
        Sing hosanna . . .

4   Give me peace in my heart,
        keep me resting,
    give me peace in my heart, I pray;
    give me peace in my heart,
        keep me resting,
    keep me resting till the break of day.
        Sing hosanna . . .

51 © 1986 Greg Leavers

Glory to God in the highest,
peace upon earth,
Jesus Christ has come to earth;
that's why we sing,
'Jesus the King,
Jesus has come for you.'

1 The shepherds who were sitting there
were suddenly filled with fear;
the dark night was filled with light,
angels singing everywhere.
Glory to God . . .

2 The next time we hear a song
of worship from a heavenly throng,
will be when Jesus comes again,
then with triumph we'll all sing:
Glory to God . . .

52 Thomas Ken (1637–1711)
© in this version The Jubilate Group

1 **Glory to You, my God, this night**
for all the blessings of the light;
keep me, O keep me, King of kings,
beneath Your own almighty wings.

2 Forgive me, Lord, through Your dear Son,
the wrong that I this day have done,
that peace with God and man may be,
before I sleep, restored to me.

3 Teach me to live, that I may dread
the grave as little as my bed;
teach me to die, that so I may
rise glorious at the awesome day.

4 O may my soul on you repose
and restful sleep my eyelids close;
sleep that shall me more vigorous make
to serve my God when I awake.

5 If in the night I sleepless lie,
my mind with peaceful thoughts supply;
let no dark dreams disturb my rest,
no powers of evil me molest.

6 Praise God from whom all blessings flow
in heaven above and earth below;
one God, three persons, we adore –
to Him be praise for evermore!

53 Anon
Copyright control

1 **God is so good,**
God is so good,
God is so good,
He's so good to me.

2 He took my sin,
He took my sin,
He took my sin,
He's so good to me.

3 Now I am free,
now I am free,
now I am free,
He's so good to me.

4 God is so good,
He took my sin,
now I am free,
He's so good to me.

54 Carol Owens
© 1972 Kevin Mayhew Ltd

1 **God forgave my sin in Jesus' name;**
I've been born again in Jesus' name,
and in Jesus' name I come to you
to share His love as He told me to.
He said:
'Freely, freely you have received,
freely, freely give;
go in My name
and because you believe,
others will know that I live.'

2 All power is given in Jesus' name
in earth and heaven in Jesus' name;
and in Jesus' name I come to you
to share His power as He told me to.
He said . . .

55 Graham Kendrick
© 1985 Thankyou Music

God is good – we sing and shout it,
God is good – we celebrate;
God is good – no more we doubt it,
God is good – we know it's true!

And when I think of His love for me,
my heart fills with praise
and I feel like dancing;
for in His heart there is room for me,
and I run with arms opened wide.

God is good – we sing and shout it,
God is good – we celebrate;
God is good – no more we doubt it,
God is good – we know it's true! *Hey!*

3   God is our hope, our joy
         and our salvation,
    His love alone transforms the sinful heart.
    Lord, how we sought Your Spirit's
         sweet renewing:
    Your healing touch has filled our hearts
         with praise.
    We come and worship Jesus,
         Lord and Saviour,
    His love alone must fill our earthly days.

4   God is our strength,
         our rock and our redeemer
    in times of trouble and in times of joy.
    Lord, may our lives be full
         of sure thanksgiving,
    our lips be full of symphonies of praise.
    You gave us love, a risen, living Saviour,
    we bring ourselves, a sacrifice of praise.

56 © Christopher Porteous / The Jubilate Group

1   **God is our guide, our light
         and our deliverer,**
    He holds our hand,
         He walks beside the way.
    Lord, may our feet tread
         in the steps You taught us
    to follow firmly as by faith each day,
    Your word a light,
         a lamp to lead our footsteps –
    we love the hours
         when You beside us stay.

2   God is our peace,
         our help and our protector,
    we find His presence in the hour of need.
    Lord, though the storms of life
         may leave us trembling,
    Your words of comfort
         bring us peace within.
    When we are weak
         and fear to face the future
    we find such comfort in Your loving arms.

57 Arthur Campbell Ainger (1841–1919)
© in this version The Jubilate Group

1   **God is working His purpose out,**
    as year succeeds to year:
    God is working His purpose out,
    and the time is drawing near:
    nearer and nearer draws the time,
    the time that shall surely be,
    when the earth shall be filled
    with the glory of God,
    as the waters cover the sea.

2   From utmost east to utmost west
    wherever man has trod,
    by the mouth of many messengers
    rings out the voice of God:
    listen to me, you continents,
    you islands, look to me,
    that the earth may be filled
    with the glory of God,
    as the waters cover the sea.

3 We shall march in the strength of God,
with the banner of Christ unfurled,
that the light of the glorious gospel
    of truth
may shine throughout the world;
we shall fight with sorrow and sin
to set their captives free,
that the earth may be filled
with the glory of God,
as the waters cover the sea.

4 All we can do is nothing worth
unless God blesses the deed;
vainly we hope for the harvest-tide
till God gives life to the seed:
nearer and nearer draws the time,
the time that shall surely be,
when the earth shall be filled
with the glory of God,
as the waters cover the sea.

58 Gloria and William J Gaither
© 1971 Coronation Music Publishing /
Thankyou Music

1 **God sent His Son, they call Him Jesus;**
He came to love, heal, and forgive;
He lived and died to buy my pardon,
an empty grave is there
    to prove my Saviour lives.
    Because He lives I can face tomorrow;
    because He lives all fear is gone;
    because I know, I know
        He holds the future,
    and life is worth the living
        just because He lives.

2 How sweet to hold a new-born baby,
and feel the pride and joy he gives;
but greater still the calm assurance,
this child can face uncertain days
        because He lives.
    Because He lives . . .

3 And then one day I'll cross the river;
I'll fight life's final war with pain;
and then as death gives way to victory,
I'll see the lights of glory
        and I'll know He lives.
    Because He lives . . .

59 © 1986 Peter Horrobin

1 **God so loved the world**
    He sent to us Jesus,
God so loved the world He sent His Son.
Alleluia, Jesus, Lord Jesus, Jesus,
alleluia, Jesus, God sent His Son.

2 Jesus showed the world
        the love of the Father,
Jesus showed the world
        how we must love.
Alleluia, Jesus, Lord Jesus, Jesus,
alleluia, Jesus, God sent His Son.

60 Anon
Altered © 1986 Horrobin/Leavers

God's not dead (no),
He is alive,
God's not dead (no),
He is alive,
God's not dead (no),
He is alive!
Serve Him with my hands,
follow with my feet,
love Him in my heart,
know Him in my life;
for He's alive in me.

61 John Arlott (1914–91)
© Mrs B M Arlott / W S V Kennard

1 **God, whose farm is all creation,**
take the gratitude we give;
take the finest of our harvest,
crops we grow that men may live.

2 Take our ploughing, seeding, reaping,
hopes and fears of sun and rain,
all our thinking, planning, waiting,
ripened in this fruit and grain.

3 All our labour, all our watching,
all our calendar of care,
in these crops of Your creation,
take, O God; they are our prayer.

62

1 **God whose Son
was once a man on earth**
gave His life that men may live.
Risen, our ascended Lord
fulfilled His promised word.
*When the Spirit came,
the Church was born,
God's people shared
in a bright new dawn.
They healed the sick,
they taught God's word,
they sought the lost,
they obeyed the Lord.
And it's all because the Spirit came
that the world will never be the same,
because the Spirit came.*

2 God whose power
fell on the early church,
sent to earth from heaven above;
Spirit-led, by Him ordained,
they showed the world God's love.
When the Spirit came . . .

3 Pour Your Spirit on the church today,
that Your life through me may flow;
Spirit-filled, I'll serve Your name
and live the truth I know.
*When the Spirit comes, new life is born,
God's people share
in a bright new dawn.
We'll heal the sick,
we'll teach God's word,
we'll seek the lost,
we'll obey the Lord.
And it's all because the Spirit came
that the world will never be the same,
because the Spirit came.*

63

1 **God, who made the earth,**
the air, the sky, the sea,
who gave the light its birth,
will care for me.

2 God, who made the grass,
the flower, the fruit, the tree,
the day and night to pass,
will care for me.

3 God, who made the sun,
the moon, the stars, is He
who, when life's clouds come on,
will care for me.

4 God, who sent His son
to die on Calvary,
He, if I lean on Him,
will care for me.

5 God, who gave me life
His servant here to be,
has promised in His word
to care for me.

64

1 **Great is Your faithfulness,
O God my Father,**
You have fulfilled all Your promise to me;
You never fail
and Your love is unchanging;
all You have been You for ever will be.
*Great is Your faithfulness,
great is Your faithfulness;
morning by morning
new mercies I see;
all I have needed
Your hand has provided –
great is Your faithfulness,
Father, to me!*

2 Summer and winter,
and spring-time and harvest,
sun, moon and stars
in their courses above,
join with all nature in eloquent witness
to Your great faithfulness, mercy and love.
Great is Your faithfulness . . .

3 Pardon for sin, and a peace everlasting,
    Your living presence
        to cheer and to guide;
    strength for today
        and bright hope for tomorrow,
    these are the blessings
        Your love will provide.
        Great is Your faithfulness . . .

66 Dale Garratt
© 1972 Scripture in Song /
Integrity's Hosanna! Music / Thankyou Music

**Hallelujah! for the Lord our God
    the almighty reigns.**
Hallelujah! for the Lord our God
    the almighty reigns.
Let us rejoice and be glad and give
    the glory unto Him.
Hallelujah! for the Lord our God
    the almighty reigns.

65 © Geoffrey Marshall-Taylor / The Jubilate Group

Go, tell it on the mountain,
over the hills and everywhere;
go, tell it on the mountain
that Jesus is His name.

1 He possessed no riches,
        no home to lay His head;
    He saw the needs of others
        and cared for them instead.
        Go, tell it on the mountain . . .

2 He reached out and touched them,
        the blind, the deaf, the lame;
    He spoke and listened gladly
        to anyone who came.
        Go, tell it on the mountain . . .

3 Some turned away in anger,
        with hatred in the eye;
    they tried Him and condemned Him,
        then led Him out to die.
        Go, tell it on the mountain . . .

4 'Father, now forgive them' –
        those were the words He said;
    in three more days He was alive
        and risen from the dead.
        Go, tell it on the mountain . . .

5 He still comes to people,
        His life moves through the lands;
    He uses us for speaking,
        He touches with our hands.
        Go, tell it on the mountain . . .

67 Anon
Copyright control

Hallelu, hallelu, hallelu, hallelujah;
we'll praise the Lord;
hallelu, hallelu, hallelu, hallelujah;
we'll praise the Lord!
We'll praise the Lord, hallelujah,
we'll praise the Lord, hallelujah,
we'll praise the Lord, hallelujah,
we'll praise the Lord!

68 Philip Doddridge (1702–51)
altered © 1986 Horrobin/Leavers

1 **Hark, the glad sound!
    the Saviour comes,**
    the Saviour promised long;
    let every heart prepare a throne,
    and every voice a song.

2 He comes, the prisoners to release
    in Satan's bondage held;
    the chains of sin before Him break,
    the iron fetters yield.

3 He comes the broken heart to bind,
    the wounded soul to cure;
    and with the treasures of His grace
    to enrich the humble poor.

4 Our glad hosannas, Prince of peace,
    Your welcome shall proclaim;
    and heaven's eternal arches ring
    with Your belovèd name.

69 Charles Wesley (1707–88) and others

1 **Hark! the herald-angels sing,**
'Glory to the new-born King!
Peace on earth, and mercy mild,
God and sinners reconciled.'
Joyful, all you nations rise,
join the triumph of the skies;
with the angelic host proclaim,
'Christ is born in Bethlehem!'
  Hark! the herald-angels sing,
  'Glory to the new-born King!'

2 Christ by highest heaven adored,
Christ, the everlasting Lord,
late in time behold Him come,
offspring of a virgin's womb!
Veiled in flesh the Godhead see!
Hail, the incarnate Deity!
Pleased as man with man to dwell,
Jesus, our Immanuel.
  Hark! the herald-angels sing,
  'Glory to the new-born King!'

3 Hail, the heaven-born Prince of peace!
Hail, the Sun of righteousness!
Light and life to all He brings,
risen with healing in His wings.
Mild He lays His glory by,
born that man no more may die;
born to raise the sons of earth,
born to give them second birth.
  Hark! the herald-angels sing,
  'Glory to the new-born King!'

70 Ira F Stanphill

1 **Happiness is to know the Saviour,**
living a life within His favour,
having a change in my behaviour,
happiness is the Lord.

2 Happiness is a new creation,
Jesus and me in close relation,
having a part in His salvation,
happiness is the Lord.
  Real joy is mine,
  no matter if teardrops start;
  I've found the secret –
  it's Jesus in my heart!

3 Happiness is to be forgiven,
living a life that's worth the living,
taking a trip that leads to heaven,
happiness is the Lord,
happiness is the Lord,
happiness is the Lord!

71

1 **Have you heard the raindrops**
drumming on the rooftops?
Have you heard the raindrops
  dripping on the ground?
Have you heard the raindrops
  splashing in the streams
and running to the rivers all around?
  There's water, water of life,
  Jesus gives us the water of life,
  there's water, water of life,
  Jesus gives us the water of life.

2 There's a busy workman
  digging in the desert,
digging with a spade that
  flashes in the sun;
soon there will be water
  rising in the wellshaft,
spilling from the bucket as it comes.
  There's water . . .

3 Nobody can live who hasn't any water,
when the land is dry
  then nothing much grows;
Jesus gives us life if we drink
  the living water,
sing it so that everybody knows.
  There's water . . .

72 © P A Taylor

1 **Have you seen the pussy cat
    sitting on the wall?**
Have you heard his beautiful purr? (*purr*)
Have you seen the lion
        stalking round his prey?
Have you heard his terrible roar? (*roar*)
    One so big, one so small,
    our heavenly Father cares for them all,
    one so big, one so small,
    our heavenly Father cares.

2 Have you seen the children
        coming home from school?
Have you heard them shout,
        'Hurray!' (*Hurray!*)
Have you seen the grown-ups
        coming home from work,
saying, 'What a horrible day!'
        (*What a horrible day!*)
    Some so big, some so small,
    our heavenly Father cares for them all,
    some so big, some so small,
    our heavenly Father cares.

73 Anon
       Copyright control

1 **He brought me to His banqueting
    house**
    and His banner over me is love,
    He brought me to His banqueting house
    and His banner over me is love,
    He brought me to His banqueting house
    and His banner over me is love,
    His banner over me is love.
        God loves you and I love you
        and that's the way it should be.
        God loves you and I love you
        and that's the way it should be.

2 He feeds me at His banqueting table . . .
    God loves you . . .

3 He lifts me up to the heavenly places . . .
    God loves you . . .

4 There's one way to peace through the
        power of the cross . . .
    God loves you . . .

5 Jesus is the rock of my salvation . . .
    God loves you . . .

74 Alan Pinnock
       © 1970 Campbell Connelly & Co Ltd

1 **He gave me eyes so I could see**
    the wonders of the world.
    Without my eyes I could not see
    the other boys and girls.
    He gave me ears so I could hear
    the wind and rain and sea.
    I've got to tell it to the world,
    He made me!

2 He gave me lips so I could speak,
    and say what's in my mind.
    Without my lips I could not speak
    a single word or line.
    He made my mind so I could think
    and choose what I should be.
    I've got to tell it to the world,
    He made me!

3 He gave me hands so I could touch,
    and hold a thousand things.
    I need my hands to help me write,
    to help me fetch and bring.
    These feet He made so I could run,
    He meant me to be free.
    I've got to tell it to the world,
    He made me!

75 Marvin Frey
       Copyright control

1 **He is Lord, He is Lord,**
    He is risen from the dead
    and He is Lord!
    Every knee shall bow,
    every tongue confess
    that Jesus Christ is Lord.

2 He's my Lord, He's my Lord,
    He is risen from the dead
    and He's my Lord!
    And my knee shall bow
    and my tongue confess
    that Jesus is my Lord.

76 © Archie Hall

He made the stars to shine,
He made the rolling sea,
He made the mountains high,
and He made me.
But this is why I love Him –
for me He bled and died,
the Lord of all creation
became the crucified.

77 Anon
Copyright control

He paid a debt He did not owe,
I owed a debt I could not pay.
I needed someone to wash my sins away,
and now I sing a brand new song,
'Amazing grace!' the whole day long,
for Jesus paid a debt that I could never pay.

78 Anon
© HarperCollins*Religious* / CopyCare

1 **He's got the whole wide world
   in His hands,**
   He's got the whole wide world
   in His hands,
   He's got the whole wide world
   in His hands,
   He's got the whole world in His hands.

2 He's got everybody here in His hands . . .

3 He's got the tiny little baby
   in His hands . . .

4 He's got you and me, brother,
   in His hands . . .

79 © 1986 Peter Horrobin and Greg Leavers

1 **He's great! He's God!**
   Jesus Christ is Lord.
   He's great! He's God!
   Trust His word.

2 His word is truth,
   for He cannot lie.
   His word is truth,
   to live by.

3 His love is strong,
   and will never end.
   His love is strong,
   praise His name.

4 He lives evermore
   as the King of kings.
   He lives evermore!
   Worship Him.

80 Percy Dearmer (1867–1936)
after John Bunyan (1628–88)
© Oxford University Press

1 **He who would valiant be**
   'gainst all disaster,
   let him in constancy
   follow the Master.
   There's no discouragement
   shall make him once relent
   his first avowed intent
   to be a pilgrim.

2 Who so beset him round
   with dismal stories,
   do but themselves confound –
   his strength the more is.
   No foes shall stay his might,
   though he with giants fight:
   he will make good his right
   to be a pilgrim.

3 Since, Lord, Thou dost defend
   us with Thy Spirit,
   we know we at the end
   shall life inherit.
   Then fancies flee away!
   I'll fear not what men say,
   I'll labour night and day
   to be a pilgrim.

81 Israeli traditional song

Hévénu shalom aléchem,
Hévénu shalom aléchem,
Hévénu shalom aléchem,
Hévénu shalom,
shalom, shalom aléchem.

82 Anon
Copyright control

How great is our God,
how great is His name,
how great is His love
forever the same.

He rolled back the waters
of the mighty Red Sea,
and He said, 'I'll never leave you,
put your trust in Me.'

83 Hugh Mitchell
© 1973 Zondervan Corporation /
Fine Balance Music / CopyCare

How did Moses cross the Red Sea?
How did Moses cross the Red Sea?
How did Moses cross the Red Sea?
How did he get across?
Did he swim? No! No!
Did he row? No! No!
Did he jump? No! No! No! No!
Did he drive? No! No!
Did he fly? No! No!
How did he get across?
God blew with His wind, puff, puff, puff, puff.
He blew just enough, 'nough, 'nough,
          'nough, 'nough,
and through the sea He made a path –
that's how he got across.

84 Leonard E Smith Jnr
© 1974, 1978 New Jerusalem Music /
Thankyou Music

1 **How lovely on the mountains**
      are the feet of him
   who brings good news, good news,
   proclaiming peace,
         announcing news of happiness:
   our God reigns, our God reigns!
      Our God reigns, our God reigns,
      our God reigns, our God reigns!

2 You watchmen,
         lift your voices joyfully as one,
   shout for your King, your King.
   See eye to eye the Lord restoring Zion:
   your God reigns, your God reigns!
      Your God reigns, your God reigns,
      your God reigns, your God reigns!

3 Waste places of Jerusalem
         break forth with joy,
   we are redeemed, redeemed.
   The Lord has saved
         and comforted His people:
   your God reigns, your God reigns!
      Your God reigns, your God reigns,
      your God reigns, your God reigns!

4 Ends of the earth,
         see the salvation of your God,
   Jesus is Lord, is Lord.
   Before the nations
         He has bared His holy arm:
   your God reigns, your God reigns!
      Your God reigns, your God reigns,
      your God reigns, your God reigns!

85 James Drummond Burns (1823–64)
altered © 1986 Horrobin/Leavers

1 **Hushed was the evening hymn,**
   the temple courts were dark;
   the lamp was burning dim
   before the sacred ark,
   when suddenly a voice divine
   rang through the silence of the shrine.

2 The old man, meek and mild,
the priest of Israel, slept;
his watch the temple child,
the little Samuel, kept:
and what from Eli's sense was sealed
the Lord to Hannah's son revealed.

3 O give me Samuel's ear,
the open ear, O Lord,
alive and quick to hear
each whisper of Your word –
like him to answer at Your call,
and to obey You first of all.

4 O give me Samuel's heart,
a lowly heart, that waits
to serve and play the part
You show us at Your gates,
by day and night, a heart that still
moves at the breathing of Your will.

5 O give me Samuel's mind,
a sweet, unmurmuring faith,
obedient and resigned
to You in life and death,
that I may read with childlike eyes
truths that are hidden from the wise.

86 Frances Ridley Havergal (1836–79)

1 **I am trusting You, Lord Jesus,**
You have died for me;
trusting You for full salvation,
great and free.

2 I am trusting You for pardon,
at Your feet I bow;
for Your grace and tender mercy,
trusting now.

3 I am trusting You for cleansing,
Jesus, Son of God;
trusting You to make me holy
by Your blood.

4 I am trusting You to guide me;
You alone shall lead,
every day and hour supplying
all my need.

5 I am trusting You for power,
Yours can never fail;
words which You Yourself shall give me
must prevail.

6 I am trusting You, Lord Jesus;
never let me fall;
I am trusting You for ever,
and for all.

87 Graham Kendrick
© 1985 Thankyou Music

I am a lighthouse,
a shining and bright house,
out in the waves of a stormy sea.
The oil of the Spirit keeps my lamp burning:
Jesus my Lord is the light in me.
And when people see
the good things that I do,
they'll give praise to God
who has sent us Jesus.
We'll send out a lifeboat
of love and forgiveness
and give them a hand to get in.
I am a lighthouse . . .

While the storm is raging, whoosh, whoosh,
and the wind is blowing, oooh, oooh,
and the waves are crashing,
crash! crash! crash! crash!

I am a lighthouse,
a shining and bright house,
out in the waves of a stormy sea.
The oil of the Spirit keeps my lamp burning:
Jesus my Lord is the light in me.

88 Philip Paul Bliss (1838–76)

1 **I am so glad that our Father in heaven**
tells of His love in the book He has given:
wonderful things in the Bible I see;
this is the dearest, that Jesus loves me.
I am so glad that Jesus loves me,
Jesus loves me, Jesus loves me,
I am so glad that Jesus loves me,
Jesus loves even me.

2 Though I forget Him, and wander away,
He'll always love me wherever I stray;
back to His dear loving arms do I flee,
when I remember that Jesus loves me.
I am so glad . . .

3 Oh, if there's only one song I can sing,
when in His beauty I see the great King,
this shall my song in eternity be:
'O what a wonder that Jesus loves me!'
I am so glad . . .

4 If one should ask of me, 'How can I tell?'
Glory to Jesus, I know very well;
God's Holy Spirit with mine does agree,
constantly witnessing: Jesus loves me.
I am so glad . . .

89 Anon
Copyright control

'I am the way, the truth and the life,'
that's what Jesus said.
'I am the way, the truth and the life,'
that's what Jesus said.
Without the way there is no going,
without the truth there is no knowing,
without the life there is no living.
'I am the way, the truth and the life,'
that's what Jesus said.

90 Anon
Copyright control

I can run through a troop
and leap over a wall.
Hallelujah (glory, glory), hallelujah.
He's my Prince of peace,
He gives power to all.
Hallelujah (glory, glory), hallelujah.
Now there is no condemnation,
Jesus is the rock of my salvation.
I can run through a troop
and leap over a wall.
Hallelujah (glory, glory), hallelujah.

91 Sydney Carter
© 1963 Stainer & Bell Ltd

1 **I danced in the morning**
when the world was begun
and I danced in the moon
and the stars and the sun,
and I came down from heaven
and I danced on the earth –
at Bethlehem I had my birth.
Dance, then, wherever you may be,
I am the Lord of the dance, said He,
and I'll lead you all,
wherever you may be,
and I'll lead you all in the dance,
said He.

2 I danced for the scribe and the pharisee,
but they would not dance
and they wouldn't follow me.
I danced for the fishermen,
for James and John –
they came with me and the dance went
on.
Dance, then . . .

92 Alfred B Smith and Eugene Clarke
© 1958 Brentwood Benson Catalogue

1 **I do not know what lies ahead,**
the way I cannot see;
yet one stands near to be my guide,
He'll show the way to me:
I know who holds the future,
and He'll guide me with His hand;
with God things don't just happen,
everything by Him is planned.
So as I face tomorrow,
with its problems large and small,
I'll trust the God of miracles,
give to Him my all.

2 I do not know how many days
of life are mine to spend;
but one who knows and cares for me
will keep me to the end:
I know who holds . . .

3   I do not know the course ahead,
     what joys and griefs are there;
     but one is near who fully knows,
     I'll trust His loving care:
       I know who holds . . .

93   Rick Founds and Todd Collins
       © 1982 Maranatha! Music / CopyCare

I'll be still and know that You are God;
I'll be still and know You are the Lord;
I'll be still to worship and adore You,
blessèd One, Emmanuel, Jesus.

94   Brian Howard
       © 1974 Mission Hills Music / CopyCare

1   **If I were a butterfly,**
     I'd thank You, Lord, for giving me wings.
     And if I were a robin in a tree,
     I'd thank You, Lord, that I could sing.
     And if I were a fish in the sea,
     I'd wiggle my tail and I'd giggle with glee,
     but I just thank you, Father,
       for making me 'me'.
     For You gave me a heart
     and You gave me a smile,
     You gave me Jesus
     and You made me Your child,
     and I just thank you, Father,
       for making me 'me'.

2   If I were an elephant,
     I'd thank You, Lord, by raising my trunk.
     And if I were a kangaroo
     You know I'd hop right up to You.
     And if I were an octopus,
     I'd thank You, Lord, for my fine looks,
     but I just thank You, Father,
       for making me 'me'.
     For You gave me a heart . . .

3   If I were a wiggly worm,
     I'd thank You, Lord, that I could squirm,
     and if I were a billy goat,
     I'd thank You, Lord, for my strong throat,
     and if I were a fuzzy wuzzy bear,
     I'd thank You, Lord, for my fuzzy wuzzy
       hair,
     but I just thank You, Father,
       for making me 'me'.
     For You gave me a heart . . .

95   Annie and Neil Simpson

1   **If you see someone lying in the road,**
     don't leave him there, give him a hand.
     If you see someone crying in the road,
     don't leave him there, give him a hand.
     Doesn't matter who you are;
     you might be a tramp or a movie star.
     Just remember, whoever you are,
     that it's Jesus lying there,
     that it's Jesus crying there.

2   If Jesus sees you lying in the road,
     He won't leave you there,
       he'll give you a hand.
     If Jesus sees you crying in the road,
     He won't leave you there,
       he'll give you a hand.
     Doesn't matter who you are;
     you might be a tramp or a movie star.
     Just remember, whoever you are,
     that He sees you lying there,
     and He sees you crying there.

96   Joseph Carlson
       Copyright control

If you want joy, real joy, wonderful joy,
let Jesus come into your heart.
If you want joy, real joy, wonderful joy,
let Jesus come into your heart.
Your sins He'll take away,
your night He'll turn to day,
your heart He'll make over anew,
and then come in to stay.
If you want joy, real joy, wonderful joy,
let Jesus come into your heart.

97

1 **I gotta home in gloryland
that outshines the sun,**
I gotta home in gloryland
that outshines the sun,
I gotta home in gloryland
that outshines the sun,
way beyond the blue.
Do, Lord, O do, Lord,
O do remember me;
do, Lord, O do, Lord,
O do remember me;
do, Lord, O do, Lord,
O do remember me,
way beyond the blue.

2 I took Jesus as my Saviour,
you take Him too . . .
Do, Lord, O do, Lord . . .

3 If you will not bear a cross,
you can't wear a crown . . .
Do, Lord, O do, Lord . . .

98

1 **I have decided to follow Jesus,**
(3 times)
no turning back, no turning back.

2 The world behind me, the cross before
me, *(3 times)*
no turning back, no turning back.

3 Though none go with me, I still will follow,
(3 times)
no turning back, no turning back.

4 Will you decide now to follow Jesus?
(3 times)
no turning back, no turning back.

99

1 **I have seen the golden sunshine,**
I have watched the flowers grow,
I have listened to the song birds
and there's one thing now I know:
they were all put there for us to share
by someone so divine,
and if you're a friend of Jesus
(*clap, clap, clap, clap*)
you're a friend of mine.
I've seen the light, I've seen the light,
and that's why my heart sings.
I've known the joy, I've known the joy
that loving Jesus brings.

2 I have seen the morning sunshine,
I have heard the oceans roar,
I have seen the flowers of springtime
and there's one thing I am sure:
they were all put there for us to share
by someone so divine,
and if you're a friend of Jesus
(*clap, clap, clap, clap*)
you're a friend of mine.
I've seen the light . . .

100

I hear the sound of the army of the Lord;
I hear the sound of the army of the Lord;
it's the sound of praise,
it's the sound of war;
the army of the Lord,
the army of the Lord,
the army of the Lord is marching on.

101 Anon
Copyright control

I may never march in the infantry,
ride with the cavalry, shoot with the artillery,
I may never zoom o'er the enemy,
for I'm in the Lord's army.
I'm in the Lord's army (Yes, sir!),
I'm in the Lord's army (Yes, sir!).
I may never march in the infantry,
ride with the cavalry, shoot with the artillery,
I may never zoom o'er the enemy,
for I'm in the Lord's army.

102 Anon
Copyright control

I met Jesus at the crossroads,
where the two ways meet.
Satan too was standing there,
and he said, 'Come this way!
Lots and lots of pleasures
I can give to you today.'
But I said, 'No, there's Jesus here,
just see what He offers me.
Down here, my sins forgiven,
up there, a home in heaven.
Praise God! That's the way for me.'

103 Eric A Thorn
© Christian Music Ministries

1 **I met You at the cross,**
    Jesus, my Lord;
    I heard You from that cross:
    my name You called –
    asked me to follow You all of my days,
    asked me for evermore
        Your name to praise.

2 I saw You on the cross
    dying for me;
    I put You on that cross:
    but Your one plea –
    would I now follow You all of my days,
    and would I evermore
        Your great name praise?

3 Jesus, my Lord and King,
    Saviour of all,
    Jesus the King of kings,
    You heard my call –
    that I would follow You all of my days,
    and that for evermore
        Your name I'd praise.

104 Anon
altered © 1986 Horrobin/Leavers

I'm feeding on the living bread,
I'm drinking at the fountain head;
for all who drink, so Jesus said,
will never, never thirst again.
What, never thirst again?
No! never thirst again.
What, never thirst again?
No! never thirst again.
For all who drink, so Jesus said,
will never, never thirst again.

105 Oswald J Smith
© 1952 Zondervan Corporation /
Fine Balance Music / CopyCare

1 **I'm singing for my Lord**
        everywhere I go,
    singing of His wondrous love,
        that the world may know
    how He saved a wretch like me
        by His death on Calvary:
    I'm singing for my Lord everywhere I go.

2 I'm singing, but sometimes
        heavy is the rod,
    for this world is not a friend
        to the grace of God.
    Yet I sing the whole day long,
        for He fills my heart with song,
    I'm singing for my Lord everywhere I go.

3 I'm singing for the lost
        just because I know
    Jesus Christ, whose precious blood
        washes white as snow.
    If my songs to Him can bring
        some lost soul I'll gladly sing:
    I'm singing for my Lord everywhere I go.

4 I'm singing for the saints
        as they journey home;
   soon they'll reach that happy land
        where they'll never roam.
   And with me they'll join and sing
        praises to our Lord and King:
   I'm singing for my Lord everywhere I go.

106 Graham Kendrick
         © 1986 Thankyou Music

I'm special because God has loved me,
for He gave the best thing that He had
        to save me:
His own Son Jesus,
        crucified to take the blame,
for all the bad things I have done.

Thank You, Jesus, thank You, Lord,
for loving me so much;
I know I don't deserve anything,
help me feel Your love right now,
to know deep in my heart
        that I'm Your special friend.

107 Alice M Pullen
         © Church of Scotland

1 **I'm very glad of God:**
   His love takes care of me.
   In every lovely thing I see
   God smiles at me.

2 I'm very glad of God:
   His love takes care of me.
   In every lovely sound I hear
   God speaks to me.

108 W G Wills (1841–91)
         altered © 1986 Horrobin/Leavers

1 **In our work and in our play,**
   Jesus, ever with us stay;
   may we serve You all our days,
   true and faithful in our ways.

2 May we in Your strength subdue
   evil tempers, words untrue,
   thoughts impure and deeds unkind,
   all things hateful to Your mind.

3 Jesus, from Your throne above,
   fill anew our hearts with love;
   so that what we say and do
   shows that we belong to You.

4 Children of the King are we,
   may we loyal to Him be:
   try to please Him every day,
   in our work and in our play.

109 Gordon Brattle (1917–91)
         © D H Brattle

In my need Jesus found me,
put His strong arm around me,
brought me safe home,
into the shelter of the fold.

Gracious shepherd that sought me,
precious life-blood that bought me;
out of the night,
into the light and near to God.

110 From a Polish carol
         tr. E M G Reed (1885–1933)
         Copyright control

1 **Infant holy, infant lowly,**
   for His bed a cattle stall;
   oxen lowing, little knowing
   Christ the babe is Lord of all.
   Swift are winging angels singing,
   nowells ringing, tidings bringing:
   Christ the babe is Lord of all;
   Christ the babe is Lord of all!

2 Flocks were sleeping, shepherds keeping
   vigil till the morning new,
   saw the glory, heard the story –
   tidings of a gospel true.
   Thus rejoicing, free from sorrow,
   praises voicing, greet the morrow:
   Christ the babe was born for you;
   Christ the babe was born for you!

111 Anon
Copyright control

In the name of Jesus,
in the name of Jesus,
we have the victory.
In the name of Jesus,
in the name of Jesus,
demons will have to flee.
Who can tell what God can do?
Who can tell of His love for you?
In the name of Jesus, Jesus,
we have the victory.

112 Ralph Carmichael
© 1964 Bud John Songs / Alliance Media Ltd /
CopyCare

In the stars His handiwork I see,
on the wind He speaks with majesty;
though He's ruling over land and sea,
what is that to me?
I will celebrate nativity,
for it has a place in history,
sure, Christ came to set His people free.
What is that to me?

Then by faith I met Him face to face,
and I felt the wonder of His grace.
Then I knew that He was more
          than just a god
who didn't care, who lived away up there.
And now He lives within me day by day,
ever watching o'er me lest I stray,
helping me to find the narrow way.
He's everything to me.

113 Alfred Henry Ackley (1887–1960)
© 1933 Renewed 1961 Word Music, LLC /
CopyCare

1   **I serve a risen Saviour,**
    He's in the world today;
    I know that He is living,
    whatever men may say.
    I see His hand of mercy,
    I hear His voice of cheer;
    and just the time I need Him,
    He's always near.

He lives, He lives,
Christ Jesus lives today!
He walks with me and talks with me
along life's narrow way.
He lives, He lives,
salvation to impart!
You ask me how I know He lives?
He lives within my heart.

2   In all the world around me
    I see His loving care,
    and though my heart grows weary
    I never will despair;
    I know that He is leading,
    through all the stormy blast,
    the day of His appearing
    will come at last.
        He lives . . .

3   Rejoice, rejoice, O Christian,
    lift up your voice and sing
    eternal hallelujahs
    to Jesus Christ the King!
    The hope of all who seek Him,
    the help of all who find,
    none other is so loving,
    so good and kind.
        He lives . . .

114 Anon
Copyright control

Isaiah heard the voice of the Lord
and he said, 'Here am I, send me!'
He loved to do the will of the Lord,
so he said, 'Here am I, send me;
here am I, send me anywhere for Thee.'
So when I hear the voice of the Lord
I will say, 'Here am I, send me!'

115

1   **I sing a song of the saints of God,**
    patient and brave and true,
    who toiled and fought and lived and died
    for the Lord they loved and knew.
    And one was a doctor,
        and one was a queen,
    and one was a shepherdess
        on the green:
    they were all of them saints of God;
        and I mean,
    God helping, to be one too.

2   They loved their God so good and dear,
    and His love made them strong;
    and they followed the right,
        for Jesus' sake,
    the whole of their good lives long.
    And one was a soldier,
        and one was a priest,
    and one was slain by a fierce wild beast:
    and there's not any reason, no,
        not in the least,
    why I shouldn't be one too.

3   They lived not only in ages past,
    there are hundreds of thousands still;
    the world is bright with the joyous saints
    who love to do Jesus' will.
    You can meet them in school,
        or in lanes, or at sea,
    in church, or in trains,
        or in shops, or at tea,
    for the saints of God began just like me,
    and I mean to be one too.

116

1   **It came upon the midnight clear,**
    that glorious song of old,
    from angels bending near the earth
    to touch their harps of gold:
    'Peace on the earth, goodwill to men
    from heaven's all-gracious King!'
    The world in solemn stillness lay
    to hear the angels sing.

2   With sorrow brought by sin and strife
    the world has suffered long,
    and, since the angels sang, have passed
    two thousand years of wrong;
    for man at war with man hears not
    the love-song which they bring:
    O hush the noise, you men of strife,
    and hear the angels sing!

3   And those whose journey now is hard,
    whose hope is burning low,
    who tread the rocky path of life
    with painful steps and slow:
    O listen to the news of love
    which makes the heavens ring!
    O rest beside the weary road
    and hear the angels sing!

4   And still the days are hastening on –
    by prophets seen of old –
    towards the fulness of the time
    when comes the age foretold:
    then earth and heaven renewed shall see
    the Prince of peace, their King;
    and all the world repeat the song
    which now the angels sing.

117

1   **It is a thing most wonderful,**
    almost too wonderful to be,
    that God's own Son
        should come from heaven
    and die to save a child like me.

2   And yet I know that it is true;
    He came to this poor world below
    and wept, and toiled, and mourned,
        and died,
    only because He loved us so.

3   I cannot tell how He could love
    a child so weak and full of sin;
    His love must be so wonderful,
    if He could die my love to win.

4   I sometimes think about the cross,
    and shut my eyes and try to see
    the cruel nails and crown of thorns,
    and Jesus crucified for me.

5   But even could I see Him die,
    I could but see a little part
    of that great love, which, like a fire,
    is always burning in His heart.

6   How wonderful it is to know
    His love for me so free and sure;
    but yet more wonderful to see
    my love for Him so faint and poor.

7   And yet I want to love You, Lord;
    O teach me how to grow in grace,
    that I may love You more and more,
    until I see You face to face.

118 Gary Pfeiffer

1   **It's a happy day and I praise God
    for the weather.**
    It's a happy day, living it for my Lord.
    It's a happy day, things are going
        to get better,
    living each day by the promises
        in God's word.

2   It's a grumpy day and I can't stand
        the weather.
    It's a grumpy day, living it for myself.
    It's a grumpy day and things aren't going
        to get better,
    living each day with my Bible
        up on my shelf.

3   It's a happy day and I praise God
        for the weather.
    It's a happy day, living it for my Lord.
    It's a happy day, things are going
        to get better,
    living each day by the promises
        in God's word.

119 Traditional

    It's me, it's me, it's me, O Lord,
    standin' in the need of prayer.
    It's me, it's me, it's me, O Lord,
    standin' in the need of prayer.

1   Not my brother or my sister,
        but it's me, O Lord,
    standin' in the need of prayer.
    Not my brother or my sister,
        but it's me, O Lord,
    standin' in the need of prayer.
        It's me, it's me . . .

2   Not my mother or my father,
        but it's me, O Lord,
    standin' in the need of prayer.
    Not my mother or my father,
        but it's me, O Lord,
    standin' in the need of prayer.
        It's me, it's me . . .

3   Not my stranger or my neighbour,
        but it's me, O Lord,
    standin' in the need of prayer.
    Not my stranger or my neighbour,
        but it's me, O Lord,
    standin' in the need of prayer.
        It's me, it's me . . .

120 Spiritual

**I've got peace like a river,
    peace like a river,**
I've got peace like a river in my soul;
I've got peace like a river, peace like a river,
I've got peace like a river in my soul.

121 George W Cooke

1   **I've got that joy, joy, joy, joy**
    down in my heart, (where?)
    down in my heart, (where?)
    down in my heart.
    I've got that joy, joy, joy, joy
    down in my heart, (where?)
    down in my heart to stay.
        And I'm so happy,
        so very happy,
        I've got the love of Jesus in my heart,
        and I'm so happy,
        so very happy,
        I've got the love of Jesus in my heart.

2 I've got the peace
       that passes understanding
   down in my heart, (where?)
   down in my heart, (where?)
   down in my heart.
   I've got the peace
       that passes understanding
   down in my heart, (where?)
   down in my heart to stay.
       And I'm so happy . . .

124

1 **I want to walk with Jesus Christ,**
   all the days I live of this life on earth;
   to give to Him complete control
   of body and of soul.
       Follow Him, follow Him,
       yield your life to Him –
       He has conquered death,
       He is King of kings;
       accept the joy which He gives to those
       who yield their lives to Him.

2 I want to learn to speak to Him,
   to pray to Him, confess my sin,
   to open my life and let Him in,
   for joy will then be mine.
       Follow Him, follow Him . . .

3 I want to learn to speak of Him –
   my life must show that He lives in me;
   my deeds, my thoughts, my words
       must speak
   all of His love for me.
       Follow Him, follow Him . . .

4 I want to learn to read His word,
   for this is how I know the way
   to live my life as pleases Him,
   in holiness and joy.
       Follow Him, follow Him . . .

5 O Holy Spirit of the Lord,
   enter now into this heart of mine;
   take full control of my selfish will
   and make me wholly Thine!
       Follow Him, follow Him . . .

122

1 **I want to live for Jesus every day
       (every day).**
   I want to live for Jesus, come what may
       (come what may).
   Take the world and all its pleasure,
   I've got a more enduring treasure.
   I want to live for Jesus every day.

2 I'm gonna live for Jesus every day
       (every day).
   I'm gonna live for Jesus, come what may
       (come what may).
   Take the world and all its pleasure,
   I've got a more enduring treasure.
   I'm gonna live for Jesus every day.

123

I will make you fishers of men,
fishers of men, fishers of men,
I will make you fishers of men
if you follow Me.
If you follow Me, if you follow Me,
I will make you fishers of men
if you follow Me.

125

1 **I was lost but Jesus found me,**
   found the sheep that went astray,
   threw His loving arms around me,
   drew me back into His way.
       Alleluia, alleluia,
       alleluia, alleluia.

2 Glory, glory, alleluia,
come and bless the Lord our King.
Glory, glory, alleluia,
with His praise all heaven rings.
Alleluia . . .

126 Max Dyer
© 1975 Celebration /
Thankyou Music

1 **I will sing, I will sing a song
unto the Lord,** (*3 times*)
alleluia, glory to the Lord.
*Allelu, alleluia, glory to the Lord,
allelu, alleluia, glory to the Lord,
allelu, alleluia, glory to the Lord,
alleluia, glory to the Lord.*

2 We will come, we will come as one
before the Lord, (*3 times*)
alleluia, glory to the Lord.
Allelu, alleluia . . .

3 If the Son, if the Son shall make you free,
(*3 times*)
you shall be free indeed.
Allelu, alleluia . . .

4 They that sow in tears shall reap in joy,
(*3 times*)
alleluia, glory to the Lord!
Allelu, alleluia . . .

5 Every knee shall bow and every
tongue confess, (*3 times*)
that Jesus Christ is Lord.
Allelu, alleluia . . .

6 In His name, in His name we have
the victory. (*3 times*)
Alleluia, glory to the Lord.
Allelu, alleluia . . .

127 Francis Harold Rowley (1854–1952)
© HarperCollins*Religious* / CopyCare

1 **I will sing the wondrous story**
of the Christ who died for me –
how He left the realms of glory
for the cross on Calvary.
Yes, I'll sing the wondrous story
of the Christ who died for me –
sing it with His saints in glory,
gathered by the crystal sea.

2 I was lost: but Jesus found me,
found the sheep that went astray,
raised me up and gently led me
back into the narrow way.
Days of darkness still may meet me,
sorrow's path I oft may tread;
but His presence still is with me,
by His guiding hand I'm led.

3 He will keep me till the river
rolls its waters at my feet:
then He'll bear me safely over,
made by grace for glory meet.
Yes, I'll sing the wondrous story
of the Christ who died for me –
sing it with His saints in glory,
gathered by the crystal sea.

128 Susan Warner (1819–85)

1 **Jesus bids us shine**
with a pure, clear light,
like a little candle
burning in the night.
In this world is darkness,
so let us shine,
you in your small corner
and I in mine.

2 Jesus bids us shine
first of all for Him.
Well He sees and knows it,
if our light grows dim.
He looks down from heaven
to see us shine,
you in your small corner
and I in mine.

3 Jesus bids us shine, then,
for all around;
many kinds of darkness
in the world are found –
sin and want and sorrow –
so we must shine,
you in your small corner
and I in mine.

129 Anon
Copyright control

Jesus Christ is alive today,
I know, I know it's true.
Sovereign of the universe,
I give Him homage due.
Seated there at God's right hand,
I am with Him in the promised land.
Jesus lives and reigns in me,
that's how I know it's true.

130 *Lyra Davidica*, 1708

1 **Jesus Christ is risen today, *hallelujah!***
our triumphant holy day, *hallelujah!*
who did once upon the cross, *hallelujah!*
suffer to redeem our loss, *hallelujah!*

2 Hymns of praise then let us sing,
hallelujah!
unto Christ our heavenly King, *hallelujah!*
who endured the cross and grave,
hallelujah!
sinners to redeem and save, *hallelujah!*

3 But the pains which He endured,
hallelujah!
our salvation have procured, *hallelujah!*
now in heaven above He's King,
hallelujah!
Where the angels ever sing, *'hallelujah!'*

131 From the German (15th century)
Michael Perry (1942–1996)
© Mrs B Perry / The Jubilate Group

1 **Jesus Christ the Lord is born,**
all the bells are ringing!
Angels greet the Holy One
and shepherds hear them singing,
and shepherds hear them singing.

2 'Go to Bethlehem today,
find your King and Saviour:
glory be to God on high,
to earth His peace and favour,
to earth His peace and favour!'

3 Held within a cattle stall,
loved by love maternal,
see the Master of us all,
our Lord of lords eternal,
our Lord of lords eternal!

4 Soon shall come the wise men three,
rousing Herod's anger;
mothers' hearts shall broken be
and Mary's Son in danger,
and Mary's Son in danger.

5 Death from life and life from death,
our salvation story;
let all living things give breath
to Christmas songs of glory,
to Christmas songs of glory!

132 Anon
Copyright control

Jesus died for all the children,
all the children of the world.
Red and yellow, black and white,
all are precious in His sight:
Jesus died for all the children of the world.

133 David Bolton
© 1975 Thankyou Music

Jesus, how lovely You are!
You are so gentle, so pure and kind,
You shine like the morning star:
Jesus, how lovely You are.

1 Alleluia, Jesus is my Lord and King;
alleluia, Jesus is my everything.
Jesus, how lovely . . .

2 Alleluia, Jesus died and rose again;
alleluia, Jesus forgave all my sin.
Jesus, how lovely . . .

3 Alleluia, Jesus is meek and lowly;
alleluia, Jesus is pure and holy.
Jesus, how lovely . . .

4 Alleluia, Jesus is the bridegroom;
alleluia, Jesus will take His bride soon.
Jesus, how lovely . . .

134 Margaret Cropper
© Stainer & Bell Ltd

1 **Jesus' hands were kind hands,**
doing good to all,
healing pain and sickness,
blessing children small,
washing tired feet
and saving those who fall;
Jesus' hands were kind hands
doing good to all.

2 Take my hands, Lord Jesus,
let them work for You,
make them strong and gentle,
kind in all I do.
Let me watch You, Jesus,
till I'm gentle too,
till my hands are kind hands,
quick to work for You.

135 Gordon Brattle (1917–91)
© D H Brattle

Jesus is knocking, patiently waiting,
outside your heart's closed door.
Do not reject Him, simply accept Him,
now and for evermore.

136 Paul Mazak
© 1974, 1975 Celebration /
Kingsway's Thankyou Music

1 **Jesus is a friend of mine,**
praise Him!
Jesus is a friend of mine,
praise Him!
Praise Him! Praise Him!
Jesus is a friend of mine,
praise Him!

2 Jesus died to set us free,
praise Him!
Jesus died to set us free,
praise Him!
Praise Him! Praise Him!
Jesus died to set us free,
praise Him!

3 Jesus is the King of kings,
praise Him!
Jesus is the King of kings,
praise Him!
Praise Him! Praise Him!
Jesus is the King of kings,
praise Him!

137 David J Mansell
© 1982 Authentic Publishing / CopyCare

1 **Jesus is Lord!**
    Creation's voice proclaims it,
for by His power each tree and flower
    was planned and made.
Jesus is Lord! The universe declares it;
sun, moon and stars in heaven cry:
    'Jesus is Lord!'
    Jesus is Lord! Jesus is Lord!
    Praise Him with hallelujahs,
    for Jesus is Lord!

2 Jesus is Lord! Yet from His throne eternal
in flesh He came to die in pain
    on Calvary's tree.
Jesus is Lord!
    From Him all life proceeding,
yet gave His life a ransom
    thus setting us free.
    Jesus is Lord . . .

3   Jesus is Lord!
        O'er sin the mighty conqueror,
    from death He rose and all His foes
        shall own His name.
    Jesus is Lord! God sends His Holy Spirit
    to show by works of power
        that Jesus is Lord.
        Jesus is Lord . . .

138 Roger Jones
© 1979 Christian Music Ministries /
Sovereign Music UK

Jesus, I will come with You,
I will follow in Your way.
I will trust You,
I will bring You all I have today.
Jesus, You're the way,
Jesus, You're the truth,
Jesus, You're the life,
praise Your name.

139 H W Rattle
© Scripture Union

Jesus' love is very wonderful,
Jesus' love is very wonderful,
Jesus' love is very wonderful,
O wonderful love!
So high you can't get over it,
so low you can't get under it,
so wide you can't get round it,
O wonderful love!

140 Anna Warner (1827–1915)

1   **Jesus loves me! this I know,**
    for the Bible tells me so.
    Little ones to Him belong;
    they are weak, but He is strong.
        Yes, Jesus loves me!
        Yes, Jesus loves me!
        Yes, Jesus loves me!
        The Bible tells me so.

2   Jesus loves me! He who died,
    heaven's gate to open wide;
    He will wash away my sin,
    let His little child come in.
        Yes, Jesus loves me . . .

3   Jesus loves me! He will stay
    close beside me all the way;
    then His little child will take
    up to heaven, for His dear sake.
        Yes, Jesus loves me . . .

141 Naida Hearn
© 1974 Scripture in Song / Maranatha! Music /
CopyCare

Jesus, name above all names,
beautiful Saviour, glorious Lord;
Emmanuel, God is with us,
blessèd Redeemer, living Word.

142 Anon
Copyright control

1   **Jesus said that whosoever will,**
    whosoever will, whosoever will,
    Jesus said that whosoever will,
    whosoever will may come.

2   I'm so glad that He included me,
    He included me, He included me,
    I'm so glad that He included me,
    when Jesus said that whosoever
        will may come.

143 Spiritual

    Joshua fit the battle of Jericho,
    Jericho, Jericho,
    Joshua fit the battle of Jericho
    and the walls came tumbling down.

1   You may talk about your king of Gideon,
    you may talk about your man of Saul,
    but there's none like good old Joshua
    at the battle of Jericho.

2 Up to the walls of Jericho
   he marched with spear in hand.
   'Go, blow them ram-horns,' Joshua cried,
   ''cause the battle am in my hand!'

3 Then the ram-sheep's horns began to
        blow,
   trumpets began to sound.
   Joshua commanded the children to shout
   and the walls came tumbling
        down that morning.
        Joshua fit the battle . . .

144 Anon
Copyright control

**Joy is the flag flown high from the castle
        of my heart,**
from the castle of my heart,
from the castle of my heart,
joy is the flag flown high from the castle
        of my heart
when the King is in residence there.
        So let it fly in the sky,
            let the whole world know,
        let the whole world know,
        let the whole world know,
        so let it fly in the sky,
            let the whole world know
        that the King is in residence there.

145 From Psalm 100, Fred Dunn (1909–79)
© 1977, 1980 Thankyou Music

Jubilate, everybody,
serve the Lord in all your ways, and
come before His presence singing:
enter now His courts with praise.
For the Lord our God is gracious,
and His mercy everlasting.
Jubilate, jubilate,
jubilate Deo!

146 Marianne Farningham (1834–1909)
altered © 1986 Horrobin/Leavers

1 **Just as I am, Your child to be,**
   friend of the young, who died for me,
   to give my life wholeheartedly,
   O Jesus Christ, I come.

2 While I am still a child today,
   I give my life, my work and play
   to Him alone, without delay,
   with all my heart I come.

3 I see in Jesus Christ the light,
   with Him as Lord, and in His might
   I turn from sin to what is right,
   My Lord, to You I come.

4 Lord, take my dreams of fame and gold,
   I accept now a life controlled
   by faith in You, as days unfold,
   with my whole life I come.

5 Just as I am, young, strong and free,
   to be the best that I can be,
   that others may see You in me,
   Lord of my life, I come.

147 Kate Barclay Wilkinson (1858–1928)
Copyright control

Keep me shining, Lord,
keep me shining, Lord,
in all I say or do,
that the world may see
Christ lives in me,
and learn to love Him too.

148 Sophie Conty and Naomi Batya
© 1980 Maranatha! Music / CopyCare

King of kings and Lord of lords,
        glory, hallelujah!
King of kings and Lord of lords,
        glory, hallelujah!
Jesus, Prince of peace,
        glory, hallelujah!
Jesus, Prince of peace,
        glory, hallelujah!

149
Traditional

1 **Kum ba yah, my Lord, kum ba yah,**
kum ba yah, my Lord, kum ba yah,
kum ba yah, my Lord, kum ba yah,
O Lord, kum ba yah.

2 Someone's crying, Lord . . .

3 Someone's singing, Lord . . .

4 Someone's praying, Lord . . .

5 Hear our prayer, O Lord, hear our prayer.
Keep our friends, O Lord, in Your care,
keep our friends, O Lord, in Your care,
O Lord, kum ba yah.

150
H Buffum Jr
Copyright control

Let's talk about Jesus,
the King of kings is He,
the Lord of lords, supreme
through all eternity,
the great I AM, the way, the truth,
the life, the door.
Let's talk about Jesus, more and more.

151
Graham Kendrick
© 1983 Make Way Music

1 **Led like a lamb to the slaughter,**
in silence and shame,
there on Your back You carried a world
of violence and pain.
Bleeding, dying, bleeding, dying.
You're alive,
You're alive,
You have risen!
Alleluia!
And the power
and the glory
is given,
Alleluia!
Jesus, to You.

2 At break of dawn, poor Mary,
still weeping she came,
when through her grief
she heard Your voice,
now speaking her name.
Mary! Master! Mary! Master!
You're alive . . .

3 At the right hand of the Father,
now seated on high,
You have begun Your eternal reign
of justice and joy.
Glory, glory, glory, glory.
You're alive . . .

152
James E Seddon (1915–83)
© 1969 Mavis Seddon / The Jubilate Group

1 **Let us praise God together,**
let us praise.
Let us praise God together,
Him proclaim.
He is faithful in all His ways,
He is worthy of all our praise,
His name be exalted on high.

2 Let us seek God together,
let us pray.
Let us seek His forgiveness
as we pray.
He will cleanse us from all sin,
He will help us the fight to win,
His name be exalted on high.

3 Let us serve God together,
let us serve.
Let our lives show His goodness
as we work.
Christ the Lord is the world's true light,
let us serve Him with all our might.
His name be exalted on high.

153 Marcus Uzilevsky
Copyright control

Live, live, live,
live, live, live,
Jesus is living in my soul.
Live, live, live,
live, live, live,
Jesus is living in my soul.

1   Hanging on the tree
    He prayed for you and me.
    Jesus is living in my soul.
    To His spirit yield –
    by His stripes we're healed.
    Jesus is living in my soul.
        Live, live, live . . .

2   He took me out of darkness
    and He set me free.
    Jesus is living in my soul.
    Once I was blind,
    now I can see.
    Jesus is living in my soul.
        Live, live, live . . .

3   Gonna shout and sing,
    let the hallelujah ring.
    Jesus is living in my soul.
    I'm gonna shout and sing,
    there's healing in His wing.
    Jesus is living in my soul.
        Live, live, live . . .

154 John Milton (1608–74)

1   **Let us with a gladsome mind**
    praise the Lord for He is kind;
        For His mercies still endure,
        ever faithful, ever sure.

2   He, with all-commanding might,
    filled the new-made world with light:
        For His mercies . . .

3   All things living He does feed,
    His full hand supplies their need:
        For His mercies . . .

4   Let us then with gladsome mind,
    praise the Lord for He is kind!
        For His mercies . . .

155 John Fawcett (1740–1817)
altered © 1986 Horrobin/Leavers

1   **Lord, dismiss us with Your blessing,**
    fill our hearts with joy and peace.
    Let us each, Your love possessing,
    triumph in redeeming grace.
    O refresh us, O refresh us
    as to serve we leave this place.

2   Thanks we give and adoration
    for Your gospel's joyful sound;
    may the fruits of Your salvation
    in our hearts and lives abound;
    so Your presence, so Your presence
    will with us be always found.

156 Patrick Appleford
© 1960 Josef Weinberger Ltd

1   **Lord Jesus Christ,**
        You have come to us,
    You are one with us, Mary's Son;
    cleansing our souls from all their sin,
    pouring Your love and goodness in:
    Jesus, our love for You we sing –
        living Lord!

2   Lord Jesus Christ, now and every day
    teach us how to pray, Son of God;
    You have commanded us to do
    this in remembrance, Lord, of You:
    into our lives
        Your power breaks through –
        living Lord!

3   Lord Jesus Christ, You have come to us,
    born as one of us, Mary's Son;
    led out to die on Calvary,
    risen from death to set us free:
    living Lord Jesus, help us see
        You are Lord!

4   Lord Jesus Christ, I would come to You,
    live my life for You, Son of God;
    all Your commands I know are true,
    Your many gifts will make me new:
    into my life Your power breaks through –
        living Lord!

157
Jan Struther (1901–53)
From *Enlarged Songs of Praise*
by permission of Oxford University Press

1 **Lord of all hopefulness, Lord of all joy,**
whose trust, ever childlike,
   no cares could destroy,
be there at our waking,
   and give us, we pray,
Your bliss in our hearts, Lord,
   at the break of the day.

2 Lord of all eagerness, Lord of all faith,
whose strong hands were skilled
   at the plane and the lathe,
be there at our labours,
   and give us, we pray,
Your strength in our hearts, Lord,
   at the noon of the day.

3 Lord of all kindliness, Lord of all grace,
Your hand swift to welcome,
   Your arms to embrace,
be there at our homing,
   and give us, we pray,
Your love in our hearts, Lord,
   at the eve of the day.

4 Lord of all gentleness, Lord of all calm,
whose voice is contentment,
   whose presence is balm,
be there at our sleeping,
   and give us, we pray,
Your peace in our hearts, Lord,
   at the end of the day.

158 © 1986 Andy Silver

Love, joy, peace and patience, kindness,
goodness, meekness, faith, self-control.
These are the fruit of God's Holy Spirit
and against such there is no law.
Those who belong to Christ should now
   live this way,
walking in the Spirit each day,
so praise Him, praise Him,
   give Him all the glory,
walking in the Spirit each day.

159
Robert Lowry (1826–99)

1 **Low in the grave He lay,**
Jesus, my Saviour;
waiting the coming day,
Jesus, my Lord.
   Up from the grave He arose,
   with a mighty triumph o'er His foes;
   He arose a victor from the dark domain,
   and He lives for ever
      with His saints to reign:
   He arose! He arose! Hallelujah!
      Christ arose!

2 Vainly they watch His bed,
Jesus, my Saviour;
vainly they seal the dead,
Jesus, my Lord.
   Up from the grave . . .

3 Death cannot keep his prey,
Jesus, my Saviour,
He tore the bars away,
Jesus, my Lord.
   Up from the grave . . .

160
Jack Hayford
© 1981 Brentwood Benson Catalogue

Majesty, worship His majesty;
unto Jesus be glory, honour and praise.
Majesty, kingdom authority,
   flows from His throne
unto His own, His anthem raise.
So exalt, lift up on high the name of Jesus,
magnify, come, glorify Christ Jesus the King.
Majesty, worship His majesty,
Jesus who died, now glorified,
   King of all kings.

161
Sebastian Temple
© 1967 OCP Publications

1 **Make me a channel of Your peace.**
Where there is hatred
   let me bring Your love;
where there is injury, Your pardon, Lord;
and where there's doubt, true faith in You.

O Master, grant that I may never seek
so much to be consoled as to console;
to be understood as to understand;
to be loved, as to love with all my soul.

2   Make me a channel of Your peace.
    Where there's despair in life
        let me bring hope;
    where there is darkness, only light;
    and where there's sadness, ever joy.
        O Master . . .

3   Make me a channel of Your peace.
    It is in pardoning that we are pardoned,
    in giving to all men that we receive;
    and in dying that we're born to eternal life.

162   Kelly Willard
© 1982 Maranatha! Music / CCCM Music /
CopyCare

Make me a servant, humble and meek.
Lord, let me lift up those who are weak.
And may the prayer of my heart always be:
'Make me a servant, make me a servant,
make me a servant today.'

163   R Hudson Pope (1879–1967)
© Scripture Gift Mission

Make the book live to me, O Lord,
show me Yourself within Your word,
show me myself and show me my Saviour
and make the book live to me.

164   © 1986 Andy Silver

Mary had a little baby,
    Mary had a little baby;
here and there and everywhere
    the angels sang:
'Praise the Lord!'
Mary had a little baby, Mary had a little baby;
here and there and everywhere
    the angels sang:
'Praise the Lord!'

Glory, glory, glory, glory,
everybody sing the song.
Glory, glory, glory, glory,
God's Son has come to earth.

Mary had a little baby, Mary had a little baby;
here and there and everywhere
    the angels sang:
'Praise the Lord!'

165   Kate Barclay Wilkinson (1859–1928)
Copyright control

1   **May the mind of Christ my Saviour**
    live in me from day to day,
    by His love and power controlling
    all I do or say.

2   May the word of God dwell richly
    in my heart from hour to hour,
    so that all may see I triumph
    only through His power.

3   May the peace of God my Father
    rule my life in everything,
    that I may be calm to comfort
    sick and sorrowing.

4   May the love of Jesus fill me,
    as the waters fill the sea;
    Him uplifting, self denying,
    this is victory.

5   May I run the race before me,
    strong and brave onward I go,
    looking only unto Jesus,
    as in Him I grow.

166   Eleanor Farjeon (1881–1965)
© David Higham Associates Ltd

1   **Morning has broken**
    like the first morning;
    blackbird has spoken
    like the first bird.
    Praise for the singing!
    Praise for the morning!
    Praise for them, springing
    fresh from the Word!

2 Mine is the sunlight!
   Mine is the morning,
   here in the bright light
   of this fair day!
   Praise with elation,
   praise every morning
   God's re-creation
   of the new day!

167 Anon
Copyright control

1 **Mister Noah built an ark,**
   the people thought it such a lark.
   Mister Noah pleaded so,
   but into the ark they would not go.
   Down came the rain in torrents
       (splish, splash),
   down came the rain in torrents
       (splish, splash),
   down came the rain in torrents,
   and only eight were saved.

2 The animals went in two by two,
   elephant, giraffe and kangaroo.
   All were safely stowed away
   on that great and awful day.
   Down came the rain . . .

   Whenever you see a rainbow,
   whenever you see a rainbow,
   whenever you see a rainbow,
   remember God is love.

168 Thomas Toke Lynch (1818–71)
altered © 1986 Horrobin/Leavers

1 **My faith is like a staff of oak,**
   the traveller's well-loved aid;
   my faith, it is a weapon strong,
   the soldier's trusty blade.
   I'll travel on, and still be stirred
   to action at my Master's word;
   by all life's perils undeterred,
   a soldier unafraid.

2 My faith is like a staff of oak,
   O let me on it lean!
   My faith, it is a sharpened sword,
   may falsehood find it keen!
   Now fill me with Your Spirit, Lord,
   teach and change me through Your word,
   and by Your love may I be stirred,
   as all true saints have been.

169 Anon
Copyright control

1 **My God is so big, so strong**
   and so mighty
   there's nothing that He cannot do.
   My God is so big, so strong
       and so mighty
   there's nothing that He cannot do.
   The rivers are His, the mountains are His,
   the stars are His handiwork too.
   My God is so big, so strong
       and so mighty
   there's nothing that He cannot do.

2 My God is so big, so strong
       and so mighty
   there's nothing that He cannot do.
   My God is so big, so strong
       and so mighty
   there's nothing that He cannot do.
   He's called you to live for Him every day
   in all that you say and you do.
   My God is so big, so strong
       and so mighty,
   He can do all things through you.

170 Ian Smale
© 1981 Thankyou Music

My Lord is higher than a mountain,
He is stronger than an army,
He is wiser than any man can tell.
My Lord is faster than a rocket,
can see more than a telescope,
is bigger than the universe as well.
His love is warmer than the burning sun,
closer than the nearest friend,
more real than any truth can be.
My Lord, He knows about the past,
and He knows about the future,
and He also knows all about me.

171 John Keble (1792–1866)

1 **New every morning is the love**
   our waking and uprising prove:
   through sleep and darkness
        safely brought,
   restored to life and power and thought.

2 New mercies, each returning day,
   surround Your people as they pray:
   new dangers past, new sins forgiven,
   new thoughts of God,
        new hopes of heaven.

3 If in our daily life our mind
   be set to honour all we find,
   new treasures still, of countless price,
   God will provide for sacrifice.

4 The trivial round, the common task,
   will give us all we ought to ask:
   room to deny ourselves, a road
   to bring us daily nearer God.

5 Prepare us, Lord, in Your dear love
   for perfect rest with You above,
   and help us, this and every day,
   to grow more like You as we pray.

172 J H Cansdale (d 1995)
© Michael Cansdale
altered 1985 Horrobin/Leavers

Now be strong and very courageous,
for I have commanded you.
Be not afraid,
be not dismayed;
you will have victory.
I will be with you unto the end,
captain and leader,
guide and friend.

173 Sabine Baring-Gould (1834–1924)
altered © 1986 Horrobin/Leavers

1 **Now the day is over,**
   night will soon be here,
   help me to remember
   You are always near.

2 As the darkness gathers,
   stars shine overhead,
   creatures, birds and flowers
   rest their weary heads.

3 Father, give all people
   calm and peaceful rest;
   through Your gracious presence
   may our sleep be blessed.

4 Comfort every sufferer
   watching late in pain;
   those who plan some evil
   from their sin restrain.

5 When the morning wakes me,
   ready for the day,
   help me, Lord, to serve You,
   walking in Your way.

6 Glory to the Father,
   glory to the Son,
   and to the Holy Spirit,
   blessing everyone.

174
J M C Crum (1872–1958)
From the *Oxford Book of Carols*
by permission of Oxford University Press

1 **Now the green blade riseth**
   from the buried grain,
   wheat that in the dark earth
      many days has lain.
   Love lives again,
      that with the dead has been.
   Love is come again,
      like wheat that springeth green.

2 In the grave they laid Him,
      Love whom men had slain,
   thinking that never He would wake again.
   Laid in the earth like grain
      that sleeps unseen,
   Love is come again,
      like wheat that springeth green.

3 Forth He came at Easter,
      like the risen grain,
   He that for three days
      in the grave had lain.
   Quick from the dead
      my risen Lord is seen;
   Love is come again,
      like wheat that springeth green.

4 When our hearts are wintry,
      grieving or in pain,
   Your touch can call us back to life again.
   Fields of our hearts
      that dead and bare have been;
   Love is come again,
      like wheat that springeth green.

175
Martin Rinkart (1586–1649)
tr. Catherine Winkworth (1829–78)
altered © 1986 Horrobin/Leavers

1 **Now thank we all our God,**
   with hearts, and hands, and voices;
   who wondrous things has done,
   in whom His world rejoices;
   who, from our mothers' arms,
   has blessed us on our way
   with countless gifts of love,
   and still is ours today.

2 We thank You, then, O God
   that through our life You're near us,
   for joy that fills our hearts,
   which, with Your peace, restores us.
   Lord, keep us in Your grace,
   and guide us when perplexed,
   that we may love Your ways,
   in this world and the next.

3 All praise and thanks to God
   the Father now be given,
   the Son, and Him who reigns
   with Them in highest heaven;
   the one eternal God,
   whom earth and heaven adore;
   for thus it was, is now,
   and shall be evermore.

176
From the Latin (18th century)
tr. Frederick Oakley (1802–80)
altered © 1986 Horrobin/Leavers

1 **O come, all you faithful,**
   joyful and triumphant,
   O come now, O come now to Bethlehem;
   come and behold Him,
   born the King of angels:
      O come, let us adore Him,
      O come, let us adore Him,
      O come, let us adore Him,
      Christ the Lord!

2 True God of true God,
   light of light eternal,
   He, who abhors not the virgin's womb;
   Son of the Father,
   begotten not created:
      O come, let us adore Him . . .

3 Sing like the angels,
   sing in exultation,
   sing with the citizens of heaven above,
   'Glory to God,
   glory in the highest':
      O come, let us adore Him . . .

4 Yes, Lord, we greet You,
   born that happy morning,
   Jesus, to You be glory given!
   Word of the Father,
   then in flesh appearing:
      O come, let us adore Him . . .

177
From the Latin (12th century)
tr. John Mason Neale (1818–66)
© in this version The Jubilate Group

1 **O come, O come, Emmanuel,**
and ransom captive Israel,
who mourns in lonely exile here
until the Son of God draws near.
Rejoice, rejoice! Emmanuel
shall come to you, O Israel.

2 O come, true Branch of Jesse, free
Your children from this tyranny;
from depths of hell Your people save,
to rise victorious from the grave.
Rejoice, rejoice . . .

3 O come, bright Daybreak, come and
cheer
our spirits by Your advent here;
dispel the long night's lingering gloom
and pierce the shadows of the tomb.
Rejoice, rejoice . . .

4 O come, strong key of David, come
and open wide our heavenly home;
make safe the path that leads on high,
and close the path to misery.
Rejoice, rejoice . . .

5 O come, O come, great Lord of might,
who long ago on Sinai's height
gave all Your tribes the ancient law
in cloud and majesty and awe.
Rejoice, rejoice . . .

178
Philip Doddridge (1702–51)
altered © 1986 Horrobin/Leavers

1 **O happy day! that fixed my choice**
on You, my Saviour and my God!
Well may this grateful heart rejoice,
and tell of Christ's redeeming blood.
O happy day! O happy day!
when Jesus washed my sins away;
He taught me how to watch and pray,
and live rejoicing every day;
(hallelujah!)
O happy day! O happy day!
when Jesus washed my sins away.

2 It's done, the great transaction's done!
I am my Lord's and He is mine!
He led me, and I followed on,
responding to the voice divine.
O happy day . . .

3 Now rest, my long-divided heart,
in Jesus Christ who loves you, rest;
and never from your Lord depart,
enriched by Him, by Him possessed.
O happy day . . .

4 So God, who heard the solemn vow,
in daily prayer shall hear my voice,
till in my final breath I bow,
and bless the day that fixed my choice.
O happy day . . .

179
Russian hymn
tr. Stuart Wesley Keene Hine (1899–1989)
© 1953 Thankyou Music

1 **O Lord my God!**
when I in awesome wonder
consider all the works
Thy hand hath made,
I see the stars, I hear the mighty thunder,
the power throughout the universe
displayed;
Then sings my soul,
my Saviour God, to Thee,
how great Thou art, how great Thou art!
Then sings my soul,
my Saviour God, to Thee,
how great Thou art, how great Thou art!

2 When through the woods
and forest glades I wander
and hear the birds sing sweetly
in the trees;
when I look down
from lofty mountain grandeur,
and hear the brook,
and feel the gentle breeze;
Then sings my soul . . .

3 And when I think
    that God, His Son not sparing,
sent Him to die – I scarce can take it in,
that on the cross
    my burden gladly bearing,
He bled and died to take away my sin:
    Then sings my soul . . .

4 When Christ shall come
    with shout of acclamation
and take me home –
    what joy shall fill my heart!
Then shall I bow in humble adoration
and there proclaim,
    my God, how great Thou art!
    Then sings my soul . . .

180 Anon
Copyright control

O! O! O! how good is the Lord,
O! O! O! how good is the Lord,
O! O! O! how good is the Lord,
I never will forget
    what He has done for me.

1 He gives me salvation,
    how good is the Lord,
He gives me salvation,
    how good is the Lord,
He gives me salvation,
    how good is the Lord,
I never will forget
    what He has done for me.
    O! O! O! . . .

2 He gives me His blessings . . .
    O! O! O! . . .

3 He gives me His Spirit . . .
    O! O! O! . . .

4 He gives me His healing . . .
    O! O! O! . . .

5 He gives me His glory . . .
    O! O! O! . . .

OTHER SUITABLE VERSES MAY BE ADDED
He gives us each other . . .
He gives us His body . . .
He gives us His freedom . . . *etc.*

181 William Reed Newell (1868–1956)
Copyright control

O the love that drew salvation's plan!
O the grace that brought it down to man!
O the mighty gulf that God did span
    at Calvary.
Mercy there was great and grace was free,
pardon there was multiplied to me,
there my burdened soul found liberty,
    at Calvary.

182 Phillips Brooks (1835–93)

1 **O little town of Bethlehem,**
    how still we see you lie!
Above your deep and dreamless sleep
    the silent stars go by:
yet in your dark streets shining
    is everlasting light;
the hopes and fears of all the years
    are met in you tonight.

2 O morning stars, together
    proclaim the holy birth,
and praises sing to God the King,
    and peace to men on earth.
For Christ is born of Mary;
    and, gathered all above,
while mortals sleep, the angels keep
    their watch of wondering love.

3 How silently, how silently,
    the wondrous gift is given!
So God imparts to human hearts
    the blessings of His heaven.
No ear may hear His coming;
    but in this world of sin,
where meek souls will receive Him, still
    the dear Christ enters in.

4 O holy Child of Bethlehem,
    descend to us, we pray;
cast out our sin, and enter in;
    be born in us today.
We hear the Christmas angels
    the great glad tidings tell;
O come to us, abide with us,
    our Lord Immanuel.

183
A W Edsor
© Thankyou Music

On Calvary's tree He died for me,
that I His love might know.
To set me free He died for me –
that's why I love Him so.

184 Traditional

1 **Oh, the Lord looked down
    from His window in the sky,**
  said, 'I created man
      but I can't remember why!
  Nothing but fighting since creation day.
  I'll send a little water
      and wash them all away.'
  Oh, the Lord came down and looked
      around a spell.
  There was Mr Noah behaving mighty well.
  And that is the reason,
      the Scriptures record,
  Noah found grace in the eyes of the Lord.
    *Noah found grace in the eyes
      of the Lord,
    Noah found grace in the eyes
      of the Lord,
    Noah found grace in the eyes
      of the Lord,
    and He left him high and dry.*

2 The Lord said, 'Noah, there's going
      to be a flood,
  there's going to be some water,
      there's going to be some mud.
  So take off your hat, Noah,
      take off your coat,
  get Shem and Ham and Japheth
      and build yourself a boat.'
  Noah said, 'Lord, I don't believe I could.'
  The Lord said, 'Noah, get yourself
      some wood.
  You never know what you can do
      till you try.
  Build it fifty cubits wide
      and thirty cubits high.'
    Noah found grace . . .

3 Noah said, 'There she is,
      there she is, Lord!'
  The Lord said, 'Noah, it's time
      to get aboard.
  Take of each creature a he and a she,
  and of course take Mrs Noah
      and the whole family.'
  Noah said, 'Lord, it's getting mighty dark.'
  The Lord said, 'Noah, get those creatures
      in the ark.'
  Noah said, 'Lord, it's beginning to pour.'
  The Lord said, 'Noah, hurry up
      and close the door.'
    Noah found grace . . .

4 The ark rose up
      on the bosom of the deep.
  After forty days Mr Noah took a peep.
  He said, 'We're not moving, Lord,
      where are we at?'
  The Lord said, 'You're sitting right
      on Mount Ararat.'
  Noah said, 'Lord,
      it's getting nice and dry.'
  The Lord said, 'Noah, see my rainbow
      in the sky.
  Take all your creatures
      and people the earth,
  and be sure you're not more trouble
      than you're worth.'
    Noah found grace . . .

185 Cecil Frances Alexander (1818–95)

1 **Once in royal David's city,**
    stood a lowly cattle shed,
    where a mother laid her baby,
    in a manger for His bed.
    Mary was that mother mild,
    Jesus Christ her little child.

2 He came down to earth from heaven,
    who is God and Lord of all;
    and His shelter was a stable,
    and His cradle was a stall:
    with the poor and mean and lowly
    lived on earth our Saviour holy.

3 And through all His wondrous childhood
  He would honour and obey,
  love, and watch the lowly mother,
  in whose gentle arms He lay:
  Christian children all should be,
  kind, obedient, good as He.

4 For He is our childhood's pattern:
  day by day like us He grew;
  He was little, weak, and helpless,
  tears and smiles like us He knew;
  and He feels for all our sadness,
  and He shares in all our gladness.

5 And our eyes at last shall see Him,
  through His own redeeming love;
  for that child, so dear and gentle,
  is our Lord in heaven above;
  and He leads His children on
  to the place where He is gone.

6 Not in that poor lowly stable,
  with the oxen standing by,
  we shall see Him, but in heaven,
  set at God's right hand on high;
  there His children gather round,
  bright like stars, with glory crowned.

186 Charles Coffin (1676–1749)
       tr. John Chandler (1806–76)
       altered © 1986 Horrobin/Leavers

1 **On Jordan's bank the Baptist's cry**
  announces that the Lord is nigh;
  come then and listen for he brings
  glad tidings from the King of kings.

2 Then cleansed be every heart from sin;
  make straight the way for God within;
  prepare we in our hearts a home,
  where such a mighty guest may come.

3 For You are our salvation, Lord,
  our refuge and our great reward;
  without Your grace we waste away,
  like flowers that wither and decay.

4 To Him who left the throne of heaven
  to save mankind, all praise be given;
  to God the Father, voices raise,
  and Holy Spirit, let us praise.

187 J Wilbur Chapman (1859–1918)

1 **One day when heaven was filled
     with His praises,**
  one day when sin
     was as black as could be,
  Jesus came down to be born of a virgin,
  lived among men, my example is He!
     Living, He loved me;
        dying, He saved me;
     buried, He carried my sins far away,
     rising, He justified freely for ever:
     one day He's coming: O glorious day.

2 One day they led Him
     up Calvary's mountain,
  one day they nailed Him
     to die on the tree;
  suffering anguish, despised and rejected;
  bearing our sins, my Redeemer is He!
     Living, He loved me . . .

3 One day they left Him alone
     in the garden,
  one day He rested, from suffering free;
  angels came down o'er His tomb
     to keep vigil;
  hope of the hopeless, my Saviour is He!
     Living, He loved me . . .

4 One day the grave could conceal Him
     no longer,
  one day the stone rolled away
     from the door;
  then He arose,
     over death He had conquered;
  now is ascended, my Lord evermore!
     Living, He loved me . . .

5 One day the trumpet will sound
     for His coming,
  one day the skies with His glory will shine;
  wonderful day, my beloved ones bringing;
  glorious Saviour, this Jesus is mine!
     Living, He loved me . . .

188 Sydney Carter
© 1971 Stainer & Bell Ltd

1 **One more step along the world I go,**
one more step along the world I go,
from the old things to the new
keep me travelling along with You.
    And it's from the old I travel to the new,
    keep me travelling along with You.

2 Round the corners of the world I turn,
more and more about the world I learn.
And the new things that I see
You'll be looking at along with me.
    And it's from the old . . .

3 As I travel through the bad and good
keep me travelling the way I should.
Where I see no way to go
You'll be telling me the way, I know.
    And it's from the old . . .

4 Give me courage
    when the world is rough,
keep me loving,
    though the world is tough.
Leap and sing in all I do,
keep me travelling along with You.
    And it's from the old . . .

5 You are older than the world can be.
You are younger than the life in me.
Ever old and ever new,
keep me travelling along with you.
    And it's from the old . . .

189 Lisa Mazak
© 1974, 1975 Celebration / Thankyou Music

    One, two, three, Jesus loves me.
    One, two, Jesus loves you.

1 Three, four, He loves you more
than you've ever been loved before.
    One, two, three . . .

2 Five, six, seven, we're going to heaven.
Eight, nine, it's truly divine.
    One, two, three . . .

3 Nine, ten, it's time to end,
but instead we'll sing it again
LAST TIME
(there's no time to sing it again).

190 Anon
Copyright control

Only a boy called David,
only a rippling brook;
only a boy called David,
five little stones he took.
Then one little stone went in the sling,
and the sling went round and round,
one little stone went in the sling,
and the sling went round and round.
Round and round and round and round
and round and round and round;
one little stone went up, up, up,
and the giant came tumbling down!

191 © Roland Meredith

1 **Our eyes have seen the glory**
of our Saviour, Christ the Lord;
He is seated at His Father's side
in love and full accord;
from there upon the sons of men
His Spirit is outpoured,
all hail, ascended King!
    Glory, glory, hallelujah,
    glory, glory, hallelujah,
    glory, glory, hallelujah,
    all hail, ascended King!

2 He came to earth at Christmas
and was made a man like us;
He taught, He healed, He suffered –
and they nailed Him to the cross;
He rose again on Easter Day –
our Lord victorious,
all hail, ascended King!
    Glory, glory . . .

3 The good news of His kingdom
   must be preached to every shore,
   the news of peace and pardon,
   and the end of strife and war;
   the secret of His kingdom
   is to serve Him evermore,
   all hail, ascended King!
   Glory, glory . . .

4 His kingdom is a family
   of men of every race,
   they live their lives in harmony,
   enabled by His grace;
   they follow His example
   till they see Him face to face,
   all hail, ascended King!
   Glory, glory . . .

192 © 1979 Stainer & Bell / The Methodist Church Division of Education and Youth

1 **Our Father who is in heaven,**
   hallowed be Your name,
   Your kingdom come, Your will be done,
   hallowed be Your name.

2 On earth as it is in heaven,
   hallowed be Your name,
   give us this day our daily bread,
   hallowed be Your name.

3 Forgive us all our trespasses,
   hallowed be Your name,
   as we forgive those
        who trespass against us,
   hallowed be Your name.

4 And lead us not into temptation,
   hallowed be Your name,
   but deliver us from all that is evil,
   hallowed be Your name.

5 For Yours is the kingdom,
        the power and the glory,
   hallowed be Your name,
   for ever and for ever and ever,
   hallowed be Your name.

6 Amen, amen, it shall be so,
   hallowed be Your name,
   amen, amen, it shall be so,
   hallowed be Your name.

193 Eric A Thorn © Christian Music Ministries

1 **Our harvest day is over
   for yet another year.**
   The gifts we've brought to Jesus
        are now before us here.
   Before we go, again we raise
        our thanks to God above
   for all that He provides us with
        from His great hand of love.

2 We thank God for providing
        fresh air for us to breathe.
   Thirst-quenching water, also,
        to us He does bequeath.
   Fresh fruit and daily bread as well
        are gifts from God above,
   tinned foods, and eggs, and poultry
        come from our great God of love.

3 Our clothes and health come also
        from God's all-gracious hand;
   our happiness is something
        which He again has planned.
   But something more important still
        comes to us through God's love –
   eternal life, through His dear Son;
        all praise to God above.
        All praise to God above!

194 Spiritual

   O sinner man, where will you run to,
   O sinner man, where will you run to,
   O sinner man, where will you run to,
   all on that day?

1 Run to the rocks, rocks,
        won't you hide me,
   run to the rocks, rocks,
        won't you hide me,
   run to the rocks, rocks,
        won't you hide me,
   all on that day?
        O sinner man . . .

2 Run to the sea, sea is a-boiling,
run to the sea, sea is a-boiling,
run to the sea, sea is a-boiling,
all on that day.
O sinner man . . .

3 Run to the Lord, Lord, won't you hide me,
run to the Lord, Lord, won't you hide me,
run to the Lord, Lord, won't you hide me,
all on that day?
O sinner man . . .

4 O sinner man, should bin a-praying,
O sinner man, should bin a-praying,
O sinner man, should bin a-praying,
all on that day.
O sinner man . . .

195 Traditional

1 **O when the saints go marching in,**
O when the saints go marching in,
O Lord, I want to be among the number
when the saints go marching in!

2 O when they crown Him Lord of all,
O when they crown Him Lord of all,
O Lord, I want to be among the number
when they crown Him Lord of all.

3 O when all knees bow at His name,
O when all knees bow at His name,
O Lord, I want to be among the number
when all knees bow at His name.

4 O when they sing the Saviour's praise,
O when they sing the Saviour's praise,
O Lord, I want to be among the number
when they sing the Saviour's praise.

5 O when the saints go marching in,
O when the saints go marching in,
O Lord, I want to be among the number
when the saints go marching in!

196 Graham Kendrick
© 1979 Thankyou Music

1 **Peace I give to you,**
I give to you My peace;
peace I give to you,
I give to you My peace.
Let it flow to one another,
let it flow, let it flow;
let it flow to one another,
let it flow, let it flow.

2 Love I give to you, I give to you My love;
love I give to you, I give to you My love.
Let it flow . . .

3 Hope I give to you, I give to you My hope;
hope I give to you, I give to you My hope.
Let it flow . . .

4 Joy I give to you, I give to you My joy;
joy I give to you, I give to you My joy.
Let it flow . . .

197 Anon
Copyright control

1 **Peter and James and John in a**
sailboat,
Peter and James and John in a sailboat,
Peter and James and John in a sailboat,
out on the beautiful sea.

2 They fished all night
but they caught nothing,
they fished all night
but they caught nothing,
they fished all night
but they caught nothing,
out on the beautiful sea.

3 Along came Jesus walking on the water,
along came Jesus walking on the water,
along came Jesus walking on the water,
out on the beautiful sea.

4 He said, 'Throw your nets over
on the other side!'
He said, 'Throw your nets over
on the other side!'
He said, 'Throw your nets over
on the other side!'
out on the beautiful sea.

5 The nets were filled with great big fishes,
the nets were filled with great big fishes,
the nets were filled with great big fishes,
out on the beautiful sea.

6 The lesson of this story is,
'listen to the Lord',
the lesson of this story is,
'listen to the Lord',
the lesson of this story is,
'listen to the Lord',
wherever you may be.

praise Him on the loud cymbals,
praise Him on the loud cymbals;
let everything that has breath
praise the Lord!

Hallelujah, praise the Lord;
hallelujah, praise the Lord:
let everything that has breath
praise the Lord!

Hallelujah, praise the Lord;
hallelujah, praise the Lord:
let everything that has breath
praise the Lord!

198 Anon
Copyright control

1 **Peter and John went to pray,**
they met a lame man on the way;
he asked for alms and held out his palms,
and this is what Peter did say:

2 'Silver and gold have I none,
but such as I have I give you.
In the name of Jesus Christ of Nazareth,
rise up and walk!'

3 He went walking and leaping
and praising God,
walking and leaping and praising God.
'In the name of Jesus Christ of Nazareth,
rise up and walk!'

199 Thomas Ken (1637–1711)

Praise God from whom all blessings flow;
praise Him all creatures here below,
praise Him above, you heavenly hosts;
praise Father, Son, and Holy Ghost.

200 John Kennett
© 1981 Thankyou Music

Praise Him on the trumpet,
the psaltery and harp;
praise Him on the timbrel and the dance;
praise Him with stringed instruments too;

201 Anon, c1890
Copyright control

1 **Praise Him, praise Him,**
all you little children,
God is love, God is love.
Praise Him, praise Him,
all you little children,
God is love, God is love.

2 Love Him, love Him, all you little children,
God is love, God is love.
Love Him, love Him, all you little children,
God is love, God is love.

3 Thank Him, thank Him,
all you little children,
God is love, God is love.
Thank Him, thank Him,
all you little children,
God is love, God is love.

202 Anon
Copyright control

1 **Praise Him, praise Him,**
praise Him in the morning,
praise Him in the noontime,
praise Him, praise Him,
praise Him as the sun goes down.

2 Thank Him . . .

3 Love Him . . .

4 Serve Him . . .

203 Fanny J Crosby (1820–1915)
altered © 1986 Horrobin/Leavers

1 **Praise Him, praise Him!**
      Jesus, our blessèd Redeemer!
   Sing, O earth –
      His wonderful love proclaim!
   Hail Him, hail Him!
      highest archangels in glory;
   strength and honour
      give to his holy name!
   Like a shepherd,
      Jesus will guard His children,
   in His arms He carries them all day long.
      Praise Him, praise Him!
      tell of His excellent greatness;
      praise Him, praise Him
      ever in joyful song!

2 Praise Him, praise Him!
      Jesus, our blessèd Redeemer!
   For our sins He suffered,
      and bled, and died;
   He – our rock,
      our hope of eternal salvation,
   hail Him, hail Him! Jesus the crucified!
   Sound His praises –
      Jesus who bore our sorrows,
   love unbounded, wonderful,
      deep and strong.
      Praise Him . . .

3 Praise Him, praise Him!
      Jesus, our blessèd Redeemer!
   All in heaven, let their hosannas ring!
   Jesus, Saviour, reigning for ever and ever:
   crown Him, crown Him!
      Prophet, and Priest, and King!
   Christ is coming,
      over the world victorious,
   power and glory unto the Lord belong.
      Praise Him . . .

204 Henry Francis Lyte (1793–1847)

1 **Praise, my soul, the King of heaven;**
   to His feet your worship bring;
   ransomed, healed, restored, forgiven,
   we do now His praises sing.
      Praise Him! Praise Him!
      Praise Him! Praise Him!
   Praise the everlasting King.

2 Praise Him for His grace and favour
   to our fathers, in distress;
   praise Him, still the same for ever;
   merciful, He waits to bless.
      Praise Him! Praise Him!
      Praise Him! Praise Him!
   Glorious in His faithfulness.

3 Father-like He loves and spares us;
   well our weaknesses He knows;
   in His hands He gently bears us,
   rescues us from all our foes.
      Praise Him! Praise Him!
      Praise Him! Praise Him!
   Widely as His mercy flows.

4 Angels, help us to adore Him;
   you behold Him face to face;
   sun and moon, bow down before Him;
   dwellers all in time and space.
      Praise Him! Praise Him!
      Praise Him! Praise Him!
   Praise with us the God of grace.

205 Estelle White
© McCrimmon Publishing Co Ltd

Praise to the Lord our God,
      let us sing together,
lifting our hearts and our voices to sing
      with joy and gladness.
Come along, along, along
      and sing with praise.

206

This song has been withdrawn
for copyright-related reasons

207 Percy Dearmer (1867–1936)
© Oxford University Press

1 **Remember all the people**
   who live in far off lands,
   in strange and lovely cities,
   or roam the desert sands,
   or farm the mountain pastures,
   or till the endless plains
   where children wade through rice fields
   and watch the camel trains.

2 Some work in sultry forests
   where apes swing to and fro,
   some fish in mighty rivers,
   some hunt across the snow.
   Remember all God's children
   who yet have never heard
   the truth that comes from Jesus,
   the glory of His word.

3 God bless the men and women
   who serve Him oversea:
   God raise up more to help them
   to set the nations free,
   till all the distant people
   in every foreign place
   shall understand His kingdom
   and come into His grace.

208 From Philippians 4
Copyright control

Rejoice in the Lord always,
and again I say rejoice!
Rejoice in the Lord always,
and again I say rejoice!
Rejoice, rejoice, and again I say rejoice!
Rejoice, rejoice, and again I say rejoice!

209 Henry Hart Milman (1791–1868)
© in this version The Jubilate Group

1 **Ride on, ride on in majesty**
   as all the crowds, 'Hosanna!' cry:
   through waving branches slowly ride,
   O Saviour, to be crucified.

2 Ride on, ride on in majesty,
   in lowly pomp ride on to die:
   O Christ, your triumph now begin
   with captured death and conquered sin!

3 Ride on, ride on in majesty –
   the angel armies of the sky
   look down with sad and wondering eyes
   to see the approaching sacrifice.

4 Ride on, ride on in majesty,
   the last and fiercest foe defy:
   the Father on His sapphire throne
   awaits His own anointed Son.

5 Ride on, ride on in majesty,
   in lowly pomp ride on to die:
   bow Your meek head to mortal pain,
   then take, O God, Your power and reign!

210 Traditional

   Rise and shine and give God
      His glory, glory,
   rise and shine and give God
      His glory, glory,
   rise and shine and give God
      His glory, glory,
   children of the Lord.

1 The Lord said to Noah,
      'There's gonna be a floody, floody.'
   Lord said to Noah,
      'There's gonna be a floody, floody.
   Get those children out of the muddy,
      muddy,
   children of the Lord.'
      Rise and shine . . .

2 The Lord told Noah to build Him
      an arky, arky,
   the Lord told Noah to build Him
      an arky, arky,
   build it out of gopher barky, barky,
   children of the Lord.
      Rise and shine . . .

3 The animals, the animals,
    they came on by twosies, twosies,
the animals, the animals,
    they came on by twosies, twosies,
elephants and kangaroosies, 'roosies,
children of the Lord.
    Rise and shine . . .

4 It rained and poured for
    forty daysies, daysies,
it rained and poured for
    forty daysies, daysies,
almost drove those animals crazies,
    crazies,
children of the Lord.
    Rise and shine . . .

5 The sun came out and dried up the
    landy, landy,
the sun came out and dried up the
    landy, landy.
Everything was fine and dandy, dandy,
children of the Lord.
    Rise and shine . . .

4 Said Jesus to Mary, 'Your love is so deep,
today you may do as you will;
tomorrow, you say, I am going away,
but My body I leave with you still,'
    He said,
'My body I leave with you still.'

5 'The poor of the world are My body,'
    He said,
'to the end of the world they shall be;
the bread and the blankets
    you give to the poor
you'll find you have given to Me,' He said,
'you'll find you have given to Me.'

6 'My body will hang on the cross
    of the world
tomorrow,' He said, 'and today,
and Martha and Mary will find Me again
and wash all My sorrow away,' He said,
'and wash all my sorrow away.'

211

Sydney Carter
© 1964 Stainer & Bell Ltd

1 **Said Judas to Mary,**
    'Now what will you do
with your ointment so rich and so rare?'
'I'll pour it all over the feet of the Lord
and I'll wipe it away with my hair,'
    she said,
'I'll wipe it away with my hair.'

2 'O Mary, O Mary, O think of the poor –
this ointment it could have been sold,
and think of the blankets
    and think of the bread
you could buy with the silver and gold,'
    he said,
'you could buy with the silver and gold.'

3 'Tomorrow, tomorrow I'll think of the poor,
tomorrow,' she said, 'not today;
for dearer than all of the poor of the world
is my love who is going away,' she said,
'is my love who is going away.'

212

This song has been withdrawn
for copyright-related reasons

213

Edward Caswall (1814–78)
altered © 1986 Horrobin/Leavers

1 **See, amid the winter snow,**
born for us on earth below;
see, the Son of God appears,
promised from eternal years.
    Hail, O ever-blessèd morn!
    Hail, redemption's happy dawn!
    Sing through all Jerusalem,
    Christ is born in Bethlehem!

2 Low within a manger lies
He who built the starry skies,
He who, throned in heaven's height
reigns in power and glorious light.
    Hail, O ever-blessèd morn . . .

3 Say, you humble shepherds, say,
what's your joyful news today?
Tell us why you left your sheep
on the lonely mountain steep:
   Hail, O ever-blessèd morn . . .

4 'As we watched at dead of night,
all around us shone a light:
angels singing, "Peace on earth!"
told us of a Saviour's birth.'
   Hail, O ever-blessèd morn . . .

5 Sacred baby, King most dear,
what a tender love was here!
Down He came from glory high
in a manger there to lie.
   Hail, O ever-blessèd morn . . .

6 Holy Saviour, born on earth,
teach us by Your lowly birth;
grant that we may ever be
taught by such humility.
   Hail, O ever-blessèd morn . . .

214 Michael Perry (1942–96)
© Mrs B Perry / The Jubilate Group

1 **See Him lying on a bed of straw:**
a draughty stable with an open door;
Mary cradling the babe she bore –
the Prince of glory is His name.
   O now carry me to Bethlehem
   to see the Lord appear to men –
   just as poor as was the stable then,
   the Prince of glory when He came.

2 Star of silver, sweep across the skies,
show where Jesus in the manger lies;
shepherds, swiftly from your stupor rise
to see the Saviour of the world!
   O now carry . . .

3 Angels, sing the song that you began,
bring God's glory to the heart of man;
sing that Bethl'em's little baby can
be salvation to the soul.
   O now carry . . .

4 Mine are riches, from Your poverty,
from Your innocence, eternity;
mine forgiveness by Your death for me,
child of sorrow for my joy.
   O now carry . . .

215 Karen Lafferty
© 1972 Maranatha! Music / CCCM Music /
CopyCare

1 **Seek ye first the kingdom of God,**
and His righteousness,
and all these things
   shall be added unto you.
Allelu, alleluia.
Seek ye first . . .

2 Man shall not live by bread alone,
but by every word
that proceeds from the mouth of God.
Allelu, alleluia.
Man shall not . . .

3 Ask and it shall be given unto you,
seek and ye shall find;
knock and the door shall be opened
   up to you.
Allelu, alleluia.
Ask and it shall . . .

216 © 1986 Greg Leavers

Saviour of the world,
thank You for dying on the cross.
All praise to You, our risen Lord,
hallelujah! Jesus.

1 In the garden of Gethsemane
   Jesus knelt and prayed;
for He knew the time was near
   when He would be betrayed.
God gave Him the strength to cope with
   all that people did to hurt Him;
soldiers laughed and forced a crown of
   thorns upon His head.
   Saviour of the world . . .

2 On a cross outside the city
      they nailed Jesus high;
innocent, but still He suffered
      as they watched Him die.
Nothing that the soldiers did could make
      Him lose control, for Jesus
knew the time to die, then,
      'It is finished!' was His cry.
    Saviour of the world . . .

3 Three days later by God's power
      He rose up from the dead,
for the tomb could not hold Jesus,
      it was as He'd said;
victor over sin and death, He conquered
      Satan's power; so let us
celebrate that Jesus is alive for evermore.
    Saviour of the world . . .

3 All shall be well in His kingdom of peace,
freedom and wisdom
      and love shall not cease;
foe shall be friend
      when His triumph we sing,
sword shall be sickle when Jesus is King.
    Come let us sing . . .

4 Souls shall be saved
      from the burden of sin;
doubt shall not darken his witness within;
hell has no terrors,
      and death has no sting;
love is victorious, when Jesus is King.
    Come let us sing . . .

5 Kingdom of Christ,
      for your coming we pray;
hasten, O Father, the dawn of the day
when this new song
      Your creation shall sing,
Satan is conquered and Jesus is King.
    Come let us sing . . .

217 Michael Lehr
© Stainer & Bell Ltd

Shalōm, my friend, shalōm, my friend,
shalōm, shalōm.
Till we meet again, till we meet again,
shalōm, shalōm.

218 Charles Silvester Horne (1865–1914)

1 **Sing we the King**
    who is coming to reign,
glory to Jesus, the Lamb that was slain;
life and salvation His coming shall bring,
joy to the nations when Jesus is King.
    Come let us sing: praise to our King.
    Jesus our King, Jesus our King:
    this is our song, who to Jesus belong:
    glory to Jesus, to Jesus our King.

2 All men who dwell in His marvellous light,
races long severed His love shall unite;
justice and truth
      from His sceptre shall spring,
wrong shall be ended
      when Jesus is King.
    Come let us sing . . .

219 Joseph Mohr (1792–1848)
tr. Stopford Augustus Brooke (1832–1916)

1 **Silent night, holy night!**
Sleeps the world; hid from sight,
Mary and Joseph in stable bare
watched o'er the child belovèd and fair
    sleeping in heavenly rest,
    sleeping in heavenly rest.

2 Silent night, holy night!
Shepherds first saw the light,
heard resounding clear and long,
far and near, the angel-song:
    'Christ the Redeemer is here,
    Christ the Redeemer is here.'

3 Silent night, holy night!
Son of God, O how bright
love is smiling from Your face!
Strikes for us now the hour of grace,
    Saviour, since You are born,
    Saviour, since You are born.

220 Anon
Copyright control

1 **Someone's brought a loaf of bread,**
   someone's brought a loaf of bread,
   someone's brought a loaf of bread
   to put on the harvest table.

2 Someone's brought a jar of jam,
   someone's brought a jar of jam,
   someone's brought a jar of jam
   to put on the harvest table.

Other verses may be added

Last verse:

   Thank You, Lord, for all Your gifts,
   thank You, Lord, for all Your gifts,
   thank You, Lord, for all Your gifts
   to put on the harvest table.

221 Andrae Crouch
© 1978 Kevin Mayhew Ltd

1 **Soon, and very soon,**
   we are going to see the King;
   soon, and very soon,
   we are going to see the King;
   soon, and very soon,
   we are going to see the King;
      alleluia, alleluia,
      we're going to see the King!

2 No more crying there . . .
      alleluia . . .

3 No more dying there . . .
      alleluia . . .
      Alleluia, alleluia, alleluia, alleluia.

4 Soon and very soon . . .
      alleluia . . .
      Alleluia, alleluia, alleluia, alleluia.

222 Daniel Iverson
© 1963 Kevin Mayhew Ltd

Spirit of the living God,
   fall afresh on me;
Spirit of the living God,
   fall afresh on me;
break me, melt me,
   mould me, fill me;
Spirit of the living God,
   fall afresh on me.

223 Alfred B Smith and John W Peterson
© 1954 Brentwood Benson Catalogue

Surely goodness and mercy
      shall follow me
all the days, all the days of my life;
surely goodness and mercy shall follow me
all the days, all the days of my life.
And I shall dwell in the house
         of the Lord forever,
and I shall feast at the table spread for me.
Surely goodness and mercy shall follow me
all the days, all the days of my life.

224 © 1986 Andy Silver

Stand up and bless the Lord your God,
stand up and bless the Lord;
His name is exalted above all names;
stand up and bless the Lord.

For our God is good to us,
always ready to forgive;
He is gracious and merciful,
slow to anger and very kind.

So, stand up and bless the Lord your God,
stand up and bless the Lord;
stand up and bless the Lord your God,
stand up.

225 Roger Dyer
© 1970 Campbell Connelly & Co Ltd

Stand up, clap hands, shout,
* 'Thank You, Lord,*
thank You for the world I'm in.'
Stand up, clap hands, shout,
* 'Thank You, Lord,*
for happiness and peace within.'

1 I look around and the sun's in the sky,
I look around and then I think, 'Oh, my!'
The world is such a wonderful place,
and all because of the good Lord's grace.
Stand up, clap hands . . .

2 I look around and the creatures I see,
I look around and it amazes me
that every fox and bird and hare
must fit in a special place somewhere.
Stand up, clap hands . . .

3 I look around at all the joy I've had,
I look around and then it makes me glad
that I can offer thanks and praise
to Him who guides me through my days.
Stand up, clap hands . . .

226 George Duffield (1818–88)
© in this version The Jubilate Group

1 **Stand up! stand up for Jesus!**
you soldiers of the cross,
lift high His royal banner;
it must not suffer loss.
From victory unto victory
His army He shall lead,
till evil is defeated
and Christ is Lord indeed.

2 Stand up! stand up for Jesus!
the trumpet-call obey;
then join the mighty conflict
in this His glorious day.
Be strong in faith and serve Him
against unnumbered foes;
let courage rise with danger,
and strength to strength oppose.

3 Stand up! stand up for Jesus!
stand in His power alone;
for human might will fail you,
you dare not trust your own.
Put on the gospel armour,
keep watch with constant prayer;
where duty calls, or danger,
be never failing there.

4 Stand up! stand up for Jesus!
the fight will not be long;
this day the noise of battle,
the next the victor's song.
To everyone who conquers
a crown of life shall be;
we with the King of glory
shall reign eternally.

227 Arabella Catherine Hankey (1834–1911) altd.

1 **Tell me the old, old story**
of unseen things above,
of Jesus and His glory,
of Jesus and His love.
Tell me the story simply,
as to a little child,
for I am weak and weary,
and helpless and defiled.
Tell me the old, old story,
tell me the old, old story,
tell me the old, old story
of Jesus and His love.

2 Tell me the story slowly,
that I may take it in –
that wonderful redemption,
God's remedy for sin.
Tell me the story often,
for I forget so soon:
the early dew of morning
has passed away at noon.
Tell me the old . . .

3 Tell me the story softly,
with earnest tones and grave;
Remember! I'm the sinner
whom Jesus came to save.
Tell me the story always,
if you would really be,
in any time of trouble,
a comforter to me.
Tell me the old . . .

4 Tell me the same old story,
when you have cause to fear
that this world's empty glory
is costing me too dear.
Yes, and when that world's glory
is dawning on my soul,
tell me the old, old story;
'Christ Jesus makes you whole.'
Tell me the old . . .

228 William Henry Parker (1845–1929)
v.6 Hugh Martin (1890–1964)
adapted Horrobin/Leavers by permission of
the National Christian Education Council

1 **Tell me the stories of Jesus**
I love to hear;
things I would ask Him to tell me
if He were here;
scenes by the wayside,
tales of the sea,
stories of Jesus,
tell them to me.

2 First let me hear how the children
stood round His knee;
that I may know of His blessing
resting on me;
words full of kindness,
deeds full of grace,
signs of the love found
in Jesus' face.

3 Tell me, in words full of wonder,
how rolled the sea,
tossing the boat in a tempest
on Galilee.
Jesus then doing
His Father's will,
ended the storm saying,
'Peace, peace, be still.'

4 Into the city I'd follow
the children's band,
waving a branch of the palm-tree
high in my hand;
worshipping Jesus,
yes, I would sing
loudest hosannas,
for He is King!

5 Show me that scene in the garden,
of bitter pain;
and of the cross where my Saviour
for me was slain;
and, through the sadness,
help me to see
how Jesus suffered
for love of me.

6 Gladly I'd hear of His rising
out of the grave,
living and strong and triumphant,
mighty to save:
and how He sends us
all men to bring
stories of Jesus,
Jesus, their King.

229 © Timothy Dudley-Smith / OUP

1 **Tell out, my soul,**
   the greatness of the Lord;
unnumbered blessings
   give my spirit voice;
tender to me the promise of His word;
in God my Saviour shall my heart rejoice.

2 Tell out, my soul,
   the greatness of His name!
Make known His might,
   the deeds His arm has done;
His mercy sure,
   from age to age the same;
His holy name – the Lord,
   the Mighty One.

3 Tell out, my soul,
   the greatness of His might!
powers and dominions lay their glory by;

proud hearts and stubborn wills
    are put to flight,
the hungry fed, the humble lifted high.

4   Tell out, my soul, the glories of His word!
    firm is His promise, and His mercy sure:
    tell out, my soul,
        the greatness of the Lord
    to children's children and for evermore!

230 M G Schneider
tr. and adpt. S Lonsdale and Michael Baughen
© Bosworth & Co Ltd

1   **Thank You for every new good
    morning,**
    thank You for every fresh new day,
    thank You that I may cast my burdens
    wholly on to You.

2   Thank You for every friend I have, Lord,
    thank You for everyone I know,
    thank You when I can feel forgiveness
    to my greatest foe.

3   Thank You for leisure and employment,
    thank You for every heartfelt joy,
    thank You for all that makes me happy
    and for melody.

4   Thank You for every shade and sorrow,
    thank You for comfort in Your word,
    thank You that I am guided by You
    everywhere I go.

5   Thank You for grace to know Your gospel,
    thank You for all Your Spirit's power,
    thank You for Your unfailing love
    which reaches far and near.

6   Thank You for free and full salvation,
    thank You for grace to hold it fast.
    Thank You, O Lord, I want to thank You
    that I'm free to thank!
    Thank You, O Lord, I want to thank You
    that I'm free to thank!

231 Anon
Copyright control

1   **Thank You, thank You, Jesus,**
    thank You, thank You, Jesus,
    thank You, thank You, Jesus, in my heart.
    Thank You, thank You, Jesus,
    O thank You, thank You, Jesus,
    thank You, thank You, Jesus, in my heart.

2   You can't make me doubt Him,
    you can't make me doubt Him,
    you can't make me doubt Him in my
        heart.
    You can't make me doubt Him,
    O you can't make me doubt Him,
    thank You, thank You, Jesus, in my heart.

3   I can't live without Him,
    I can't live without Him,
    I can't live without Him in my heart.
    I can't live without Him,
    O I can't live without Him,
    thank You, thank You, Jesus, in my heart.

4   Glory, hallelujah,
    glory, hallelujah,
    glory, hallelujah in my heart!
    Glory, hallelujah,
    O glory, hallelujah,
    thank You, thank You, Jesus, in my heart.

232 Diane Davis Andrew
© 1971, 1975 Celebration / Thankyou Music

1   **Thank You, Lord, for this fine day,**
    thank You, Lord, for this fine day,
    thank You, Lord, for this fine day,
    right where we are.
        Alleluia, praise the Lord!
        Alleluia, praise the Lord!
        Alleluia, praise the Lord,
        right where we are.

2   Thank You, Lord, for loving us,
    thank You, Lord, for loving us,
    thank You, Lord, for loving us,
    right where we are.
        Alleluia . . .

3 Thank You, Lord, for giving us peace,
  thank You, Lord, for giving us peace,
  thank You, Lord, for giving us peace,
  right where we are.
    Alleluia . . .

4 Thank You, Lord, for setting us free,
  thank You, Lord, for setting us free,
  thank You, Lord, for setting us free,
  right where we are.
    Alleluia . . .

233
Anon
Copyright control

Thank You, God, for sending Jesus;
thank You, Jesus, that You came;
Holy Spirit, won't You tell us
more about His wondrous name?

234
P Bilhorn (1865–1936)
Copyright control

1 **The best book to read is the Bible,**
  the best book to read is the Bible;
  if you read it every day
  it will help you on your way,
  Oh, the best book to read is the Bible.

2 The best friend to have is Jesus,
  the best friend to have is Jesus;
  He will hear me when I call,
  He will keep me lest I fall,
  Oh, the best friend to have is Jesus.

3 The best thing to do is to trust Him,
  the best thing to do is to trust Him;
  and if you on Him depend,
  He will keep you to the end;
  Oh, the best thing to do is to trust Him.

235
Alison Huntley
© 1978 Thankyou Music

1 **Thank You, Jesus, thank You, Jesus,**
  thank You, Lord, for loving me.
  Thank You, Jesus . . .

2 You went to Calvary,
    there You died for me,
  thank You, Lord, for loving me.
  You went to Calvary . . .

3 You rose up from the grave,
    to me new life You gave,
  thank You, Lord, for loving me.
  You rose up from the grave . . .

4 You're coming back again,
    and we with You shall reign,
  thank You, Lord, for loving me.
  You're coming back again . . .

236
John Ellerton (1826–93)
© in this version The Jubilate Group

1 **The day You gave us, Lord, is ended,**
  the sun is sinking in the west;
  to You our morning hymns ascended,
  Your praise shall sanctify our rest.

2 We thank You
    that Your Church, unsleeping
  while earth rolls onward into light,
  through all the world
    her watch is keeping,
  and rests not now by day or night.

3 As to each continent and island
  the dawn proclaims another day,
  the voice of prayer is never silent,
  nor dies the sound of praise away.

4 The sun, that bids us rest, is waking
  Your church beneath the western sky;
  fresh voices hour by hour are making
  Your mighty deeds resound on high.

5 So be it, Lord, Your throne shall never,
  like earth's proud empires, pass away;
  Your kingdom stands, and grows for ever,
  until there dawns that glorious day.

237 © Michael Baughen / The Jubilate Group

1 **The fields are white unto harvest time,**
   look up and see,
   the fields are white unto harvest time,
   look up and see!
   Pray to the Lord of the harvest,
   Christ says, 'Pray!'
   Pray to the Lord for the workers
   which we need in this day.

2 The harvest truly is fit to reap
   but workers few,
   the harvest truly is fit to reap
   but workers few.
   Pray to the Lord . . .

3 Who else will go into all the world
   to preach the word?
   Who else will go into all the world
   to preach the word?
   Pray to the Lord . . .

4 The Lord's return may be very soon,
   the time is short,
   the Lord's return may be very soon,
   the time is short!
   Pray to the Lord . . .

238 Anon (17th century)
© in this version The Jubilate Group

1 **The first nowell the angel did say,**
   was to Bethlehem's shepherds
       in fields as they lay;
   in fields where they
       lay keeping their sheep
   on a cold winter's night that was so deep:
   Nowell, nowell, nowell, nowell,
   born is the King of Israel!

2 Then wise men from a country far
   looked up and saw a guiding star;
   they travelled on by night and day
   to reach the place where Jesus lay:
   Nowell, nowell . . .

3 At Bethlehem they entered in,
   on bended knee they worshipped Him;
   they offered there in His presence
   their gold and myrrh and frankincense:
   Nowell, nowell . . .

4 Then let us all with one accord
   sing praises to our heavenly Lord;
   for Christ has our salvation wrought
   and with His blood mankind has bought:
   Nowell, nowell . . .

239 Mark Pendergrass
© 1977 Kevin Mayhew Ltd

1 **The greatest thing in all my life**
       is knowing You;
   the greatest thing in all my life
       is knowing You;
   I want to know You more;
       I want to know You more.
   The greatest thing in all my life
       is knowing You.

2 The greatest thing in all my life
       is loving You;
   the greatest thing in all my life
       is loving You;
   I want to love You more;
       I want to love You more.
   The greatest thing in all my life
       is loving You.

3 The greatest thing in all my life
       is serving You;
   the greatest thing in all my life
       is serving You;
   I want to serve You more;
       I want to serve You more.
   The greatest thing in all my life
       is serving You.

240 Alliene Vale
© 1978 His Eye Music / Multisongs /
Joy of the Lord Music / Alliance Media Ltd /
CopyCare

1 **The joy of the Lord is my strength,**
   the joy of the Lord is my strength,
   the joy of the Lord is my strength,
   the joy of the Lord is my strength.

2 If you want joy you must sing for it,
if you want joy you must sing for it,
if you want joy you must sing for it,
the joy of the Lord is my strength.

3 If you want joy you must shout for it,
if you want joy you must shout for it,
if you want joy you must shout for it,
the joy of the Lord is my strength.

4 If you want joy you must jump for it,
if you want joy you must jump for it,
if you want joy you must jump for it,
the joy of the Lord is my strength.

242
Cecil J Allen
© F R Allen

The Lord has need of me,
His soldier I will be;
He gave Himself my life to win,
and so I mean to follow Him,
and serve Him faithfully.
So although the fight be fierce and long,
I'll carry on: He makes me strong;
and then one day His face I'll see,
and O the joy when He says to me,
'Well done, my brave crusader!'

241
Henry Williams Baker (1821–77)
© in this version The Jubilate Group

1 **The King of love my shepherd is,**
whose goodness fails me never;
I nothing lack if I am His
and He is mine for ever.

2 Where streams of living water flow,
a ransomed soul, He leads me;
and where the fertile pastures grow
with food from heaven feeds me.

3 Perverse and foolish I have strayed;
but in His love He sought me,
and on His shoulder gently laid,
and home, rejoicing, brought me.

4 In death's dark vale I fear no ill
with You, dear Lord, beside me;
Your rod and staff my comfort still,
Your cross before to guide me.

5 You spread a banquet in my sight
of love beyond all knowing,
and O the gladness and delight
from Your pure chalice flowing!

6 And so through all the length of days
Your goodness fails me never;
Good Shepherd, may I sing Your praise
within Your house for ever!

243
Francis Rous (1579–1659)
revised for *Scottish Psalter*, 1650
altered © 1986 Horrobin/Leavers

1 **The Lord's my shepherd, I'll not want;**
He makes me down to lie
in pastures green; He's leading me
the quiet waters by.

2 My soul He does restore again,
and me to walk does make
within the paths of righteousness,
e'en for His own name's sake.

3 Yes, though I walk
through death's dark vale,
yet will I fear no ill;
for You are with me, and Your rod
and staff me comfort still.

4 My table You have furnishèd
in presence of my foes;
my head You now with oil anoint,
and my cup overflows.

5 Goodness and mercy all my life
shall surely follow me;
and in God's house for evermore
my dwelling-place shall be.

244 From Psalm 23
Copyright control

The Lord is my shepherd,
I'll trust in Him always.
He leads me by still waters,
I'll trust in Him always.
Always, always, I'll trust in Him always.
Always, always, I'll trust in Him always.

245 Cecil Frances Alexander (1818–95)

1 **There is a green hill far away**
outside a city wall,
where the dear Lord was crucified,
who died to save us all.

2 We may not know, we cannot tell
what pains He had to bear;
but we believe it was for us
He hung and suffered there.

3 He died that we might be forgiven,
He died to make us good,
that we might go at last to heaven,
saved by His precious blood.

4 There was no other good enough
to pay the price of sin;
He only could unlock the gate
of heaven, and let us in.

5 O dearly, dearly has He loved,
and we must love Him too,
and trust in His redeeming blood,
and try His works to do.

246 John Gowans
© 1970 Salvationist Publishing and Supplies Ltd /
CopyCare

1 **There are hundreds of sparrows,**
   thousands, millions,
they're two a penny,
      far too many there must be;
there are hundreds and thousands,
      millions of sparrows,
but God knows every one
      and God knows me.

2 There are hundreds of flowers,
      thousands, millions,
and flowers fair the meadows
      wear for all to see;
there are hundreds and thousands,
      millions of flowers,
but God knows every one
      and God knows me.

3 There are hundreds of planets,
      thousands, millions,
way out in space each has a place
      by God's decree;
there are hundreds and thousands,
      millions of planets,
but God knows every one
      and God knows me.

4 There are hundreds of children,
      thousands, millions,
and yet their names are written
      on God's memory;
there are hundreds and thousands,
      millions of children,
but God knows every one
      and God knows me,
but God knows every one
      and God knows me.

247 Anon
Copyright control

ALL   **There's a song of exaltation**
       full of joy and inspiration
       echoed down through all creation,
       sing hallelujah, sing.

PART 1   Sing hallelujah,
PART 2   sing hallelujah,
PART 1   sing hallelujah,
PART 2   sing hallelujah,
PART 1   sing hallelujah,
PART 2   sing hallelujah,
ALL   sing hallelujah, sing.

248 E H Swinstead (d1976)
Copyright control

There's a way back to God
    from the dark paths of sin;
there's a door that is open
    and you may go in:
at Calvary's cross is where you begin,
when you come as a sinner to Jesus.

249 Anon
Copyright control

1 **There's new life in Jesus,**
     lift up your heart,
    there's new life in Jesus, lift up your heart.
    Lift up your heart, lift up your heart,
    there's new life in Jesus,
    lift up your heart.

2 There is healing in His love,
     lift up your heart,
    there is healing in His love,
     lift up your heart.
    Lift up your heart . . .

3 There is joy in serving Him,
     lift up your heart,
    there is joy in serving Him,
     lift up your heart.
    Lift up your heart . . .

250 Edith McNeill
© 1974 Celebration / Thankyou Music

The steadfast love of the Lord
     never ceases,
His mercies never come to an end;
they are new every morning,
     new every morning:
great is Your faithfulness, O Lord,
great is Your faithfulness.

251 Anon
Copyright control

1 **The virgin Mary had a baby boy,**
    the virgin Mary had a baby boy,
    the virgin Mary had a baby boy
    and they said that His name was Jesus.
    He come from the glory,
    He come from the glorious kingdom,
    He come from the glory,
    He come from the glorious kingdom.
    O yes, believer,
    O yes, believer,
    He come from the glory,
    He come from the glorious kingdom.

2 The angels sang
     when the baby was born,
    the angels sang when the baby was born,
    the angels sang when the baby was born,
    and proclaimed Him the Saviour Jesus.
    He come from the glory . . .

3 The wise men saw
     where the baby was born,
    the wise men saw
     where the baby was born,
    the wise men saw
     where the baby was born,
    and they saw that His name was Jesus.
    He come from the glory . . .

252 Anon
Copyright control

1 **The wise man built his house**
     upon the rock,
    the wise man built his house
     upon the rock,
    the wise man built his house
     upon the rock
    and the rain came tumbling down.
    And the rain came down and the
     floods came up,
    the rain came down and the
     floods came up,
    the rain came down and the
     floods came up
    and the house on the rock stood firm.

2 The foolish man built his house
        upon the sand,
   the foolish man built his house
        upon the sand,
   the foolish man built his house
        upon the sand
   and the rain came tumbling down.
   And the rain came down and the
        floods came up,
   the rain came down and the
        floods came up,
   the rain came down and the
        floods came up
   and the house on the sand fell flat.

253 From the *Book of Praise for Children*, 1881
        altered

1 **The wise may bring their learning,**
   the rich may bring their wealth,
   and some may bring their greatness,
   and some their strength and health.
   We too would bring our treasures
   to offer to the King;
   we have no wealth or learning,
   what gifts then shall we bring?

2 We'll bring the many duties
   we have to do each day.
   We'll try our best to please Him
   at home, at school, at play,
   and better are these treasures
   to offer to the King
   than richest gifts without them,
   yet these we all may bring.

3 We'll bring Him hearts that love Him,
   we'll bring Him thankful praise,
   and lives for ever striving
   to follow in His ways,
   and these shall be the treasures
   we offer to the King,
   and these are gifts that ever
   our grateful hearts may bring.

254 Doreen Newport
        © 1969 Stainer & Bell Ltd

1 **Think of a world without any flowers,**
   think of a world without any trees,
   think of a sky without any sunshine,
   think of the air without any breeze.
   We thank You, Lord, for flowers and trees
        and sunshine,
   we thank You, Lord, and praise
        Your holy name.

2 Think of a world without any animals,
   think of a field without any herd,
   think of a stream without any fishes,
   think of a dawn without any bird.
   We thank You, Lord, for all Your
        living creatures,
   we thank You, Lord, and praise
        Your holy name.

3 Think of a world without any people,
   think of a street with no-one living there,
   think of a town without any houses,
   no-one to love and nobody to care.
   We thank You, Lord, for families
        and friendships,
   we thank You, Lord, and praise
        Your holy name.

255 Les Garrett
        © 1967 Scripture in Song / Maranatha! Music /
        CopyCare

1 **This is the day,**
   this is the day that the Lord has made,
   that the Lord has made.
   We will rejoice,
   we will rejoice and be glad in it,
   and be glad in it.
   This is the day that the Lord has made,
   we will rejoice and be glad in it.
   This is the day,
   this is the day that the Lord has made.

2 This is the day,
   this is the day when He rose again,
   when He rose again.
   We will rejoice,
   we will rejoice and be glad in it,
   and be glad in it.

This is the day when He rose again,
we will rejoice and be glad in it.
This is the day,
this is the day when He rose again.

3 This is the day,
   this is the day when the Spirit came,
   when the Spirit came.
   We will rejoice,
   we will rejoice and be glad in it,
   and be glad in it.
   This is the day when the Spirit came,
   we will rejoice and be glad in it.
   This is the day,
   this is the day when the Spirit came.

256 Fred Pratt Green
© 1969 Stainer & Bell Ltd

1 **This joyful Eastertide,**
   what need is there for grieving?
   Cast all your care aside
   and be not unbelieving:
     Come, share our Easter joy
     that death could not imprison,
     nor any power destroy,
     our Christ, who is arisen,
     arisen, arisen, arisen!

2 No work for Him is vain,
   no faith in Him mistaken,
   for Easter makes it plain
   His kingdom is not shaken:
     Come, share our Easter joy . . .

3 Then put your trust in Christ,
   in waking or in sleeping.
   His grace on earth sufficed;
   He'll never quit His keeping:
     Come, share our Easter joy . . .

257 © 1964 Richard Bewes / The Jubilate Group

1 **Though the world has forsaken God,**
   treads a different path,
     lives a different way,
   I walk the road that the Saviour trod,
   and all may know
     I live under Jesus' sway.

     They are watching you,
       marking all you do,
     hearing the things you say;
     let them see the Saviour
       as He shines in you,
     let His power control you every day.

2 Men will look at the life I lead,
   see the side I take and the things I love;
   they judge my Lord by my every deed –
   Lord, set my affections on things above.
     They are watching you . . .

3 When assailed in temptation's hour
   by besetting sins, by the fear of man,
   then I can know Jesus' mighty power,
   and become like Him in His perfect plan.
     They are watching you . . .

4 Here on earth people walk in the night;
   with no lamp to guide
       they are dead in sin.
   I know the Lord who can give them light,
   I live, yet not I, but Christ within.
     They are watching you . . .

258 Traditional

     This little light of mine,
       I'm gonna let it shine,
     this little light of mine,
       I'm gonna let it shine.
     This little light of mine,
       I'm gonna let it shine,
     let it shine, let it shine, let it shine.

1 The light that shines is the light of love,
   lights the darkness from above.
   It shines on me and it shines on you,
   and shows what the power of love can
       do.
   I'm gonna shine my light both far and
       near,
   I'm gonna shine my light
       both bright and clear.
   Where there's a dark corner in this land
   I'm gonna let my little light shine.
     This little light of mine . . .

2 On Monday, He gave me the gift of love,
Tuesday, peace came from above.
On Wednesday He told me
    to have more faith,
on Thursday He gave me a little more
    grace.
Friday, He told me just to watch and pray,
Saturday, He told me just what to say.
On Sunday He gave me the power divine
to let my little light shine.
    This little light of mine . . .

259 Fanny J Crosby (1820–1915)

1 **To God be the glory!**
    great things He has done;
so loved He the world
    that He gave us His Son;
who yielded His life an atonement for sin,
and opened the life gate
    that all may go in.
    Praise the Lord, praise the Lord!
    let the earth hear His voice;
    praise the Lord, praise the Lord!
    let the people rejoice:
    O come to the Father,
    through Jesus the Son
    and give Him the glory;
    great things He has done!

2 O perfect redemption,
    the purchase of blood!
to every believer the promise of God;
the vilest offender who truly believes,
that moment from Jesus
    a pardon receives.
    Praise the Lord . . .

3 Great things He has taught us,
    great things He has done,
and great our rejoicing
    through Jesus the Son;
but purer, and higher, and greater will be
our wonder, our rapture,
    when Jesus we see.
    Praise the Lord . . .

260 Helen H Lemmel (1864–1961)
© 1922, 1950 Brentwood Benson Catalogue

1 **Turn your eyes upon Jesus,**
look full in His wonderful face;
and the things of earth
    will grow strangely dim
in the light of His glory and grace.

2 Keep your eyes upon Jesus,
let nobody else take His place;
so that hour by hour you will know
    His power
till at last you have run the great race.

261 © 1945 Hugh Mitchell
Copyright control

Twelve men went to spy in Canaan,
ten were bad, two were good.
What did they see when they spied
    in Canaan?
Ten were bad, two were good.
Some saw giants tough and tall,
some saw grapes in clusters fall,
some saw God was in it all,
ten were bad, two were good.

262 C C Kerr
© Scripture Union

Two little eyes to look to God,
two little ears to hear His word,
two little feet to walk in His ways,
two little lips to sing His praise,
two little hands to do His will,
and one little heart to love Him still.

263 German (15th century)
tr. Percy Dearmer (1867–1936)
From the *Oxford Book of Carols*
by permission of Oxford University Press

1 **Unto us a boy is born!**
King of all creation,
came He to a world forlorn,
    the Lord of every nation,
    the Lord of every nation.

2 Cradled in a stall was He
with sleepy cows and asses;
but the very beasts could see
  that He all men surpasses,
  that He all men surpasses.

3 Herod then with fear was filled:
'A Prince,' he said, 'in Jewry!'
All the little boys he killed
  at Bethlehem in his fury,
  at Bethlehem in his fury.

4 Now may Mary's Son, who came
so long ago to love us,
lead us all with hearts aflame
  unto the joys above us,
  unto the joys above us.

5 Alpha and Omega He!
Let the organ thunder,
while the choir with peals of glee
  doth rend the air asunder,
  doth rend the air asunder!

4 What shall we do with our life
    this morning,
what shall we do with our life
    this morning,
what shall we do with our life
    this morning?
Give it up in service!
  Jesus the King is risen . . .

265 © 1986 Margaret Parker

1 **We love to praise You, Jesus,**
we love to tell You
that You are Lord, that You are Lord.

2 We love to know You, Jesus,
we love to hear You,
say we are Yours, say we are Yours.

3 We want to thank You, Jesus,
for giving Your life
so we can live, so we can live.

264 Fred Kaan
© 1968 Stainer & Bell Ltd

1 **We have a king who rides a donkey,**
we have a king who rides a donkey,
we have a king who rides a donkey
and His name is Jesus.
  Jesus the King is risen,
  Jesus the King is risen,
  Jesus the King is risen
  early in the morning.

2 Trees are waving a royal welcome,
trees are waving a royal welcome,
trees are waving a royal welcome
for the king called Jesus.
  Jesus the King is risen . . .

3 We have a king who cares for people,
we have a king who cares for people,
we have a king who cares for people
and His name is Jesus.
  Jesus the King is risen . . .

266 Priscilla Jane Owens (1829–1907)
altered © 1986 Horrobin/Leavers

1 **We have heard a joyful sound!**
Jesus saves!
Spread the gladness all around:
Jesus saves!
Words of life for every land
must be sent across the waves;
onward! 'tis our Lord's command:
Jesus saves!

2 Sing above the toils of life:
Jesus saves!
He is with us in the strife:
Jesus saves!
Sing the truth, He died yet lives,
strengthening me through all my days.
Sing in triumph! Life He gives:
Jesus saves!

3 Let the nations hear God's voice:
Jesus saves!
So that they can then rejoice:
Jesus saves!
Shout salvation full and free
that every land may hear God's praise –
this our song of victory:
Jesus saves!

267 Matthias Claudius (1740–1815)
tr. Jane Montgomery Campbell (1817–78)
altered © 1986 Horrobin/Leavers

1 **We plough the fields and scatter**
the good seed on the land,
but it is fed and watered
by God's almighty hand;
He sends the snow in winter,
the warmth to swell the grain,
the breezes and the sunshine
and soft refreshing rain.
*All good gifts around us
are sent from heaven above,
then thank the Lord, O thank the Lord,
for all His love.*

2 He only is the maker
of all things near and far;
He paints the wayside flower,
He lights the evening star;
the wind and waves obey Him,
by Him the birds are fed;
much more to us, His children,
He gives our daily bread.
All good gifts . . .

3 We thank You then, O Father,
for all things bright and good,
the seed-time and the harvest,
our life, our health, our food.
Accept the gifts we offer
for all Your love imparts;
we come now, Lord, to give You
our humble, thankful hearts.
All good gifts . . .

268 Verses 1 and 2: Ed Baggett
© 1974 Celebration / Thankyou Music
Verse 3 after Thomas Ken (1637–1711)

We really want to thank You, Lord,
we really want to bless Your name:
hallelujah! Jesus is our King!

1 We thank You, Lord, for Your gift to us,
Your life so rich beyond compare,
the gift of Your body here on earth
of which we sing and share.
We really want . . .

2 We thank You, Lord, for our life together,
to live and move in the love of Christ,
Your tenderness which sets us free
to serve You with our lives.
We really want . . .

3 Praise God from whom all blessings flow,
praise Him all creatures here below,
praise Him above, you heavenly host,
praise Father, Son and Holy Ghost.
We really want . . .

269 American folk hymn
Copyright control

1 **Were you there**
when they crucified my Lord?
Were you there
when they crucified my Lord?
Oh! Sometimes it causes me to tremble,
tremble, tremble;
Were you there
when they crucified my Lord?

2 Were you there
when they nailed Him to the tree?
Were you there
when they nailed Him to the tree?
Oh! Sometimes it causes me to tremble,
tremble, tremble;
Were you there
when they nailed Him to the tree?

3 Were you there
        when they laid Him in the tomb?
  Were you there
        when they laid Him in the tomb?
  Oh! Sometimes it causes me to tremble,
        tremble, tremble;
  Were you there
        when they laid Him in the tomb?

4 Were you there when God raised Him
        from the dead?
  Were you there when God raised Him
        from the dead?
  Oh! Sometimes it causes me to tremble,
        tremble, tremble;
  Were you there when God raised Him
        from the dead?

270

This song has been withdrawn
for copyright-related reasons

271 John H Hopkins (1820–91)
altered © 1986 Horrobin/Leavers

1 **We three kings of Orient are,**
  bearing gifts we travel afar,
  field and fountain, moor and mountain,
  following yonder star:
      O star of wonder, star of night,
      star with royal beauty bright,
      westward leading, still proceeding,
      guide us to the perfect light.

2 Born a King on Bethlehem plain,
  gold I bring to crown Him again:
  King for ever, ceasing never,
  over us all to reign.
      O star of wonder . . .

3 Frankincense for Jesus have I,
  God on earth yet Priest on high;
  prayer and praising all men raising:
  worship is earth's reply.
      O star of wonder . . .

4 Myrrh is mine: its bitter perfume
  tells of His death and Calvary's gloom;
  sorrowing, sighing, bleeding, dying,
  sealed in a stone-cold tomb.
      O star of wonder . . .

5 Glorious now, behold Him arise,
  King, and God, and sacrifice!
  Heaven sings, 'Alleluia!',
  'Alleluia!' the earth replies.
      O star of wonder . . .

272 Colin Sterne (1862–1926)

1 **We've a story to tell to the nations,**
  that shall turn their hearts to the right;
  a story of truth and sweetness,
  a story of peace and light,
  a story of peace and light:
      For the darkness shall turn to dawning,
      and the dawning to noon-day bright,
      and Christ's great kingdom
          shall come on earth,
      the kingdom of love and light.

2 We've a song to be sung to the nations,
  that shall lift their hearts to the Lord;
  a song that shall conquer evil,
  so love will replace the sword,
  so love will replace the sword.
      For the darkness . . .

3 We've a message to give to the nations,
  that the Lord who's reigning above
  has sent us His Son to save us,
  and show us that God is love,
  and show us that God is love:
      For the darkness . . .

4 We've a Saviour to show to the nations,
  who the path of sorrow has trod,
  that all of the world may listen
  and learn of the truth of God,
  and learn of the truth of God:
      For the darkness . . .

273 Joseph Scriven (1819–86)
altered © 1986 Horrobin/Leavers

1 **What a friend we have in Jesus,**
   all our sins and griefs to bear!
   What a privilege to carry
   everything to God in prayer!
   O what peace we often forfeit,
   O what needless pain we bear –
   all because we do not carry
   everything to God in prayer!

2 Have we trials and temptations?
   Is there trouble anywhere?
   We should never be discouraged:
   take it to the Lord in prayer!
   Can we find a friend so faithful,
   who will all our sorrows share?
   Jesus knows our every weakness –
   take it to the Lord in prayer!

3 Are we weak and heavy-laden,
   cumbered with a load of care?
   Jesus only is our refuge!
   Take it to the Lord in prayer!
   Do your friends despise, forsake you?
   Take it to the Lord in prayer!
   In His arms He'll take and shield you,
   you will find His comfort there.

274 Anon
Copyright control

1 **What a wonderful Saviour is Jesus,**
   what a wonderful friend is He,
   for He left all the glory of heaven,
   came to earth to die on Calvary:
      Sing hosanna, sing hosanna,
      sing hosanna to the King of kings!
      Sing hosanna, sing hosanna,
      sing hosanna to the King.

2 He arose from the grave, hallelujah!
   and He lives never more to die,
   at the Father's right hand interceding,
   He will hear and heed our faintest cry:
      Sing hosanna . . .

3 He is coming some day to receive us,
   we'll be caught up to heaven above,
   what a joy it will be to behold Him,
   sing for ever of His grace and love.
      Sing hosanna . . .

275 Sydney Carter
© 1965 Stainer & Bell Ltd

1 **When I needed a neighbour,**
      were you there, were you there?
   When I needed a neighbour,
      were you there?
      And the creed and the colour
      and the name won't matter,
      were you there?

2 I was hungry and thirsty,
      were you there, were you there?
   I was hungry and thirsty, were you there?
      And the creed . . .

3 I was cold, I was naked,
      were you there, were you there?
   I was cold, I was naked, were you there?
      And the creed . . .

4 When I needed a shelter,
      were you there, were you there?
   When I needed a shelter, were you there?
      And the creed . . .

5 When I needed a healer, were you there,
      were you there?
   When I needed a healer, were you there?
      And the creed . . .

6 Wherever you travel, I'll be there,
      I'll be there,
   Wherever you travel, I'll be there.
      And the creed . . .

276 Spiritual, adapted Peter D Smith
© Stainer & Bell Ltd

1 **When Israel was in Egypt's land,**
   let my people go;
   oppressed so hard they could not stand,
   let my people go.

Go down, Moses, way down in
   Egypt's land,
tell old Pharaoh to let my people go.

2   The Lord told Moses what to do,
    let my people go;
    to lead the children of Israel through,
    let my people go.
    Go down . . .

3   Your foes shall not before you stand,
    let my people go;
    and you'll possess fair Canaan's land,
    let my people go.
    Go down . . .

4   O let us from all bondage flee,
    let my people go;
    and let us all in Christ be free,
    let my people go.
    Go down . . .

5   I do believe without a doubt,
    let my people go;
    that a Christian has a right to shout,
    let my people go.
    Go down . . .

278

From the German (19th century)
Edward Caswall (1814–78)
© in this version The Jubilee Group

1   **When morning gilds the skies,**
    my heart awakening cries:
        May Jesus Christ be praised!
    Alike at work and prayer
    I know my Lord is there:
        May Jesus Christ be praised!

2   When sadness fills my mind
    my strength in Him I find –
        may Jesus Christ be praised!
    When earthly hopes grow dim
    my comfort is in Him –
        may Jesus Christ be praised!

3   The night becomes as day
    when from the heart we say:
        May Jesus Christ be praised!
    The powers of darkness fear,
    when this glad song they hear:
        May Jesus Christ be praised!

4   Be this, while life is mine,
    my canticle divine:
        May Jesus Christ be praised!
    Be this the eternal song
    through all the ages long:
        May Jesus Christ be praised!

277

Isaac Watts (1674–1748)

1   **When I survey the wondrous cross**
    on which the Prince of glory died,
    my richest gain I count but loss,
    and pour contempt on all my pride.

2   Forbid it, Lord, that I should boast,
    save in the death of Christ my God:
    all the vain things that charm me most,
    I sacrifice them to His blood.

3   See from His head, His hands, His feet,
    sorrow and love flow mingled down:
    did e'er such love and sorrow meet,
    or thorns compose so rich a crown?

4   Were the whole realm of nature mine,
    that were an offering far too small,
    love so amazing, so divine,
    demands my soul, my life, my all.

279

Norman J Clayton
© 1985 Wordspring Music, LLC / CopyCare

When the road is rough and steep,
fix your eyes upon Jesus,
He alone has power to keep,
fix your eyes upon Him.
Jesus is a gracious friend,
one on whom you can depend,
He is faithful to the end,
fix your eyes upon Him.

280

1 **When the Lord in glory comes,**
   not the trumpets, not the drums,
   not the anthem, not the psalm,
   not the thunder, not the calm,
   not the shout the heavens raise,
   not the chorus, not the praise,
   not the silences sublime,
   not the sounds of space and time,
   but His voice when He appears
   shall be music to my ears;
     but His voice when He appears
     shall be music to my ears.

2 When the Lord is seen again,
   not the glories of His reign,
   not the lightnings through the storm,
   not the radiance of His form,
   not His pomp and power alone,
   not the splendours of His throne,
   not His robe and diadems,
   not the gold and not the gems,
   but His face upon my sight
   shall be darkness into light;
     but His face upon my sight
     shall be darkness into light.

3 When the Lord to human eyes
   shall bestride our narrow skies,
   not the child of humble birth,
   not the carpenter of earth,
   not the man by all denied,
   not the victim crucified,
   but the God who died to save,
   but the victor of the grave,
   He it is to whom I fall,
   Jesus Christ, my all in all;
     He it is to whom I fall,
     Jesus Christ, my all in all.

281

1 **When the trumpet of the Lord shall
        sound, and time shall be no more,**
   and the morning breaks, eternal,
        bright, and fair;
   when the saved of earth shall gather
        over on the other shore,
   and the roll is called up yonder,
        I'll be there.
   When the roll is called up yonder,
   when the roll is called up yonder,
   when the roll is called up yonder,
   when the roll is called up yonder
   I'll be there.

2 On that bright and cloudless morning
        when the dead in Christ shall rise,
   and the glory of His resurrection share;
   when His chosen ones shall gather
        to their home beyond the skies,
   and the roll is called up yonder,
        I'll be there.
   When the roll is called . . .

3 Let us labour for the Master
        from the dawn till setting sun,
   let us talk of all His wondrous love and
        care;
   then when all of life is over,
        and our work on earth is done,
   and the roll is called up yonder,
        I'll be there.
   When the roll is called . . .

282

Wherever I am, I'll praise Him,
whenever I can, I'll praise Him;
for His love surrounds me like a sea;
I'll praise the name of Jesus,
lift up the name of Jesus,
for the name of Jesus lifted me.

283 © 1986 Margaret Parker

1 **Wherever I am I will praise You, Lord,**
praise You, Lord.
Wherever I am
Your Spirit fills my life with song.

2 Whenever I can I will tell You, Lord,
I love You.
Wherever I am
Your Spirit fills my heart with love.

3 Wherever I go I will serve You, Lord,
serve You, Lord.
Wherever I am
Your Spirit fills my life with power.

4 Whatever I do I will need You, Lord,
need You, Lord.
Wherever I am
Your Spirit lives Your life through me.

284 Graham Kendrick
© 1986 Thankyou Music

1 **Whether you're one
or whether you're two**
or three or four or five,
six or seven or eight or nine,
it's good to be alive.
It really doesn't matter how old you are,
Jesus loves you whoever you are.
La, la, la, la, la, la, la, la, la,
Jesus loves us all.
La, la, la, la, la, la, la, la, la,
Jesus loves us all.

2 Whether you're big
or whether you're small
or somewhere in between,
first in the class or middle or last,
we're all the same to Him.
It really doesn't matter
how clever you are,
Jesus loves you whoever you are.
La, la, la, la . . .

285 Nahum Tate (1652–1715)

1 **While shepherds watched
their flocks by night,**
all seated on the ground,
the angel of the Lord came down
and glory shone around.

2 'Fear not,' said he – for mighty dread
had seized their troubled mind –
'Glad tidings of great joy I bring
to you and all mankind:

3 'To you in David's town this day
is born of David's line,
a Saviour, who is Christ the Lord.
And this shall be the sign:

4 'The heavenly babe you there shall find
to human view displayed,
all meanly wrapped in swaddling bands,
and in a manger laid.'

5 Thus spake the angel; and forthwith
appeared a shining throng
of angels praising God, who thus
addressed their joyful song:

6 'All glory be to God on high,
and to the earth be peace;
goodwill henceforth from heaven to men
begin and never cease!'

286 Betty Lou Mills and Russell J Mills
© 1968 B L Mills and R J Mills /
Copyright control

1 **Who took fish and bread,
hungry people fed?**
Who changed water into wine?
Who made well the sick,
who made see the blind?
Who touched earth with feet divine?
Only Jesus, only Jesus,
only He has done this:
Who made live the dead?
Truth and kindness spread?
Only Jesus did all this.

2 Who walked dusty road?
    Cared for young and old?
Who sat children on His knee?
Who spoke words so wise?
    Filled men with surprise?
Who gave all but charged no fee?
Only Jesus, only Jesus,
    only He has done this:
Who in death and grief
    spoke peace to a thief?
Only Jesus did all this.

3 Who soared through the air?
    Joined His Father there?
He has you and me in view:
He who this has done is God's only Son,
and He's interested in you.
Only Jesus, only Jesus,
    only He has done this:
He can change a heart,
    give a fresh new start,
only He can do all this.

287 Frances Ridley Havergal (1836–79)
altered © 1986 Horrobin/Leavers

1 **Who is on the Lord's side?**
Who will serve the King?
Who will be His helpers
other lives to bring?
Who will leave the world's side?
Who will face the foe?
Who is on the Lord's side?
Who for Him will go?
By His call of mercy,
now our lives we bring,
we are on the Lord's side;
Jesus, He's our King.

2 Fierce may be the conflict,
strong may be the foe,
but the King's own army
none can overthrow.
Round His standard ranging,
victory is secure,
for His truth unchanging
makes the triumph sure.
Joyfully enlisting,
now our lives we bring,
we are on the Lord's side;
Jesus, He's our King.

3 Chosen to be soldiers
in an alien land,
chosen, called, and faithful,
for our captain's band;
in the service royal
let us not grow cold;
let us be right loyal,
noble, true and bold.
Master, You will keep us,
serving You we sing:
'Always on the Lord's side,
Jesus, always King!'

288 J A P Booth
© 1980 Paul Booth / CopyCare

1 **Who put the colours in the rainbow?**
Who put the salt into the sea?
Who put the cold into the snowflake?
Who made you and me?
Who put the hump upon the camel?
Who put the neck on the giraffe?
Who put the tail upon the monkey?
Who made hyenas laugh?
Who made whales and snails and quails?
Who made hogs and dogs and frogs?
Who made bats and rats and cats?
Who made everything?

2 Who put the gold into the sunshine?
Who put the sparkle in the stars?
Who put the silver in the moonlight?
Who made Earth and Mars?
Who put the scent into the roses?
Who taught the honey bee to dance?
Who put the tree inside the acorn?
It surely can't be chance!
Who made seas and leaves and trees?
Who made snow and winds that blow?
Who made streams and rivers flow?
God made all of these!

289 Annie Bush
© Mrs A Spiers

Who's the king of the jungle?
Who's the king of the sea?
Who's the king of the universe
and who's the king of me?
I'll tell you J-E-S-U-S is,
He's the king of me,
He's the king of the universe,
the jungle and the sea.

290 Priscilla Jane Owens (1829–1907)

1 **Will your anchor hold
      in the storms of life,**
   when the clouds unfold
      their wings of strife?
   When the strong tides lift,
      and the cables strain,
   will your anchor drift, or firm remain?
      *We have an anchor that keeps the soul
      steadfast and sure while the billows roll;
      fastened to the rock
         which cannot move,
      grounded firm and deep
         in the Saviour's love!*

2 Will your anchor hold in the straits of fear,
   when the breakers roar
      and the reef is near?
   While the surges rage,
      and the wild winds blow,
   shall the angry waves
      then your life o'erflow?
      We have an anchor . . .

3 Will your anchor hold
      in the floods of death,
   when the waters cold
      chill your final breath?
   On the rising tide you can never fail,
   while your anchor holds within the veil.
      We have an anchor . . .

4 Will your eyes behold
      through the morning light,
   the city of gold and the harbour bright?
   Will you anchor safe
      by the heavenly shore,
   when life's storms are past for evermore?
      We have an anchor . . .

291 Anon
Copyright control

**With Jesus in the boat
   we can smile at the storm,**
smile at the storm, smile at the storm,
with Jesus in the boat
   we can smile at the storm
as we go sailing home.
Sailing, sailing home,
sailing, sailing home,
with Jesus in the boat
   we can smile at the storm
as we go sailing home.

292 C Austin Miles (1865–1946)
© 1917, 1945 Word Music, LLC / CopyCare

**Wide, wide as the ocean,
   high as the heaven above,**
deep, deep as the deepest sea
   is my Saviour's love.
I, though so unworthy,
   still am a child of His care,
for His word teaches me that His love
   reaches me everywhere.

293 John Hampden Gurney (1802–1862)

1 **Yes, God is good – in earth and sky,**
   from ocean depths and spreading wood,
   ten thousand voices seem to cry:
   'God made us all, and God is good!'

2 The sun that keeps his trackless way,
   and downward pours his golden flood,
   night's sparkling hosts, all seem to say
   in accents clear that God is good.

3 The joyful birds prolong the strain,
their song with every spring renewed;
the air we breathe, and falling rain,
each softly whispers: 'God is good!'

4 I hear it in the rushing breeze;
the hills that have for ages stood,
the echoing sky and roaring seas,
all swell the chorus: 'God is good!'

5 Yes, God is good, all nature says,
by God's own hand with speech endued;
and man, in louder notes of praise,
should sing for joy that God is good.

6 For all Your gifts we bless You, Lord,
but chiefly for our heavenly food,
Your pardoning grace,
   Your quickening word,
these prompt our song, that God is good.

294 Albert B Simpson (1843–1919)

Yesterday, today, for ever,
Jesus is the same;
all may change, but Jesus never,
glory to His name!
Glory to His name!
Glory to His name!
All may change, but Jesus never,
glory to His name!

295 Georgian Banov
© 1978 Brentwood Benson Catalogue

1 **Your ways are higher than mine,**
Your ways are higher than mine,
Your ways are higher than mine,
much higher.
Your ways are higher than mine,
Your ways are higher than mine,
Your ways are higher than mine,
much higher.
Higher, higher, much much higher,
higher, higher, much higher.
Higher, higher, much much higher,
higher, higher, much higher.

2 Your thoughts are wiser . . .

3 Your strength is greater . . .

   Hallelujah, hallelujah,
   hallelujah, hallelu.
   Hallelujah, hallelujah,
   hallelujah, hallelu.

296 Mavis Ford
© 1978 Authentic Publishing / CopyCare

You are the King of glory,
You are the Prince of peace,
You are the Lord of heaven and earth,
You're the Son of righteousness.
Angels bow down before You,
worship and adore,
for You have the words of eternal life,
You are Jesus Christ the Lord.
Hosanna to the Son of David!
Hosanna to the King of kings!
Glory in the highest heaven,
for Jesus the Messiah reigns!

297 John Gowans
© 1970 Salvationist Publishing and Supplies Ltd /
CopyCare

1 **You can't stop rain from falling down,**
prevent the sun from shining,
you can't stop spring from coming in,
or winter from resigning,
or still the waves or stay the winds,
or keep the day from dawning;
you can't stop God from loving you,
His love is new each morning.

2 You can't stop ice from being cold,
you can't stop fire from burning,
or hold the tide that's going out,
delay its sure returning,
or halt the progress of the years,
the flight of fame and fashion;
you can't stop God from loving you,
His nature is compassion.

3 You can't stop God from loving you,
   though you may disobey Him.
   You can't stop God from loving you,
   however you betray Him.
   From love like this no power on earth
   the human heart can sever.
   You can't stop God from loving you,
   not God, not now, not ever.

298 Edward Hayes Plumptre (1821–91)

1 **Your hand, O God, has guided**
   Your flock, from age to age;
   Your faithfulness is written
   on history's open page;
   our fathers knew Your goodness,
   and we their deeds record;
   and both to this bear witness:
   One Church, one faith, one Lord.

2 Your heralds brought the gospel
   to greatest as to least;
   they summoned men to hasten
   and share the great King's feast;
   and this was all their teaching
   in every deed and word;
   to all alike proclaiming:
   One Church, one faith, one Lord.

3 Through many days of darkness,
   through many scenes of strife,
   the faithful few fought bravely
   to guard the nation's life.
   Their gospel of redemption,
   sin pardoned, man restored,
   was all in this enfolded:
   One Church, one faith, one Lord.

4 Your mercy will not fail us,
   nor leave Your work undone;
   with Your right hand to help us,
   the victory shall be won;
   and then by earth and heaven
   Your name shall be adored,
   and this shall be their anthem:
   One Church, one faith, one Lord.

299 Edmond Budry (1854–1932)
      tr. R Birch Hoyle (1875–1939)
      © in this version The Jubilate Group

1 **Yours be the glory,**
     risen, conquering Son,
   endless is the victory over death You won;
   angels robed in splendour
     rolled the stone away,
   kept the folded grave-clothes
     where Your body lay.
   Yours be the glory,
     risen, conquering Son,
   endless is the victory
     over death You won.

2 See! Jesus meets us,
     risen from the tomb;
   lovingly He greets us,
     scatters fear and gloom;
   let the Church with gladness
     hymns of triumph sing,
   for her Lord is living;
     death has lost its sting.
   Yours be the glory . . .

3 No more we doubt You,
     glorious Prince of life;
   what is life without You?
     Aid us in our strife;
   make us more than conquerors,
     through Your deathless love:
   bring us safe through Jordan
     to Your home above.
   Yours be the glory . . .

300 Anon
      Copyright control

Zacchaeus was a very little man,
and a very little man was he.
He climbed up into a sycamore tree
for the Saviour he wanted to see.
And when the Saviour passed that way
He looked into the tree
and said, 'Now, Zacchaeus, you come down,
for I'm coming to your house to tea.'

301

© 1986 Peter Horrobin

1 **Lord, we ask now to receive
    Your blessing,**
    Lord, we ask now to receive Your love,
    Come, we pray, come, we pray
    and lead us hour by hour.
    Bless, we ask, our friends and
        close relations,
    let them feel Your touch of loving power.

2 Lord, we trust You to give us
    Your blessing,
    Lord, we trust You to give us Your love.
    As we give, as we give
    our lives afresh to You.
    Take, we ask, all that we have
        and are, Lord,
    let them now be used in service true.

3 Lord, we give to others now
    Your blessing,
    Lord, we give to others now Your love.
    As we share, as we share
    with them the life You've given.
    Yes, we will, in harmony with You, Lord,
    let them see in us a touch of heaven.

302

Paul Field
© 1991 Daybreak Music Ltd / CopyCare

1 **A naggy mum, a grumpy dad,
    a brother who's a pain.**
    A sister who takes toys and never
        gives them back again.
    *All the same, all the same,
    in sunshine and in rain.
    No matter who we are, you know,
    God loves us all the same.*

2 An auntie who cooks sprouts for tea
        and makes you eat them all.
    A grandad who tells terrible jokes
        and drives you up the wall.
    All the same . . .

3 An uncle who forgets about your birthday
        when it comes.
    A teacher who gets cross with you
        and makes you do more sums.
    All the same . . .

303

From John 13
© Roy Crabtree

A new commandment that I give to you,
is to love one another as I have loved you,
is to love one another as I have loved you.

By this shall all men know
        that you are My disciples,
if you have love one for another;
by this shall all men know
        that you are My disciples,
if you have love one for another.

304

© Timothy Dudley-Smith

1 **A purple robe, a crown of thorn,**
    a reed in His right hand;
    before the soldiers' spite and scorn
    I see my Saviour stand.

2 He bears between the Roman guard
    the weight of all our woe;
    a stumbling figure bowed and scarred
    I see my Saviour go.

3 Fast to the cross's spreading span,
    high in the sunlit air,
    all the unnumbered sins of man
    I see my Saviour bear.

4 He hangs, by whom the world was made,
    beneath the darkened sky;
    the everlasting ransom paid,
    I see my Saviour die.

5 He shares on high His Father's throne,
    who once in mercy came;
    for all His love to sinners shown
    I sing my Saviour's name.

305

© 1992 Laura and Heather Bradley
Copyright control

1 **A special star is in the sky**
    to lead the way (to lead the way);
    a tiny stable cold and lonely
    where they can stay
        (where they can stay).

But our hearts have been warm,
since the day Jesus Christ was born,
and that's the way it shall stay,
because He is the way,
  the truth and the life,
  (the truth and the life).

2 The shepherds left their flocks behind
   to see the Babe (to see the Babe);
   the angel told them to bring a gift so
   a lamb they gave (a lamb they gave).
     But our hearts . . .

3 The wise men came from lands afar,
   on camels they rode,
     (on camels they rode);
   the gifts they offered were frankincense,
   myrrh and gold (myrrh and gold).
     But our hearts . . .

306 Paul Field
         © 1991 Daybreak Music Ltd / CopyCare

1 **A wiggly waggly worm,**
     a slippery slimy slug,
   a creepy crawly buzzy thing,
     a tickly wickly bug.
   Of all the things to be,
     I'm happy that I'm me.
   Thank you, Lord, I'm happy that I'm me.

   I'm happy that I'm me, happy that I'm me.
   There's no-one else in all the world
     that I would rather be.
   A wiggly waggly worm,
     a slippery slimy slug,
   a creepy crawly buzzy thing,
     a tickly wickly bug.

2 A prickly porcupine, a clumsy kangaroo,
   A croaky frog, a hairy hog,
     a monkey in a zoo.
   Of all the things to be,
     I'm happy that I'm me.
   Thank you, Lord, I'm happy that I'm me.

   I'm happy that I'm me, happy that I'm me.
   There's no-one else in all the world
     that I would rather be.
   A prickly porcupine, a clumsy kangaroo,
   a croaky frog, a hairy hog,
     a monkey in a zoo.

307 Paul Field and Ralph Chambers
         © 1991 Daybreak Music Ltd / CopyCare

All you have to do is to ask the Lord
to forgive the wrong things you have done.
Tell Him that you're sorry you have hurt Him,
and then believe that Jesus is God's Son.
He died on the cross to be your Saviour,
rose from the dead to be your special friend.
Ask Him in your heart,
     make a brand new start.
Love and serve Him till your life shall end.

308 Anon
         Copyright control

1 **Alleluia. (*8 times*)**

2 How I love Him . . .

3 Blessèd Jesus . . .

4 My Redeemer . . .

5 Jesus, Master . . .

6 Alleluia . . .

309 Kathie Hill and Janet McMahan
         © 2003 Kathie Hill Music /
         Word Music, LLC / CopyCare

   Are you humbly grateful
   or grumbly hateful?
   What's your attitude?
   Do you grumble and groan,
   or let it be known
   you're grateful for all
   God's done for you?

1 When Jonah found himself
   in the belly of a whale,
   did he cause a riot inside?
   No!
   He headed for shore
   with his message from God
   and thanked the Lord
   for his free ride.
   Phew!
     Are you humbly grateful . . .

2 When Noah found himself
in the floating zoo,
did he ever try to jump ship?
No!
For forty long days
and for forty long nights
he cleared the deck
on that long trip!
Phew!
   Are you humbly grateful . . .

      Which one are you?
Spoken Which one are you?

3 God helps the farmers cut the corn,
He keeps the weather dry and warm,
until it's baled and brought inside,
before the start of wintertide.
   Praise the Lord . . .

4 Now once the crops are in their barns
there's work to do still on the farms.
It's time to put the crops to use
to make the different kinds of foods.
   Praise the Lord . . .

5 At harvest time we celebrate
God's gifts to us of food and drink.
Let's sing and clap to show our thanks
for all the care God takes of us.
   Praise the Lord . . .
   Praise the Lord . . .

310 Peter and Hanneke Jacobs
© 1988 Maranatha! Music / CopyCare

And we know that all things,
all things, all things work together for good,
yes, we know that all things,
all things, all things work together for good!
To them that love the Lord,
to them that love the Lord,
to them that love the Lord,
and are called according to His purpose.
And we know that all things,
all things, all things work together for good,
yes, we know that all things,
all things, all things work together for good.
Romans eight, verse twenty-eight.

312 Anon
Copyright control

Be careful, little hands, what you do,
be careful, little hands, what you do.
There's a Father up above who is
      looking down in love,
so be careful, little hands, what you do.

311 Sandie L Scarr
© Mrs S L Scarr

1 **At harvest time we celebrate**
God's gift to us of food and drink.
We thank Him for the care He's shown
for farmers and the seeds they've sown.
   Praise the Lord! Praise the Lord!
   Praise the Lord! Praise the Lord!
   Praise the Lord! Praise the Lord!
   Thank Him for harvest.

2 God's watched the fields
      through day and night,
He's given the seeds both dark and light.
He's watered them with fresh cool rain
and now there's fields and fields of grain.
   Praise the Lord . . .

313 Geoffrey Ainger
© 1964, 1972 Stainer & Bell Ltd

1 **Born in the night,**
   Mary's child,
a long way from Your home:
coming in need,
   Mary's child,
born in a borrowed room.

2 Clear shining light,
   Mary's child,
Your face lights up our way:
light of the world,
   Mary's child,
dawn on our darkened day.

3   Truth of our life,
        Mary's child,
    You tell us God is good:
    prove it is true,
        Mary's child,
    go to Your cross of wood.

4   Hope of the world,
        Mary's child,
    You're coming soon to reign:
    King of the earth,
        Mary's child,
    walk in our streets again.

314   © 1991 Alan Brown

1   **Be holy in all that you do,**
    be holy in all that you do,
    be holy in all that you do today,
    be holy in all that you do,
    you are a chosen people,
    be holy in all that you do,
    you are a chosen people,
    be holy in all that you do.

2   Be holy in all that you say . . .

3   Be holy in all that you think . . .

4   Be holy in all that you are . . .

315   Valerie Ruddle and William Horton
From *New Songs of Praise 5*
© Oxford University Press

   Bring your Christingle
   with gladness and joy!
   Sing praise to God
   who gave us His Son;
   so give Him, give Him your love.

LEADER
1   Here is an orange –
    ALL
    An orange as round as the world
        that God made.
        Bring your Christingle . . .

LEADER
2   Here is a candle –
    ALL
    A candle for Jesus, the Light of the world,
    an orange as round as the world
        that God made;
        Bring your Christingle . . .

LEADER
3   Here is red ribbon –
    ALL
    Red ribbon reminds us
        Christ died for us all;
    a candle for Jesus, the Light of the world;
    an orange as round as the world
        that God made;
        Bring your Christingle . . .

LEADER
4   Here are the fruits –
    ALL
    The fruits of the earth God has given
        us to share;
    red ribbon reminds us
        Christ died for us all;
    a candle for Jesus, the Light of the world;
    an orange as round as the world
        that God made;
        Bring your Christingle . . .

316   © Geoffrey Marshall-Taylor / The Jubilate Group

1   **Can you be sure that the rain will fall?**
    Can you be sure that birds will fly?
    Can you be sure that rivers will flow?
    Or that the sun will light the sky?
        God has promised.
        God never breaks a promise He makes.
        His word is always true.

2   Can you be sure that the tide will turn?
    Can you be sure that grass will grow?
    Can you be sure that night will come,
    or that the sun will melt the snow?
        God has promised . . .

3 You can be sure that God is near;
   you can be sure He won't let you down;
   you can be sure He'll always hear;
   and that He's given Jesus, His Son.
     God has promised . . .

Well, this experience is not imagination;
it's a fact, oh yes, it's true.
And I just can't keep it to myself;
I'll pass it on to you,
and you, and you, and you.

317 Paul Field
© 1991 Daybreak Music Ltd / CopyCare

1 **Can you count the stars shining**
   in the sky?
   Can you hold the moonlight
     in your hand?
   Can you stop the waves rolling
     on the shore?
   Or find the place where rainbows
     meet the land?
     I've got a friend, who knows how
       all these things are done,
     Jesus, Lord of all, God's only Son.

2 Up in outer space,
     planets spinning round,
   millions more than we can ever see.
   It's hard to understand how God,
     who made it all,
   still cares about someone
     like you and me.
     I've got a friend . . .

318 Jeanette Smart
© Lillenas Publishing Co / CopyCare

1 **Can you imagine how it feels to know**
   the God who made the earth
     and sky and sea?
   When He created all the universe,
   His mighty plan included you and me.
     Well, this experience is not imagination;
     it's a fact, oh yes, it's true.
     And I just can't keep it to myself;
     I'll pass it on to you.

2 Can you imagine how it feels to have
   a Friend who never slumbers,
     never sleeps?
   Can you believe that when He comes into
   your heart and says He'll live there,
     it's for keeps?

319 © Timothy Dudley-Smith / OUP

1 **Christ be my leader by night as by day;**
   safe through the darkness,
     for He is the way.
   Gladly I follow, my future His care;
   darkness is daylight when Jesus is there.

2 Christ be my teacher in age as in youth,
   drifting or doubting, for He is the truth.
   Grant me to trust Him,
     though shifting as sand;
   doubt cannot daunt me, in Jesus I stand.

3 Christ be my Saviour in calm as in strife;
   death cannot hold me, for He is the life.
   Not darkness nor doubting
     nor sin and its stain
   can touch my salvation:
     with Jesus I reign.

320 Joe E Parks
© Brentwood Benson Catalogue

1 **Children, join the celebration**
   on this happy Easter day;
   Christ the Lord is risen as He said!
   Mary on that early morning
   heard the angel gladly say:
   'Jesus lives – He is no longer dead!'

2 Praise Him now with songs of gladness,
   sing triumphant hymns of praise:
   Christ the Lord is risen as He said!
   Children, join the celebration,
   with the hosts of heaven say:
   'Jesus Christ, our Saviour, lives today!'

321
Ernie and Debbie Rettino
© Maranatha! Music / CopyCare

Christmas is a time, Christmas is a time,
Christmas is a time to love.
Christmas is a time, Christmas is a time,
Christmas is a time to love.

We often start to worry, and people get upset
if things don't all go right on Christmas day.
What we should remember in all the push
    and shove,
is Christmas is a time of love.

Christmas is a time, Christmas is a time,
Christmas is a time to love.
Christmas is a time, Christmas is a time,
Christmas is a time to love.

322
Jimmy and Carol Owens
© 1980 Bud John Songs / Alliance Media Ltd /
CopyCare

Christmas isn't Christmas
    till it happens in your heart;
somewhere deep inside you
    is where Christmas really starts.
So give your heart to Jesus;
    you'll discover when you do
that it's Christmas,
    really Christmas for you.

Jesus brings warmth like a winter fire,
a light like a candle's glow.
He's waiting now to come inside
as He did so long ago.
Jesus brings gifts of truth and life,
and makes them bloom and grow.
So welcome Him with a song of joy,
and when He comes, you'll know,

that Christmas isn't Christmas
    till it happens in your heart;
somewhere deep inside you
    is where Christmas really starts.
So give your heart to Jesus;
    you'll discover when you do
that it's Christmas, really Christmas;
Christmas, really Christmas for you.

323
Valerie Collison
© 1972 Campbell Connelly & Co Ltd

Come and join the celebration,
it's a very special day;
come and share our jubilation,
there's a new King born today!

1 See the shepherds
    hurry down to Bethlehem;
    gaze in wonder
    at the Son of God who lay before them.
    Come and join . . .

2 Wise men journey,
    led to worship by a star;
    kneel in homage,
    bringing precious gifts from lands afar, so
    Come and join . . .

3 'God is with us,'
    round the world the message bring;
    He is with us,
    'Welcome!' all the bells on earth are
      pealing.
    Come and join . . .

324
From Psalm 95
© 1987 Ruth Hooke

BOYS   **Come, let us sing**
        for joy to the Lord.

GIRLS Come, let us sing for joy to the Lord.

BOYS   We will sing, we will sing,
        we will sing.

GIRLS We will sing, we will sing,
        we will sing.

BOYS   Let us shout aloud
        to the rock of our salvation.

GIRLS Let us shout aloud
        to the rock of our salvation.

BOYS   We will shout! We will shout!
        We will shout!

GIRLS We will shout! We will shout!
        We will shout!

ALL   For the Lord is the great God,
        the great King above all gods.

BOYS   Splendour and majesty,

GIRLS   splendour and majesty,

BOYS   are before Him,

GIRLS   are before Him.

BOYS   Strength and glory,

GIRLS   strength and glory,

ALL   are in His sanctuary.

325   Patricia Morgan and Dave Bankhead
© 1984 Thankyou Music

Come on and celebrate!
His gift of love we will celebrate –
the Son of God, who loved us
and gave us life.

We'll shout Your praise, O King:
You give us joy nothing else can bring;
we'll give to You our offering
in celebration praise.

Come on and celebrate, celebrate,
celebrate and sing,
celebrate and sing to the King.
Come on and celebrate, celebrate,
celebrate and sing,
celebrate and sing to the King!

326   © Carolyn Keats

Counting, counting, one, two, three,
clap my hands and
sing for joy, for
God made ME!
Three, four, five, six,
* and number seven too;*
shout it loud, make
sure you're heard, for
God made YOU!

1   I have ten toes, ten fingers,
two legs on which I stand,
an arm on either side of me,
at the end of each a hand;
a right ear and a left ear,
a head to shake and nod,
two eyes, one nose, a mouth, a voice
to whisper or to SHOUT!
   Counting, counting . . .

2   God made me very different
from everyone I see,
my size and shape and colour,
He chose it carefully.
God is so very clever
He made the whole world too;
He put the life in everything
including me and you.
   Counting, counting . . .

327   Ian White
© Little Misty Music Ltd

1   **Crackers and turkeys and pudding**
      and cream,
toys in the windows that I've never seen.
This is the Christmas that everyone sees,
but Christmas means more to me.
   It's somebody's birthday I won't forget,
   as I open the things that I get.
   I'll remember the inn and the stable
      so bare,
   and Jesus who once lay there.

2   Everyone's out shopping late every night,
for candles and presents and
      Christmas tree lights.
This is the Christmas that everyone sees,
but Christmas means more to me.
   It's somebody's birthday . . .

3   Christmas morning, the start of the day,
there's presents to open and new games
      to play.
This is the Christmas that everyone sees,
but Christmas means more to me.
   It's somebody's birthday . . .

328 Ralph Chambers

Don't know much about the ozone layer,
rain forests seem miles away.
But each of us can be a player,
fight to save the world God has made.
This is God's world.
This is God's world,
and you're a member of the human race.
This is God's world.
This is God's world.
Let's try to make it a better place.

329 Frances Towle Rath

1 **Did you ever talk to God above?**
   Tell Him that you need a friend to love?
   Pray in Jesus' name believing
   that God answers prayer?

2 Have you told Him
        all your cares and woes?
   Every tiny little fear He knows.
   You can know He'll always hear
   and He will answer prayer.

3 You can whisper in a crowd to Him.
   You can cry when you're alone to Him.
   You don't have to pray out loud to Him;
   He knows your thoughts.

4 On a lofty mountain peak, He's there.
   In a meadow by a stream, He's there.
   Anywhere on earth you go
   He's been there from the start.

5 Find the answer in His word; it's true.
   You'll be strong
        because He walks with you.
   By His faithfulness He'll change you too.
   God answers prayer.

330 Sam Horner

1 **Even if I don't like the way things
      went today,**
   even if I'm feeling down,
      I'll praise You anyway.
   If I'm feeling lonely, if I'm feeling bad,
   I'll think about the things You've done,
      and even when I'm sad:
      I will worship You in spirit and in truth,
      I will worship You in spirit and in truth,
      I will worship You in spirit and in truth,
      I will worship You in spirit and in truth.

2 When my life is going great,
      when everything is right,
   help me not to forget You, Lord,
      or keep You out of sight.
   I don't want to leave You out,
      not even for a day,
   I want to see Your hand at work
      and hear the words You say.
      I will worship You . . .

331

1 **Every day, if you go astray,**
   stop! and turn around.
   Then don't worry if you've said sorry,
   stop! and turn around.
   When we come to Jesus
   He says He'll forgive us,
   for He cares about us.
   This is what He promises.
   When we come to Jesus
   He says He'll forgive us
   for He cares about us all.

2 Every day as we walk God's way
   stop! and praise the Lord.
   He will change us for He's living in us,
   stop! and praise the Lord.
   Jesus, You forgive us,
   then bring Your life to us
   through Your Holy Spirit.
   This is what You promise us.
   Jesus, You forgive us,
   then bring Your life to us
   through Your Spirit in our lives.

3 Jesus, Saviour, Redeemer and King,
   let's go! and live for Him.
   Son of God, our helper and friend,
   go! and live for Him.
   Jesus, how we thank You,
   Jesus, how we love You,
   Jesus, help us trust You
   till the day You come again.
   Jesus, how we thank You,
   Jesus, how we love You,
   Jesus, help us trust You more.

332 © 1992 Greg Leavers

Everybody join in singing this song,
thanking God for all the good things
*   He's done:*
showing love for us through Jesus
*   His Son,*
good and bad and the weak and
*   strong.*
Young and old all can sing along;
come on, everybody sing this song.

1 Thank God for the gift of life.
   Thank Him for His care.
   When our lives then get messed up,
   He'll clear out the bad things there.
   Everybody join in singing . . .

2 In our lives God wants to live,
   make His presence known.
   If we're sorry He'll forgive,
   then our hearts can be His home.
   Everybody join in singing . . .

333 Derek and Jackie Llewellyn
© 1990 Sandcastle Productions

Everyone in the whole wide world
matters to our friend Jesus.
Everyone, every boy or girl,
we all matter to Him.

1 Jump up if you're wearing red. (*Jump up*)
   Wave your arms if you're wearing blue.
      (*Wave*)
   Clap your hands if you're wearing green.
      (*Clap*)
   Stamp your feet if you're wearing shoes.
      (*Stamp*)
      Everyone in the whole wide world . . .

2 Jump up if you've ridden a bike. (*Jump*)
   Wave your arms if you've flown in a plane.
      (*Wave*)
   Clap your hands if you've been in a car.
      (*Clap*)
   Stamp your feet if you've been on a train.
      (*Stamp*)
      Everyone in the whole wide world . . .

334 Ian White
© Little Misty Music Ltd

Everywhere He walks with me,
and through prayer He talks with me.
He has cared enough for me,
to die to set me free.

1 Since then you have been raised
      with Christ,
   set your hearts on things above.
   Where Christ is seated
      at God's right hand,
   set your minds on things above.
      Everywhere He walks with me . . .

2 Put to death whatever is sin,
   rid yourselves of all these things.
   You have been renewed in the Lord,
   and He is all, and is in all.
      Everywhere He walks with me . . .

3 Let His peace now rule in your hearts.
   Let His word be rich in you.
   Sing psalms and hymns
      with thanks to God,
   praise Him in all that you do.
      Everywhere He walks with me . . .

335
© 1990 Greg Leavers

1 **Father, be with *her/his/their family,**
   as they cry with sadness today.
   Aching hearts feeling such a loss:
   may they know Your love.

2 Comfort them with Your love, O Lord,
   as they try to understand
   why You called *her/him/them
        to be with You;
   may they know Your peace.

* (Use the relevant word or use the child's name)

336
© 1990 Greg Leavers

1 **Father, for our friends we pray,**
   please be near to them today;
   in their sadness, through their tears,
   may they know Your peace.

2 Now that he/she is by Your side
   comfort friends when they ask why
   their dear loved one had to die;
   may they know Your love.

3 Though part of their lives has gone,
   give them strength to carry on.
   As they face the days to come,
   may they know Your care.

337
Ian Smale
© 1984 Thankyou Music

Father God, I wonder
how I managed to exist
without the knowledge
of Your parenthood
and Your loving care.
But now I am Your son,
I am adopted in Your family,
and I can never be alone
'cause, Father God,
You're there beside me.

I will sing Your praises,
I will sing Your praises,
I will sing Your praises for evermore.
I will sing Your praises,
I will sing Your praises,
I will sing Your praises for evermore.

338
Paul Crouch and David Mudie
© Daybreak Music Ltd / CopyCare

**Father, Your word is like a
        light in the darkness.**
Father, Your word is like a
        sharp, sharp sword.
Father, Your word is like a
        stream in the desert.
There's nothing that compares
        with the wisdom of Your word.

339
From Psalm 147
© Timothy Dudley-Smith / OUP

1 **Fill your hearts with joy and gladness,**
   sing and praise your God and mine!
   Great the Lord in love and wisdom,
   might and majesty divine!
   He who framed the starry heavens
   knows and names them as they shine.

2 Praise the Lord, His people, praise Him!
   wounded souls His comfort know;
   those who fear Him find His mercies,
   peace for pain and joy for woe;
   humble hearts are high exalted,
   human pride and power laid low.

3 Praise the Lord for times and seasons,
   cloud and sunshine, wind and rain;
   spring to melt the snows of winter
   till the waters flow again;
   grass upon the mountain pastures,
   golden valleys thick with grain.

4 Fill your hearts with joy and gladness,
   peace and plenty crown your days;
   love His laws, declare His judgements,
   walk in all His words and ways;
   He the Lord and we His children –
   praise the Lord, all people, praise!

340 Paul Crouch and David Mudie

**For the foolishness of God is wiser
than man's wisdom,**
and the weakness of God is stronger
than man's strength.
For the foolishness of God is wiser
than man's wisdom,
and the weakness of God is stronger
than man's strength.
For the foolishness of God is wiser
than man's wisdom,
and the weakness of God is stronger
than man's strength.
For the foolishness of God is wiser
than man's wisdom,
and the weakness of God is stronger
than man's strength.

God knows all about the world,
the things we cannot see,
the things that we don't understand
that baffle you and me.
His strength is never-ending
and we are weak and small.
His hand supports the universe
and He is in control.

For the foolishness of God . . .

341 Graham Kendrick

1 **From heaven You came, helpless babe,**
entered our world, Your glory veiled,
not to be served but to serve,
and give Your life that we might live.
*This is our God, the Servant King,
He calls us now to follow Him,
to bring our lives as a daily offering
of worship to the Servant King.*

2 There in the garden of tears
my heavy load He chose to bear;
His heart with sorrow was torn,
'Yet not my will but yours,' He said.
This is our God . . .

3 Come see His hands and His feet,
the scars that speak of sacrifice,
hands that flung stars into space
to cruel nails surrendered.
This is our God . . .

4 So let us learn how to serve
and in our lives enthrone Him,
each other's needs to prefer,
for it is Christ we're serving.
This is our God . . .

342

From my knees to my nose,
from my head to my toes,
does God know all about me?
If I'm happy or sad,
if I'm good or I'm bad,
does God know all about me?
The answer is yes
and He loves me the best,
though He knows everything about me.
The answer is yes
and He loves me the best,
and He knows that my name is . . .
(shout name)

343 C Powell and K Wood

*Get up out of bed,
have a yawn and scratch your head
and say, 'Thank you,
it's a brand new day.'*

*Stretch out, touch your toes,
blink your eyes and blow your nose
and say, 'Thank you,
it's a brand new day.'*

Actions for the chorus:
Crouch down and jump up.
Hand over mouth, scratch head.
Lift right palm upwards on the word 'Thank',
lift left palm on the word 'you'.
Arms out, bend over, touch your toes.
Clench fists and eyes, then open, hand to nose.
As before.

1 Jesus taught us all to go His way.
   Get out of bed and go with Him today.
   Get up out of bed . . .

2 Jesus showed us
         that He can make us new.
   Get out of bed and ask Him what to do.
   Get up out of bed . . .

3 Jesus loves us all just like He said.
   Get out of bed
         and shake your sleepy head.
   Get up out of bed . . .

344 Malcolm Sargent (1895–1967)
        © Oxford University Press
        in this version Word & Music / The Jubilate Group

1 **Girls and boys, leave your toys,
   make no noise,**
   kneel at His crib and worship Him.
   For this shrine, Child divine, is the sign
   our Saviour's here.
         Alleluia, the church bells ring.
         'Alleluia!' the angels sing,
         alleluia from everything –
   all must draw near!

2 On that day, far away, Jesus lay –
   angels were watching round His head.
   Holy Child, mother mild, undefiled,
   we sing Your praise.
         Alleluia . . .
   our hearts we raise.

3 Shepherds came at the fame
         of Your name,
   angels their guide to Bethlehem;
   in that place, saw Your face
         filled with grace,
   stood at Your door.
         Alleluia . . .
   love evermore.

345 Janet Morgan
        © 1989 Sandcastle Productions

   ***Give thanks to the Lord
   for He is good.***
   Give thanks to the Lord for ever.
   Give thanks to the Lord for He is good.

1 When you jump out of bed
   and you touch your toes,
   when you brush your teeth
   and put on your clothes,
         Give thanks . . .

2 When you eat your dinner
   and you're all full up,
   when your Mum says (*Name*)
   and you help wash up,
         Give thanks . . .

3 When you stretch up high
   and you touch the ground,
   when you stretch out wide
   and you turn around,
         Give thanks . . .

4 When you click your fingers
   and you stamp your feet,
   when you clap your hands
   and you slap your knees,
         Give thanks . . .
         Give thanks to the Lord. Amen.

346 © 1992 Gill Robertson

1 **God has made me, and He knows me,**
   He will listen to my prayer.
   Understanding, ever-loving,
   He's the God who's always there.
   Even though He made the world, He
   knows my name and cares for me.
   He will hear me when I call Him;
   in His heart I'll always be.

2 Help me, Lord, to understand
   that I'm a child who's loved by You.
   You'll protect me, and be with me
   in the things I have to do.
   Thank You, Lord, that I can trust You,
   thank You for the love You bring.
   Thank You that You'll never leave me;
   Father God, Your praise I sing.

347
Fred Pratt Green
© 1973 Stainer & Bell Ltd

1 **God in His love for us**
lent us this planet,
gave it a purpose in time and in space:
small as a spark from the fire of creation,
cradle of life and the home of our race.

2 Thanks be to God for its bounty
and beauty,
life that sustains us in body and mind:
plenty for all, if we learn how to share it,
riches undreamed of to fathom and find.

3 Long have the wars of man
ruined its harvest;
long has earth bowed
to the terror of force;
long have we wasted what others
have need of,
poisoned the fountain of life at its source.

4 Earth is the Lord's: it is ours to enjoy it;
ours, as His stewards,
to farm and defend.
From its pollution,
misuse and destruction,
good Lord deliver us, world without end!

348
Anon
Copyright control

God loves you, and I love you,
and that's the way it should be.
God loves you, and I love you,
and that's the way it should be.

1 You can be happy, and I can be happy,
and that's the way it should be.
You can be happy, and I can be happy,
and that's the way it should be.
God loves you . . .

2 You can be very sad, I can be very sad;
and that's the way it can be.
You can be very sad, I can be very sad;
and that's the way it can be.
God loves you . . .

3 We can love others
like sisters and brothers,
and that's the way it should be.
We can love others
like sisters and brothers,
and that's the way it should be.
God loves you . . .

349
Derek Llewellyn
© 1990 Sandcastle Productions

1 **God loves you so much,**
God wants you so much,
God wants to tell you so much
that He put it in a book for you.
And it's the Bible,
yes, it's the Bible,
oh, it's the Bible.
Yes, He put it in a letter
so we could know Him better.

2 He wants to know you so much,
He wants to show you so much,
God wants to tell you so much
that He put it in a book for you.
And it's the Bible . . .

3 God loves you so much,
God wants you so much,
God wants to tell you so much
that He put it in a book,
put it in a book for,
put it in a book for you.

350
© 1990 Fiona Inkpen
Copyright control

God of all mercy,
Your forgiveness and compassion
call forth songs from within
that fill our hearts with gladness.

351 © 1990 Greg Leavers

God told Joshua to take Jericho.
God told Joshua to take Jericho.
He said, 'Do it My way.'
Joshua said, 'OK.'
So through faith the city walls came
    down!

1 Marching round the city,
   priests are at the front,
   blowing on their trumpets,
   going round just once.
   This they did for six days,
   just as God had said;
   the priests were making all the noise, the
        rest were saying,
        God told Joshua . . .

2 God said on day seven,
   'Here is what you do:
   march around for six times,
   then do something new.
   When you're on lap seven,
   Jericho look out!
   All their walls will crumble when you give
        a great big SHOUT!!'
        God told Joshua . . .

352 © Peter Lewis

1 **God was there before the world**
      was made.
   God is here, He's with us every day.
   God is love and that will never change.
   Yesterday, today, forever
   He's the same.
   Yesterday, today, forever
   He's the same.

2 God is good, the Bible tells us so.
   God is wise,
      He knows what we don't know.
   God is true, no matter what we do.
   Yesterday, today, forever
   our life through.
   Yesterday, today, forever
   our life through.

3 God is like a Father to us all.
   God will always listen when we call.
   God's the one we worship and adore.
   Yesterday, today, forever
   He is Lord.
   Yesterday, today, forever
   He is Lord.

353 Timothy Dudley-Smith
Oxford University Press

1 **God whose love is everywhere**
   made our earth and all things fair,
   ever keeps them in His care;
      praise the God of love!
   He who hung the stars in space
   holds the spinning world in place;
      praise the God of love!

2 Come with thankful songs to sing
   of the gifts the seasons bring,
   summer, winter, autumn, spring;
      praise the God of love!
   He who gave us breath and birth
   gives us all the fruitful earth;
      praise the God of love!

3 Mark what love the Lord displayed,
   all our sins upon Him laid,
   by His blood our ransom paid;
      praise the God of love!
   Circled by that scarlet band
   all the world is in His hand;
      praise the God of love!

4 See the sign of love appear,
   flame of glory, bright and clear,
   light for all the world is here;
      praise the God of love!
   Gloom and darkness, get you gone!
   Christ the Light of life has shone;
      praise the God of love!

354 Ian White
© Little Misty Music Ltd

Going up to Jerusalem,
going up to Jerusalem,
going up to Jerusalem,
    (Jesus going up),
going up to Jerusalem,
    (Jesus going up).
Going up to Jerusalem,
going up to Jerusalem,
going up to Jerusalem,
    (Jesus going up),
going up to Jerusalem.

1 Hosanna, hosanna,
    we lay our branches down.
    Hosanna, hosanna,
    the King is coming to our town.
    Hosanna, hosanna today.

2 He's the Saviour, He's the Saviour,
    we lay our branches down.
    He's the Saviour, He's the Saviour,
    the King is coming to our town.
    Hosanna, hosanna today.

355 Paul Crouch and David Mudie
© 1989 Daybreak Music Ltd / CopyCare

1 **Grace is when God gives us**
    the things we don't deserve.
    Grace is when God gives us
    the things we don't deserve.
    He does it because He loves us.
    He does it because He loves us.
    Grace is when God gives us
    the things we don't deserve.

2 Mercy is when God gives us
    the things we don't deserve.
    Mercy is when God gives us
    the things we don't deserve.
    He does it because He loves us.
    He does it because He loves us.
    Mercy is when God gives us
    the things we don't deserve.

356 Richard J Hubbard
© 1989 Thankyou Music

1 **Hang on, stand still,**
    stay put, hold tight;
    wait for the Spirit of God.
    Don't push, don't shove,
    don't move, that's right;
    just wait for the Spirit of God.
    Hang on . . .

    For you will receive the power of God.
    You will receive the power of God.
    You will receive the power of God
    when the Holy Spirit is upon you.

2 Let go, launch out,
    press on, don't fight;
    be filled with the Spirit of God.
    Move on, make way,
    step out, that's right;
    be filled with the Spirit of God.
    Let go . . .

    For you have received the power of God.
    You have received the power of God.
    You have received the power of God
    now the Holy Spirit lives within you.

357 Mick Gisbey
© 1985 Thankyou Music

1 **Have you got an appetite?**
    Do you eat what is right?
    Are you feeding on the word of God?
    Are you fat or are you thin?
    Are you really full within?
    Do you find your strength in Him,
        or are you starving?

You and me all should be
  exercising regularly,
standing strong, all day long,
  giving God the glory.
Feeding on the living bread,
  not eating crumbs but loaves instead;
standing stronger, living longer,
  giving God the glory.
You and me all should be
  exercising regularly,
standing strong, all day long,
  giving God the glory.
Feeding on the living bread,
  not eating crumbs but loaves instead;
standing stronger, living longer,
  giving God the glory.

2 If it's milk or meat you need,
   why not have a slap-up feed,
   and stop looking like a weed
      and start to grow?
   Take the full-of-fitness food,
   taste and see that God is good,
   come on, feed on what you should
      and be healthy.
   You and me all should be
     exercising regularly,
   standing strong, all day long,
     giving God the glory.
   Feeding on the living bread,
     not eating crumbs but loaves instead;
   standing stronger, living longer,
     giving God the glory.
   You and me all should be
     exercising regularly,
   standing strong, all day long,
     giving God the glory.
   Feeding on the living bread,
     not eating crumbs but loaves instead;
   standing stronger, living longer,
     giving God the,
   giving God the, giving God the glory.

358 Ian Smale
© 1988 Thankyou Music

  Heavenly Father, we would sing out
    Your praise,
  You're everything a Father should be.
  Made us Your sons and daughters,
  made us Your own,
    children of God's family.

1 We older ones say, 'Younger ones,
   we'll love and care for you.'
   We young ones say to older ones,
   'Our love respects you too.'
   We love you.
     Heavenly Father . . .

2 Father, as a family
   we will live forever.
   Your Church is made of all ages
   who love to be together.
   We love you.
     Heavenly Father . . .

359 Denis and Nan Allen
© 1988 Pilot Point Music /
Lillenas Publishing / CopyCare

1 **He made the water wet,**
   He made the land stay dry.
   He put twinkle in the stars
   and blue in the sky.
   And when He was sure
   it worked as it should,
   God looked at His world and said,
   'That's good!'
     Good, good, good! He said,
       'That's good!'
     Good, good, good! God looked
       at His world and said,
     'That's good!'

2   He put a touch of wag
    in a puppy dog's tail,
    then put a little slow
    in a silly old snail.
    And when He was sure
    it worked as it should,
    God looked at His world and said,
    'That's good!'
        Good, good, good . . .

        That's good, that's good,
        (shouted) that's good!

360 Peter and Hanneke Jacobs
© 1988 Maranatha! Music / CopyCare

He gives me strength, yes,
    He gives me strength.
I can do all things through Christ
    who gives me strength.
Yes, He gives me strength,
    He gives me strength.
I can do all things through Christ
    who gives me strength.

361 Refrain: Frederick Whitfield
Copyright control

QUESTION   **Hey, you, (*name*) do you love**
               Jesus?
ANSWER   oh, yes, I love Jesus.
QUESTION   Are you sure you love Jesus?
ANSWER   Yes, I'm sure I love Jesus.
QUESTION   Tell me, why do you love Jesus?
ANSWER   This is why I love Jesus,
ALL   because He first loved me.
           Yes, I love Him,
               this is why I love Him.

           Oh, how I love Jesus.
           Oh, how I love Jesus.
           Oh, how I love Jesus,
           because He first loved me.
           Yes, I love Him,
               this is why I love Him.

362 Richard K Avery and Donald S Marsh
© 1967 Hope Publishing / CopyCare

Hey! Hey! Anybody listening?
Hey! Hey! Anybody there?
Hey! Hey! Anybody listening?
Anybody care?

1   We've got good news, good news,
            good news, good news:
    Christ the Lord will soon be found here!
    Good news, good news,
            good news, good news:
    let's help spread the news around here!
    If I had a drum I'd drum it,
    a mandolin I'd strum it,
    a humming-bird hum I'd hum it,
    everywhere, everywhere,
            everywhere, everywhere.
        Hey! Hey! . . .

2   People come on, come on,
            come on, come on:
    let's sing out for Mary's Son here!
    Come on, come on, come on, come on:
    He'll bring joy for everyone here!
    If I had a harp I'd twang it,
    a tambourine I'd bang it,
    a fireman's bell I'd clang it,
    everywhere, everywhere,
            everywhere, everywhere.
        Hey! Hey! . . .

3   Come on, sing out, sing out,
            sing out, sing out!
    Tell the world about His birth now!
    Sing out, sing out, sing out, sing out
    loud and clear to all the earth now!
    If I had a chime I'd ring it,
    a finger cymbal ching it,
    we've got this song let's sing it,
    everywhere, everywhere,
            everywhere, everywhere.
        Hey! Hey! . . .

363

His name was Saul of Tarsus,
a clever Pharisee;
he studied Greek and Latin
and he spoke them fluently.
The only thing he wanted
was to wipe out those who said,
'We are followers of Jesus
and His truth we want to spread!'
Saul, Saul, Saul, Saul,
you're persecuting Me;
the Christians that you're killing
are true followers of Me.
Saul, Saul, Saul, Saul,
you really need to see
I came to bring forgiveness and
to set all people free.

2 Determined to pursue them
on his way he quickly strode,
heading for Damascus
along the well-worn road.
The followers of Jesus
he wanted locked away,
but little did he know
that God would speak to him that day.
Saul, Saul . . .

3 When God had finished speaking
Saul stood and tried to find
the men who had been with him,
but the light had made him blind.
They led him to a little house,
he stayed for just three days.
When he realised what had happened
he was simply quite amazed.
Saul, Saul . . .

4 This brought about a change in Saul,
he'd never be the same;
not only had his life been changed
he'd got a different name.
The Lord had given to Paul the task
to go to everyone,
and tell them that the way to God
is only through His Son.
Saul, Saul . . .

364

His ways are not our ways
but His ways are the best.
If we follow Jesus
we know that we'll be blessed.
If we trust Him He will help us,
listen when we pray.
His ways are not our ways
but His ways are the best.

1 When I call He listens,
when I fall He's near.
He has promised He will help me,
I will never fear.
His ways . . .

2 If I ever wander, if I turn from Him,
He has promised He will help me,
I will never fear.
His ways . . .

3 He will always love me,
He will always care.
He has promised He will help me,
I will never fear.
His ways . . .

365

1 **Hosanna, hosanna,**
hosanna in the highest;
hosanna, hosanna, hosanna in the
highest.
Lord, we lift up Your name,
with hearts full of praise.
Be exalted, O Lord my God –
hosanna, in the highest.

2 Glory, glory, glory to the King of kings;
glory, glory, glory to the King of kings.
Lord, we lift up Your name,
with hearts full of praise.
Be exalted, O Lord my God –
glory to the King of kings.

366
© 1992 Greg Leavers

**I am like a house with two windows
and a door,**
but underneath I have two legs
that reach down to the floor;
two ears to hear what's happening
and a thatched roof up above,
but right inside God's given me a heart
that's full of love.
So jump up and turn around
and thank the Lord with joyful sound.
So jump up and turn around
and thank the Lord, and now sit down!

4 And when the people gather there's
singing and there's praying,
there's laughing and there's crying
sometimes, all of it saying:
I am the Church . . .

5 At Pentecost some people received
the Holy Spirit
and told the good news through the world
to all who would hear it.
I am the Church . . .

6 I count if I am ninety, or nine,
or just a baby;
there's one thing I am sure about
and I don't mean maybe:
I am the Church . . .

367
Richard K Avery and Donald S Marsh
© 1972 Hope Publishing / CopyCare

I am the Church! –
(With your thumb, point to yourself)
You are the Church! –
(Point to your partner)
We are the Church together! –
(Shake hands)
All who follow Jesus, –
(Reach out with both hands)
all around the world, –
(Circle arms over head)
yes, we're the Church together. –
(Link arms)

1 The Church is not a building,
the Church is not a steeple.
The Church is not a resting-place,
the Church is a people!
I am the Church . . .

2 We're many kinds of people
with many kinds of faces:
all colours and all ages, too,
from all times and places.
I am the Church . . .

3 Sometimes the Church is marching,
sometimes it's bravely burning,
sometimes it's riding, sometimes hiding.
Always it's learning!
I am the Church . . .

368
Peter and Hanneke Jacobs
© 1988 Maranatha! Music / CopyCare

I am the resurrection and the life.
I am the resurrection and the life.
He that believes in Me though he may die
yet shall he live again.
And whoever lives and believes in Me,
and whoever lives and believes in Me,
the Bible says in John eleven
twenty-five and twenty-six
that we shall never die.

369
Kelly Willard
© 1978 Maranatha! Music / CopyCare

1 **I cast all my cares upon You.**
I lay all of my burdens down at Your feet.
And any time that I don't know
what to do,
I will cast all my cares upon You.

2 I cast all my cares upon You.
I lay all of my burdens down at Your feet.
And any time that I don't know
what to do,
I will cast all of my cares upon You.
I will cast all my cares upon You.

370

1 **I have a friend
 who is deeper than the ocean;**
 I have a friend who is wider than the sky.
 I have a friend
  who always understands me,
 whether I'm happy, or ready to cry.

2 If I am lost
  He will search until He finds me;
 if I am scared He will help me to be brave.
 All I've to do
  is to turn to Him and ask Him.
 I know He'll keep the promise He gave:

3 'Don't be afraid,' said Jesus,
  'I am with you.'
 'Don't be afraid,' said Jesus, 'I am here.
 Now and forever, anywhere you travel,
 I shall be with you, I'll always be near.'

371

I look out through the doorway,
who's that I see before me?
My young son coming home.
I must run to meet him,
hug him when I greet him,
and say, 'Son, welcome home.'
We will have a party
and I can't wait to start.
He must have the very finest food,
the best robe, ring and sandals.
He was lost, but now is found.
Welcome home, son, welcome home.

372

I love You, Lord Jesus,
the King of all things.
You love me, Lord Jesus,
Your love never ends.
To You I am special,
Your promises are true.
You love me, Lord Jesus,
and Lord, I love You.

373

I am a sheep, baa, baa,
and I like to be well fed;
but like a sheep, baa, baa,
I'm a little stupid in the head.
I go astray most every day.
Oh, what a trouble I must be!
I'm glad I've got the good shepherd (*spoken*)
looking after me, ha, ha, ha, ha, baa, baa.

374

1 **I want to love You, Lord;**
 I want to serve You, Lord;
 I want to please You, Lord;
 this is my prayer.

2 I want to love You, Lord;
 I want to serve You, Lord;
 I want to please You, Lord;
 this is my prayer.

375

1 **I want to tell you (I want to tell you)**
 my eyes are blue (my eyes are blue),
 I want to show you (I want to show you)
 what I can do (*clap! clap!*)
  (what I can do) (*clap! clap!*).
  *There's no-one, not one,
   in the world like me.
  I'm so very, very, very, very special,
   you see.
  There's no-one, not one,
   in the world like me,
  for God made me just the way
   He wanted me to be.*

2 There are so many (there are so many)
 things I can do (things I can do).
 I don't feel useless (I don't feel useless),
 these words are true
  (these words are true).
   There's no-one . . .

3 Jesus is special (Jesus is special),
   I'm special too (I'm special too).
   He says He loves me
       (He says He loves me)
   and He loves you (and He loves you).
       There's no-one . . .

376
© 1985 Thankyou Music

**I will wave my hands in praise
   and adoration;**
I will wave my hands in praise and adoration;
I will wave my hands in praise and adoration,
praise and adoration to the living God.
For He's given me hands
       that just love clapping –
one, two, one, two, three –
and He's given me a voice
       that just loves shouting, 'Hallelujah!'
He's given me feet that just love dancing –
one, two, one, two, three –
and He's put me in a being
       that has no trouble seeing
   that whatever I am feeling
   He is worthy to be praised.

377
© 1990 Greg Leavers

I'm a footstep follower
for Jesus leads the way.
He knows the life that's best for me:
a plan for every day.
As I walk and talk with Him,
He'll never let me stray.
I'm a footstep follower
for Jesus leads the way.

378
Peter and Hanneke Jacobs
© 1988 Maranatha! Music / CopyCare

**I'm going to hide God's word
   inside my heart**
and learn each verse from memory.
I'm going to hide God's word inside my heart
until His word is part of me.

God's word will help me each and every day
to know what is right from what is wrong.
The more that I read it,
       the more I learn of Him,
and His word will make me strong.

That's why I'm going to hide God's word
       inside my heart
and learn each verse from memory.
I'm going to hide God's word inside my heart
until His word is part of me,
until His word is part of me.

379
Ian Smale
© 1981 Thankyou Music

I'm going to say my prayers,
read my Bible every morning;
going to get some fellowship,
witness every day.
I'm going to say my prayers,
read my Bible every morning;
going to get some fellowship,
witness every day.

1 I am going to pray every morning,
   I am going to pray every day.
   I am going to pray every morning,
   I am going to pray every day.
       I'm going to say . . .

2 I am going to read my Bible
       every morning,
   I am going to read my Bible every day.
   I am going to read my Bible
       every morning,
   I am going to read my Bible every day.
       I'm going to say . . .

3 I am going to fellowship every morning,
   I am going to fellowship every day.
   I am going to fellowship every morning,
   I am going to fellowship every day.
       I'm going to say . . .

4 I am going to witness every morning,
   I am going to witness every day.
   I am going to witness every morning,
   I am going to witness every day.
       I'm going to say . . .

380
Ernie and Debbie Rettino
© 1982 Maranatha! Music / CopyCare

I'm going to stand up,
I'm going to stand up,
I'm going to stand up, I'm going to stand up.

I'm going to stand up,
stand up and live for Jesus.
Do I, I'm going to stand up,
stand up and live for Him.
I'm going to give up,
give up my life for Jesus.
Do I, I'm going to give up,
give up my life for Him.

Lord, we will live our lives for You,
serve You faithfully, like You want us to.
Lord, You give us the power to live for You,
live for You.

I'm going to stand up . . .

Let's take a stand for Jesus,
let's live our lives for Jesus.
Let's give it all for Jesus.
Stand up for Jesus! Stand up for Jesus!
Stand up, stand up, stand up,
stand up, stand up!

I'm going to stand up . . .

I'm going to stand up, I'm going to stand up,
I'm going to stand up, I'm going to stand up.
Stand up!

381 © 1990 Greg Leavers

I'm going to take (*clap clap*)
a step of faith,
I'm going to put my trust in the Lord.
He has the power to carry me through.
If I listen carefully, He'll tell me what to do.
I'm going to take (*clap clap*)
a step of faith,
and put my trust in the Lord.

2 I'm going to take (*clap clap*)
a step of faith,
I'm going to put my trust in the Lord.
He made a promise He loves me so,
wherever He might lead me,
He'll never let me go.
I'm going to take (*clap clap*)
a step of faith,
and put my trust in the Lord.

382 © 1992 Greg Leavers

I'm going to set my heart
on the precious word of God;
I'm going to feed my heart
on His many promises.
His word helps me in trouble,
it teaches me to praise.
I don't want to live with a hungry heart;
I'm going to feed on the word of God.

383 © 1992 Gill Robertson

1 **I've come to a time when I must**
change,
a time when I have to choose,
to order my own life, or follow Christ,
and gain what I cannot lose.
My Lord, I come,
I'm giving my life to You.
Fill me with Your Spirit,
and make over my heart anew.

2 The ways of the past, I leave, I leave,
my life in His hands I place.
His strength will uphold me
through anything,
sufficient for me His grace.
My Lord . . .

3 The wrong that I've done, I now confess,
I know that He will forgive.
His love is far greater than all my sin,
He'll teach me the way to live.
My Lord . . .

4 From love of myself, I turn, I turn,
to serving the King of kings.
My life will be filled with the love of Christ,
whatever the future brings.
My Lord . . .

5 I've come to a time when I must change,
a time when I have to choose,
to order my own life, or follow Christ,
and gain what I cannot lose.

384 Terrye Coelho
© 1973 Maranatha! Music / CopyCare

If any man come after Me,
    let him deny himself,
pick up his cross and follow Me
    into life eternally.
Deny yourself, pick up your cross,
    and follow Jesus.
He is the way, truth, and life.

Optional 2nd part

Alleluia! Praise the Lord,
    worship Him in one accord.
Alleluia! He is King,
    Master, Lord of everything.
Jesus Christ, Lord of all,
    loving great and small;
He is the way, truth, and life.

385 © 1992 Gill Robertson

1 **If it pleases the King,**
I want to live my life for Him.
If it offers Him praise,
I will follow His ways.
Sinful I may be,
but He will welcome me.
My life to Him I'll bring,
if it pleases the King.

2 If it pleases the King,
I want to give my love to Him.
If it honours the Lord,
I will trust in His word.
I need never fear,
for He'll be ever near.
My love to Him I'll sing,
if it pleases the King.

386 Sam Horner
© 1991 Daybreak Music Ltd / CopyCare

1 **If Jesus is de vine,**
    we must be de branches.
If Jesus is de vine,
    we must be de branches.
If Jesus is de vine,
    we must be de branches,
and bear fruit in the kingdom of God.

2 If Jesus is de rock,
    we should be a little boulder.
If Jesus is de rock,
    we should be a little boulder.
If Jesus is de rock,
    we should be a little boulder,
to bear fruit in the kingdom of God.

3 If Jesus is de bread,
    is your name on the roll now?
If Jesus is de bread,
    is your name on the roll now?
If Jesus is de bread,
    is your name on the roll now?
Let's bear fruit in the kingdom of God.

387 © 1991 Andy Hughes

If you love Me you will
    obey My commandments.
If you love Me you will do what I say;
and if you love Me then every day
    you will seek Me
saying, 'Lord, what shall I do today?'

1 Just like Joshua
  standing at the Jordan's side;
  obeyed the Lord and when he started
      to cross
  the waters opened wide.
      If you love Me . . .

2 As the disciples
  obeyed and brought Him fish and bread.
  So Jesus blessed it and they handed
      it round
  and five thousand men were fed.
      If you love Me . . .

388
Derek Llewellyn
© 1989 Sandcastle Productions

1 **If you climb (*stamp stamp*)**
    to the top of a mountain,
  if you swim (*splish splish*)
      in the ocean blue,
  if you're lost (*sniff sniff*)
      in the deepest forest,
  Jesus will always find you.

2 If you fall (*scream*) into the darkest cave,
  if you fly (*zoom*) right up into the air,
  if you run (*run on the spot*)
      all around the world,
  Jesus will always be there.

3 So if you're feeling lonely,
  if you're feeling sad,
  Jesus will always be close to you,
  so you can always feel glad.

4 If you climb (*stamp stamp*)
      to the top of a mountain,
  if you swim (*splish splish*)
      in the ocean blue,
  if you're lost (*sniff sniff*)
      in the deepest forest,
  Jesus will always find you.

389
Michael Ryan
© 1975 Maranatha! Music / CCCM Music /
CopyCare

If you want to be great in God's kingdom,
learn to be the servant of all.
If you want to be great in God's kingdom,
learn to be the servant of all.
Learn to be the servant of all,
learn to be the servant of all.
If you want to be great in God's kingdom,
learn to be the servant of all.

390
© Angela Reith

If your empty tum is rumbling
you don't leave your baked beans
      (*munch munch*).
If it's lightning and it's thundering
you don't stand beneath the trees.
And if you climb a high steep hill
you don't refuse a Coke (*pshhh*).
And if your best friend's feeling ill
you don't treat it like a joke (*ha ha*).
You don't run across the high street
if you want to grow old.
You don't look down at your feet
if you want to score a goal (*clap clap*).
So don't forget to pray
if you want to follow God today.
You don't put your Bible out of sight
if you want to do what's right.
You don't put your Bible out of sight
if you want to do what's right.

391
Ian White
© Little Misty Music Ltd

In everything that I do,
      show me what Jesus would do.
In everything that I do,
      show me what Jesus would do.
I will not be afraid, for I can always pray,
show me what Jesus would do.

392
Alan J Price
© 1990 Daybreak Music Ltd / CopyCare

I'm going to shine, shine, shine,
a light in the world I'll be;
I want to shine, shine, shine,
let people see Jesus in me!

1 I want to glorify the Father
by the things I do;
be the person God has made me,
letting His love flow through!
I'm going to . . .

2 And when it's hard and it's not so easy
to know and do what's right;
I'll trust the Holy Spirit in me,
to help me win each fight!
I'm going to . . .

3 Even if I fail Him often
and my light is dim;
He has promised to forgive me,
I can come back to Him!
I'm going to . . .

393
Marjorie Allen Anderson
© 1947 Cook Communications

1 **In the morning when I rise,**
when I open up my eyes,
rain or shine or cold and ice,
God is near, God is near.

2 When I help and when I play,
He is there to show the way,
close behind me all the day,
God is near, God is near.

3 Then when I turn off the light,
when I go to sleep at night,
I am always in His sight,
God is near, God is near.

394
Harry D Clarke
© 1924 Hope Publishing / CopyCare

1 **Into my heart, into my heart,**
come into my heart, Lord Jesus.
Come in today, come in to stay;
come into my heart, Lord Jesus.

2 Rule in my heart, rule in my heart,
O King of my heart, Lord Jesus.
Make this Your throne, rule there alone;
O King of my heart, Lord Jesus.

395
Ian White
© Little Misty Music Ltd

It takes an almighty hand,
to make your harvest grow.
It takes an almighty hand,
however you may sow.
It takes an almighty hand,
the world around me shows.
It takes the almighty hand of God.

1 It takes His hand to grow your garden,
all from a secret in a seed;
part of a plan He spoke and started,
and said is 'very good indeed!'
It takes . . .

2 It takes His hand to turn the seasons,
to give the sun and snow their hour;
and in this plan we learn His reason,
His nature and eternal power.
It takes . . .

3 It took His hands to carry sorrow,
for every sin that we have done;
and on a cross He bought tomorrow,
a world of good, like He'd begun.
It takes . . .

4 And in His hands there is perfection,
that in this land we only taste;
for now we see a poor reflection,
then we shall see Him face to face.
It takes . . .

396
Joy Webb
© Salvationist Publishing & Supplies Ltd /
CopyCare

1 **It was on a starry night**
when the hills were bright,
earth lay sleeping, sleeping calm and still;
then in a cattle shed, in a manger bed
a boy was born, King of all the world.

And all the angels sang for Him,
the bells of heaven rang for Him;
for a boy was born,
    King of all the world.
And all the angels sang for Him,
the bells of heaven rang for Him;
for a boy was born,
    King of all the world.

2   Soon the shepherds came that way,
        where the baby lay,
    and were kneeling, kneeling by His side.
    And their hearts believed again,
        for the peace of men;
    for a boy was born, King of all the world.
        And all the angels . . .

    On a starry night, on a starry night.

398

© 1991 Greg Leavers

It's a song of praise,
it's a song of thankfulness;
it's a song of joy,
    for every girl and boy.

1   God gave me my hands,
    God gave me my voice;
    God gave me a thankful heart,
    so now I can rejoice.
        It's a song of praise . . .

2   God gave me my feet,
    God gave me my arms;
    the life and love He gives to me
    makes me want to dance.
        It's a song of praise . . .

397

© 1989 Andy Silver

1   **It was Jesus who taught His disciples,**
    it was Jesus who called them by name.
    Then one night on the lake came the wind
        and the rain,
    and the waves
        splashed right over the boat.
        Splish, splash, pitter pitter pat,
        down came the storm with a bang
        and a crash.
        Splish, splash, pitter pitter pat,
        down came the storm with a bang
        and a crash.

2   It was Jesus asleep in the trawler,
    it was Jesus who woke to their cries.
    'Don't you care that we drown,
        we're afraid we'll go down!'
    and the waves
        splashed right over the boat.
        Splish splash . . .

3   It was Jesus who stood to attention,
    it was Jesus who spoke to the waves.
    'You, be quiet, do no harm';
        right away there was calm.
    'Who's this man?'
        asked the men in the boat.
        Splish splash . . .

399

Alan J Price
© 1990 Daybreak Music Ltd / CopyCare

It's an adventure following Jesus,
it's an adventure learning of Him.
It's an adventure living for Jesus,
it's an adventure following Him.
Let's go where He leads us,
turn away from wrong;
for we know we can trust Him
to help us as we go along.

It's an adventure following Jesus,
it's an adventure learning of Him.
It's an adventure living for Jesus,
it's an adventure following Him.

400

Paul Crouch and David Mudie
© 1989 Daybreak Music Ltd / CopyCare

It's easy to be a believer,
because it's plain as plain can be
that Jesus came from God and went
to die at Calvary.
But three days later He rose up
and was seen by at least
        five hundred people,
and then went back to heaven
to sit at God's right hand.

401 © 1992 Greg Leavers

**It's not very nice saying,
  'Na na na na na na';**
it's not very good saying, 'It's not fair.'
It's not very kind to fight
     your sister or your brother,
or to sneer at others saying, 'I don't care.'

God doesn't like these things –
He tells us in the Bible they're called sins;
God doesn't like these things.
We do it (*Uh huh*), we know it (*That's right*),
and we need help to stop it.

402 Basil E Bridge
© Oxford University Press

1 **It's rounded like an orange,**
     this earth on which we stand;
   and we praise the God who holds it
     in the hollow of His hand.
     So Father, we would thank You
       for all that You have done,
     and for all that You have given us
       through the coming of Your Son.

2 A candle, burning brightly,
     can cheer the darkest night
   and these candles tell how Jesus
     came to bring a dark world light.
     So Father . . .

3 The ribbon round the orange
     reminds us of the cost;
   how the shepherd, strong and gentle,
     gave His life to save the lost.
     So Father . . .

4 Four seasons with their harvest
     supply the food we need,
   and the Spirit gives a harvest
     that can make us rich indeed.
     So Father . . .

5 We come with our Christingles
     to tell of Jesus' birth
   and we praise the God who blessed us
     by His coming to this earth.
     So Father . . .

403 Bacon Boyd
© 1988 Lillenas Publishing Co / CopyCare

1 **It's the little things that show
     our love for Jesus.**
   It's the little things that show
     our love for Him.
   It's in little things that we can
     truly serve Him.
   It's with little things that we begin.
     Give a little more love
       and a little more hope
       to others as you serve Him.
     Give a little more love
       and a little more hope
       to others you may meet.
     Give a little more love
       each day to those around you.
     Then a little more love
       and a little more faith,
     and a little more love
       and a little more faith
       will make you more like Him.

2 It's the little things we do
     each day for others.
   It's the little things that show
     we really care.
   It's in little things our faith
     becomes much stronger.
   It's with little things that we begin.
     Give a little more love
       and a little more hope
       to others as you serve Him.
     Give a little more love
       and a little more hope
       to others you may meet.
     Give a little more love
       each day to those around you.
     Then a little more love
       and a little more faith,
     and a little more love
       and a little more faith,
     and a little more love
       and a little more faith,
     and a little more love
       and a little more faith
       will make you more like Him.
     I want to be more like Him,
       more like Him.

404 Ian Smale
© 1987 Thankyou Music

Jehovah Jireh, God will provide.
Jehovah Rophe, God heals.
Jehovah Makeddesh, God who sanctifies.
Jehovah Nissi, God is my banner.
Jehovah Rohi, God my shepherd.
Jehovah Shalom, God is peace.
Jehovah Tsidkenu, God our righteousness.
Jehovah Shammah, God who is there.

405 © 1989 Andy Silver

1   **Jerusalem man, walking**
      from his homeland,
    when he fell among some robbers,
          poor Jerusalem man.
    They stripped him and they beat him
          with their sticks in their hands;
    poor, poor, poor, poor Jerusalem man.

2   They hastily fled as he fell down and bled,
    but a man who was a preacher
          saw the victim ahead.
    He passed him and ignored him –
          not a word had been said;
    poor, poor, poor, poor Jerusalem man.

3   Along came a man
          who was very well read,
    now he must have seen the victim
          who by now was half dead.
    He passed him and ignored him
          not a word had been said;
    poor, poor, poor, poor Jerusalem man.

4   The next man to pass, a Samaritan man,
    though he always had been taught
          to hate a true Jewish man,
    he helped him and he took him
          to an inn near his land;
    good, good, good, good Samaritan man.

406 Scott Lawrence
Copyright control

Jesus has promised my shepherd to be,
that's why I love Him so;
and to the children He said, 'Come to Me',
that's why I love Him so.

That's why I love Him, that's why I love Him,
because He first loved me;
when I'm tempted and tried,
          He is close by my side,
that's why I love Him so.

407 © Timothy Dudley-Smith / OUP

1   **Jesus, Prince and Saviour,**
    Lord of life who died:
    Christ, the friend of sinners,
    sinners crucified.
    For a lost world's ransom,
    all Himself He gave,
    lay at last death's victim,
    lifeless in the grave.
        Lord of life triumphant,
        risen now to reign!
        King of endless ages,
        Jesus lives again!

2   In His power and Godhead
    every victory won,
    pain and passion ended,
    all His purpose done:
    Christ the Lord is risen!
    sighs and sorrows past,
    death's dark night is over,
    morning comes at last!
        Lord of life . . .

3   Resurrection morning!
    sinners' bondage freed.
    Christ the Lord is risen –
    He is risen indeed!
    Jesus, Prince and Saviour,
    Lord of life who died,
    Christ the King of glory
    now is glorified!
        Lord of life . . .

408
Graham Kendrick
© 1986 Thankyou Music

1   **Jesus put this song into our hearts,**
    Jesus put this song into our hearts;
    it's a song of joy no-one can take away.
    Jesus put this song into our hearts.

2   Jesus taught us how to live in harmony,
    Jesus taught us how to live in harmony;
    different faces, different races,
      He made us one –
    Jesus taught us how to live in harmony.

3   Jesus taught us how to be a family,
    Jesus taught us how to be a family;
    loving one another
      with the love that He gives –
    Jesus taught us how to be a family.

4   Jesus turned our sorrow into dancing,
    Jesus turned our sorrow into dancing;
    changed our tears of sadness
      into rivers of joy –
    Jesus turned our sorrow into a dance.
        (*Hey!*)

409
Derek Llewellyn
© 1991 Sandcastle Productions

Jesus, send me the helper,
      send me the helper to help me.
Jesus, send me the Holy Spirit,
      send the Holy Spirit to me.
Jesus, send me the helper,
      send me the helper to help me.
Jesus, send me the Holy Spirit,
      send the Holy Spirit to me.

He gives us love to keep on loving.
He makes us brave to do what is right.
He gives us faith to keep on going.
He gives us power to keep us
      shining so bright.

Jesus, send me the helper,
      send me the helper to help me.
Jesus, send me the Holy Spirit,
      send the Holy Spirit to me.

410
Otis Skillings
© 1984 Lillenas Publishing Co / CopyCare

1   **Jesus, I love You, love You, love You.**
    Jesus, I love You; Jesus, my Lord.

2   Jesus, I serve You, serve You, serve You.
    Jesus, I serve You; Jesus, my Lord.

3   Jesus, I praise You, praise You,
          praise You.
    Jesus, I praise You; Jesus, my Lord;
    Jesus, my Lord.

411
J Watson
© Scripture Union

1   **Jesus was the Son of God,**
    He became a man.
    He was strong and good and kind,
    followed all God's plan,
    followed all God's plan.

2   When He was a strong young man
    Jesus had to die.
    All his friends were very sad,
    and they wondered why,
    and they wondered why.

3   It's so hard to understand
    why this had to be;
    but I know it was because
    He cared for you and me,
    He cared for you and me.

412
© 1990 Greg Leavers

Jesus will never, ever,
no not ever, never, ever change.
He will always, always,
that's for all days,
always be the same.
So as Son of God and
King of kings
He will forever reign.
Yesterday, today, forever,
Jesus is the same.
Yesterday, today, forever,
Jesus is the same.

413

Joseph was sold as a slave,
and later was thrown into prison;
but God helped him be very brave,
because he had done nothing wrong.
For God knows, yes, God knows,
   God knows the truth;
for God knows, yes, God knows,
   God knows the truth.

414

Kids under construction;
maybe the paint is still wet.
Kids under construction;
the Lord might not be finished yet.

1 We're more than just accidents
      without the cause;
   we're more than just bodies and brains.
   God made us on purpose,
      we're part of a plan;
   He cares and He knows us by name. Oh!
   Kids under construction . . .

2 Now, mister, I know that I get in your way;
   I'm noisy and just bug you so.
   But there's lots of questions
      I just have to ask
   if I'm ever going to know. Oh!
   Kids under construction . . .

3 Dear Jesus, please make us more
      patient and kind;
   and help us to be more like You.
   And make room for all other children
      of Yours,
   for they are still growing up, too. Oh!
   Kids under construction . . .

415

1 **Large creatures, small creatures,**
   short and tall creatures,
   come now and praise the Lord.
   Young creatures, old creatures,
   hot and cold creatures,
   come now and praise the Lord.
      Sing praise to the Father,
         sing praise to the Son,
      sing praise to the Spirit
         who makes all creatures one.
      Sing praise for the goodness
         of what the Lord has done.
      Let all creatures praise the Lord.

2 Low creatures, high creatures,
   flying in the sky creatures,
   come now and praise the Lord.
   White creatures, brown creatures,
   all the world around creatures,
   come now and praise the Lord.
      Sing praise . . .

3 Day creatures, night creatures,
   left and right creatures,
   come now and praise the Lord.
   Near creatures, far creatures,
   anywhere you are creatures,
   come now and praise the Lord.
      Sing praise . . .

416

Let's go and tell our friends
      that Jesus cares;
let's go and tell our friends that Jesus cares.
We've got to go out and tell how Jesus died
      for them;
to tell them how He loves them; (*that's right!*)
to tell them He'll forgive them; (*that's true!*)
to tell them He'll be with them; (*Amen!*)
to tell them that He wants to be their friend.

417 Alison Moon
© 1992 Daybreak Music Ltd / CopyCare

Let's praise God together,
let us clap and praise the Lord;
for He loves to hear us –
He is King for evermore.

1 Jesus, holy is Your name;
high above all others,
power and glory belong to You.
   Let's all dance together,
   let us dance and praise the Lord;
   for he loves to see us –
   He is King for evermore.

2 Jesus, mighty is Your name;
high above all others,
power and glory belong to You.
   Let's praise God together,
   let us clap and praise the Lord;
   for He loves to hear us –
   He is King for evermore.

   Let's all dance together,
   let us dance and praise the Lord;
   for he loves to see us –
   He is King for evermore.

418 Anon
Copyright control

1 **Long ago there was born,**
   in the city of David,
a sweet, holy babe who was Jesus,
   our King.
Angels sang at His birth,
   'Lullaby, peace on earth.'
Angels sang at His birth,
   'Lullaby, peace on earth.'

2 Jesus came as a child
   from His Father in heaven,
and has shown us the way to be
   loving and kind.
While the stars sang above,
   'Lullaby, God is love.'
While the stars sang above,
   'Lullaby, God is love.'

419 © 1989 Andy Silver

1 **Long, long ago before our time began**
everything was out of shape
   and nothing filled the land.
God, who saw the emptiness,
made a plan to clear the mess,
God spoke and it was done.
Day one, came the light and the
   day and night;
day two, came the clouds and the
   sea and sky;
day three, came the land and the
   plants and trees;
day four, came the sun and the
   moon and the stars.

2 God took a look and He was happy
   and was pleased.
Now the world was taking shape
   and all because God breathed;
but He thought the sky and sea
   needed some activity –
God spoke and it was done.
Day five, came the fish and the
   birds that fly;
day six, came the beasts and the animals;
and then came the people called
   Adam and Eve;
day seven, all was done and
   God rested at ease.

3 God was very glad to see the different
   forms of life,
but the part most wonderful was Adam
   and his wife.
All He wanted them to do was love
   and serve Him through and through;
God spoke and it was done.

420 Bev Gammon
© 1989 Thankyou Music

1 **Lord Jesus,**
You are faithful,
always with us,
never leaving us;
Lord Jesus.

2 Lord Jesus,
   You are blameless,
   You are perfect,
   You are sinless;
   Lord Jesus.

3 Lord Jesus,
   You are so pure,
   pure and lovely,
   pure and holy;
   Lord Jesus.

422 Ian Smale
         © 1989 Thankyou Music

Lord, we've come to worship You;
Lord, we've come to praise.
Lord, we've come to worship You
in oh, so many ways.
Some of us shout and some of us sing,
and some of us whisper the praise we bring;
but Lord, we all are gathering
to give to You our praise.

421 Paul Field
         © 1983 Daybreak Music Ltd / CopyCare

1 **Lord, make me a mountain
   standing tall for You;**
   strong and free and holy,
      in everything I do.
   Lord, make me a river of water
      pure and sweet.
   Lord, make me the servant
      of everyone I meet.

2 Lord, make me a candle
      shining with Your light;
   steadfastly unflickering,
      standing for the right.
   Lord, make me a fire burning
      strong for You.
   Lord, make me be humble
      in everything I do.

3 Lord, make me a mountain,
      strong and tall for You;
   Lord, make me a fountain
      of water clear and new.
   Lord, make me a shepherd
      that I may feed Your sheep;
   Lord, make me the servant
      of everyone I meet.

423 © 1991 Greg Leavers

1 **Lord, You are brilliant,
      champion of champions;**
   to You our thanks and praise we bring.
   You made all the world,
      no-one's as great as You;
   You know everything and all
      Your words are true.
   Lord, You are brilliant,
      champion of champions;
   so we proclaim You are the King.

2 Lord, You are brilliant,
      champion of champions;
   to You our thanks and praise we bring.
   You see everything,
      all that we say and do;
   You're incredible,
      no-one loves us like You.
   Lord, You are brilliant,
      champion of champions;
   so we proclaim You are the King.

424 © 1988 Fiona Inkpen
         Copyright control

   *Lord, You are the Light of the world,
      shine in our hearts.*
   *Let that light shine across the earth,
      Light of the world, our God.*

1 In the warmth of Your love
      we would walk in Your light.
   Lord, You are . . .

2 Midst the sorrow of man may
    Your love fill our hearts.
    Lord, You are . . .

3 Lord, the truth and the life,
    revealing Your way!
    Lord, You are . . .

425 Peter and Hanneke Jacobs
© 1988 Maranatha! Music / CopyCare

Love, joy, peace,
patience, kindness, goodness, faith,
gentleness, and self-control;
this is the fruit of the Spirit.
Love, joy, peace,
patience, kindness, goodness, faith,
gentleness and self-control;
the fruit of the Spirit of God.

You'll find it in Galatians, chapter five,
verse twenty-two.
And if you're walking close to God,
this fruit will grow in you.

And you'll have love, joy, peace,
patience, kindness, goodness, faith,
gentleness, and self-control;
this is the fruit of the Spirit.
Love, joy, peace,
patience, kindness, goodness, faith,
gentleness and self-control;
the fruit of the Spirit of God,
the fruit of the Spirit of God.

426 © 1992 Gill Robertson

1 **M-m-m-m-must I really go and visit
    him?**
    I'd n-not be very good at it, you know.
    Surely there's s-someone else
        who's w-w-willing to;
    I'm a-f-f-fraid to go!

2 He's been p-p-persecuting Your followers,
    some have been k-killed, and some were
        thrown in jail.
    Please d-d-don't make me go
        and v-v-visit him;
    I'll be sh-sh-sure to fail.

    Listen, Ananias, I've chosen this man
    to be a witness for Me.
    Through him, the good news
        will spread to many nations,
    bringing life and liberty.

3 If I really must, Lord, I'll be o-b-bedient;
    I know You'll go with me,
        You'll s-see me through.
    Even when the task is hard
        or d-d-dangerous,
    help me to t-trust in You.

427 Graham Kendrick
© 1986 Thankyou Music

1 **Make way, make way,**
    for Christ the King in splendour arrives;
    fling wide the gates
    and welcome Him into your lives.
        Make way, make way,
        for the King of kings;
        make way, make way,
        and let His kingdom in!

2 He comes the broken hearts to heal,
    the prisoners to free;
    the deaf shall hear, the lame shall dance,
    the blind shall see.
        Make way . . .

3 And those who mourn with heavy hearts,
    who weep and sigh,
    with laughter, joy and royal crown
    He'll beautify.
        Make way . . .

4 We call you now to worship Him
    as Lord of all;
    to have no gods before Him,
    their thrones must fall!
        Make way . . .

428

© 1990 Andy Silver

1 **Matthew had been sitting in his little
    hut,**
  collecting lots of money from the Jews.
  He had a reputation, dealing in deception,
  working for the Inland Revenue.
  Jesus had been walking on the shore
      that day,
  and called out, 'Matthew,
      come and follow Me!'
  There was no hesitation,
      he didn't even question,
  he left his hut and followed straight away.
    Come, let's have a party,
    come and meet the Lord who called
        and found me;
    bring your friends and neighbours
        to the party.
    Come, let's have a P.A.R.T.Y.

2 Jesus heard the whispers
      from the Pharisees,
  'See Him eating with these wicked men.'
  They didn't stop complaining,
      gossiping and jeering,
  thinking they were holy, righteous men.
  Jesus spoke directly to the Pharisees:
  'What sort of people need a doctor's
      help?
  The healthy do not need him, but people
      sick and ailing;
  I've come to call all sinners to repent!'
    Come, let's have . . .

429

Carol Gaddy
© 1980 Lillenas Publishing Co / CopyCare

1 **Maybe you can't draw or sing
    or be a football star;**
  but just remember, be yourself,
  He made you like you are.
    It'll be a big thing when Jesus
        takes control,
    even though it seems like something
        very slim.
    From a tiny lunch He blessed the bread
        and fed the multitudes;
    and He'll use us, too,
        when we give ourselves to Him.

2 You may not have the brightest smile
      or make the highest score;
  but if you give Him what you have,
  He'll make it something more.
    It'll be a big . . .

3 If you love our blessèd Lord
      and want to do your part,
  don't worry if you've nothing else –
  the best gift is your heart.
    It'll be a big . . .

430

Mavis Ford
© 1984 Authentic Publishing / CopyCare

Mighty in victory, glorious in majesty:
every eye shall see Him when He appears,
coming in the clouds with power and glory.
    Hail to the King!
We must be ready, watching and praying,
serving each other, building His kingdom;
then every knee shall bow,
      then every tongue confess,
    Jesus is Lord!

431

Eugene Greco
© 1989 Integrity's Hosanna! Music /
Integrity Praise! / Sovereign Music UK

Mighty is our God,
mighty is our King.
Mighty is our Lord,
ruler of everything.
Glory to our God,
glory to our King.
Glory to our Lord,
ruler of everything.

His name is higher,
higher than any other name.
His power is greater,
for He has created *everything.

Mighty is our God . . .

* throw arm up in the air

432

© Peter Lewis

Noah was the only good man,
Noah was the only good man,
Noah was the only good man,
and everyone else was bad.

1 The Lord looked at the world He made
and He was very sad,
as almost everyone He saw
was wicked and was bad.
So God said He would send a flood
to wash them all away,
and He said, 'Noah, build an ark
to float upon the waves!'
Noah was . . .

2 So Noah built a wooden ark
the way God told him to,
and took his family safe inside
with animals two by two.
So God saved Noah from the flood
and promised then and there
that He would never send again
a flood upon the earth.
Noah was . . .

3 God made a rainbow in the sky
of yellow, blue and red,
so no-one ever would forget
the flood and what He said.
And when we see the rainbow now
remember God's own words:
that He would never send again
a flood upon the earth.
Noah was . . .

2 Now all Jesse's family
were handsome and strong,
and when Samuel asked them,
they all came along;
and Samuel was wondering
as in they all trod,
which one of the brothers
was chosen by God.

3 He looked on Eliab,
and he was impressed
with the curls of his hair
and the breadth of his chest;
but God said to Samuel,
'That's not where I start –
you look on his body, but I see his heart!'

4 So six more fine offspring
of Jesse's passed by
but each was rejected by God
the Most High;
then Samuel asked Jesse,
'Are those all you've got?'
He answered, 'There's David –
the babe of the lot!'

5 Now David, the shepherd,
the youngest of eight,
was out with the sheep
on the hills until late.
He had to be sent for;
and when he came in,
the Lord said, 'Rise up and
anoint him as king!'

6 You may be dressed smartly,
your face may be fair,
but God's not concerned with
your clothes or your hair;
your outward appearance is only a part –
when God looks upon you,
He looks on your heart.

433

© 1992 Gill Robertson

1 **Now Saul was rejected**
as king of the land,
so God spoke to Samuel,
'Now hear my command.
Go straight down to Bethlehem,
there worship Me;
anoint one of Jesse's sons as king to be!'

434

Joanne Pond
© 1980 Thankyou Music

O give thanks to the Lord,
all you His people;
O give thanks to the Lord,
 for He is good.
Let us praise, let us thank,
let us celebrate and dance;
O give thanks to the Lord,
 for He is good.

435

Ian Smale
© 1985 Thankyou Music

1 **O Lord, You're great, You are fabulous.**
   We love You more than any words can
    sing, sing, sing.
   O Lord, You're great, You are so
    generous;
   You lavish us with gifts
    when we don't deserve a thing.
   Allelu, alleluia, praise You, Lord.
   Alleluia, praise You, Lord,
    alleluia, praise You, Lord.
   Allelu, alleluia, praise You, Lord.
   Alleluia, praise You, Lord,
    alleluia, praise You, Lord.

2 O Lord, You're great, You are so powerful;
   You hold the mighty universe in Your
    hand, hand, hand.
   O Lord, You're great, You are so
    wonderful,
   You've poured out Your love
    on this undeserving land.
   Allelu, alleluia . . .

436

Kurt Kaiser
© 1975 Word Music, LLC / CopyCare

1 **Oh, how He loves you and me;**
   oh, how He loves you and me.
   He gave His life –
   what more could He give?
    Oh, how He loves you;
    oh, how He loves me;
    oh, how He loves you and me.

2 Jesus to Calvary did go,
   His love for sinners to show.
   What He did there
   brought hope from despair.
    Oh, how He . . .

437

© 1991 Greg Leavers

Oh no! The wine's all gone!
How can the wedding feast now go on?
Oh dear! What can be done?
Just listen to Jesus, Mary's Son.
Oh yes! We'll do what He says –
fill the stone jars with water that's fresh.
Oh my! They're pouring it out!
What, wine? That's a miracle!
            without a doubt!

438

Angela Flynn
© 1989 Sandcastle Productions

1 **Oh, oh, oh, oh, oh, oh, oh, oh.**
   Oh, oh, oh, oh, oh, oh, oh, oh.

2 Hallelujah, hallelujah.
   Hallelujah, hallelujah.

3 Christ died and rose. He will come again.
   Christ died and rose. He will come again.

4 Praise the Lord.
   Praise the Lord.

439

Sam Horner
© 1992 Daybreak Music Ltd / CopyCare

   Oh, yes I am, oh, yes I am,
   I am saved and kept secure
    in Jesus' hand.
   Oh, yes I am, oh, yes I am,
   I am saved and kept secure
    in Jesus' hand.

1 I'm redeemed, the price was paid by Him;
   justified, just as if I'd never sinned;
   sanctified, holy, set apart;
   and it's all because of Jesus' loving heart.
    Oh, yes I am . . .

2 I am saved, from death and sin and hell.
I'm empowered, by the Spirit of God as
   well.
I'm born again, I've got a brand new start;
and it's all because of Jesus' loving heart.
   Oh, yes I am . . .

3 I belong to my Father who's above.
I am kept by His never-ending love.
I will survive the devil's fiery darts;
and it's all because of Jesus' loving heart.
   Oh, yes I am . . .

4 For forty days they were afloat –
pitter patter, pitter patter, splosh!
But they were safe inside God's boat –
pitter patter, pitter patter, splosh!
So trust God here, believe God there,
here believe, there trust,
everywhere believe God;
wail, wail here . . .
flush, flush here . . .
'ha ha' here . . .
saw, saw here . . .

440 Anon
Copyright control

1 **Old man Noah built an ark –**
hammer, hammer, bang, bang, ow!
And that old ark was built of wood –
hammer, hammer, bang, bang, ow!
With a saw, saw, here and a nail, nail,
   there;
here a nail, there a saw,
everywhere a nail, nail;
Old man Noah built an ark –
hammer, hammer, bang, bang, ow!

2 The ark had a door without a knocker –
hammer, hammer, bang, bang, ow!
Everyone said, 'Noah's off his rocker' –
hammer, hammer, bang, bang, ow!
With a 'ha ha' here, and a 'ho ho' there,
here a 'ha', there a 'ho',
everywhere a 'ha ha';
saw, saw here . . .

3 God shut the door and sent the rain –
pitter patter, pitter patter, splosh!
But all the people cried in vain –
pitter patter, pitter patter, splosh!
With a wail, wail here, and a shout,
   shout there,
here a shout, there a wail,
everywhere a shout, shout;
flush, flush here . . .
'ha ha' here . . .
saw, saw here . . .

441 Traditional

1 **On Christmas night all Christians sing**
to hear the news the angels bring:
on Christmas night all Christians sing
to hear the news the angels bring:
news of great joy, news of great mirth,
news of our merciful King's birth.

2 Then why should we on earth be so sad,
since our Redeemer made us glad?
Then why should we on earth be so sad,
since our Redeemer made us glad;
when from our sin He set us free,
all for to gain our liberty?

3 When sin departs before His grace,
then life and health come in its place;
When sin departs before His grace,
then life and health come in its place;
angels and men with joy may sing,
all for to see the new-born King.

4 All out of darkness we have light,
which made the angels sing this night:
all out of darkness we have light,
which made the angels sing this night:
'Glory to God and peace to men,
now and for evermore. Amen.'

442 Anthony Welsh
© 1986 Kevin Mayhew Ltd

1 **On the road to Damascus**
   the Lord appeared
        as a man was riding by:
   his name was Saul.
   I saw him fall
   at a blinding flash from the sky.
   'Saul! Saul! Do not persecute Me!
   Saul! Saul! Do not persecute Me!'

2 On the road to Damascus
   the Lord cried out to the man
        who could not see.
   I heard Him call,
   'Now tell Me, Saul,
   just why do you persecute Me?
   Saul! Saul! Do not persecute Me!
   Saul! Saul! Do not persecute Me!'

3 On the road to Damascus
   the Lord's voice came to the man
        whose eyes were blind.
   I heard Him call
   'Now hear Me, Saul,
   I will change your name and your mind.
   Saul! Saul! Do not persecute Me!
   Saul! Saul! Do not persecute Me!'

4 On the road to Damascus
   I saw him fall to his knees
        before the Lord.
   I heard Him call,
   'Your name is Paul,
   you must go out and spread My word!
   Paul! Paul! Teach the world of Jesus!
   Paul! Paul! Teach the world of Jesus!'

5 On the road to Damascus
   yes, I was there when the Lord's
        great power He showed.
   I watched as Paul
   received God's call
   and then on my back he rode!
   'Paul! Paul! Teach the world of Jesus!
   Paul! Paul! Teach the world of Jesus!'

443 © 1988 Andy Silver

1 **Once upon a time –**
   it was many years ago –
   Jesus told a story of a man
        that you should know.
   He grew up on a farm and
        he had a hundred sheep;
   the sheep would eat and eat
        and eat and eat.
        'You're the sheep,' Jesus said,
        'far from home, all alone.
        I have come, God's own Son,
        to find you and to bring you back to
        Him.'

2 When the sun went down
        he would lead them safely home;
   one and two and three and four,
        he'd count them on his own.
   Then one night he had a fright –
        he counted ninety-nine.
   ninety, ninety, ninety, ninety-nine.
        'You're the sheep . . .

3 Out he went to find where the
        missing sheep had strayed;
   searching high and low,
        he was feeling quite dismayed.
   Then he thought he heard a noise,
        it sounded like a bleat –
   he'd found the silly, sad and sorry sheep.
        'You're the sheep . . .

444 Ian White
© Little Misty Music Ltd

1 **Once there was a house,**
   a busy little house;
   and this is all about the busy little house.

2 Jesus Christ had come, teaching
        everyone;
   so everyone had to run
        to the busy little house.

3 Everyone was there,
        you couldn't find a chair;
   in fact you had to fight for air,
        in the busy little house.

4 A man who couldn't walk,
     was carried to the spot;
but the place was chock-a-block,
     in the busy little house.

5 Whatever shall we do,
     whatever shall we do?
We'll never get him through
     into the busy little house.

6 We'll open up the roof,
     we'll open up the roof;
and then we'll put him through
     into the busy little house.

7 Then Jesus turned His eyes,
     and saw to His surprise,
the man coming from the skies
     into the busy little house.

8 Then Jesus turned and said,
     'Get up and take your bed,
and run along instead!'
     from the busy little house.

445 © 1991 Greg Leavers

One and two and three and four,
counting sheep in through the door;
fifty-one and fifty-two –
one is lost, what shall I do?
Ninety-eight and ninety-nine,
I will search until I find.
I will keep on looking just because I care.
There he is, caught in some thorns
     way over there,
he was lost but now is found.
So it's ninety-eight, ninety-nine,
     (*click fingers*) one hundred;
yes, it's ninety-eight, ninety-nine,
     (*click fingers*) one hundred!

446 Ian Smale
© 1982 Thankyou Music

1 **Praise Him, praise Him,**
bring praises to the Lord our God.
All God's faithful children
must learn to praise Him.
Praise Him, praise Him,
bring praises to the Lord our God.
All God's faithful children
must learn to praise Him.
    Sing hallelu, hallelu,
    sing hallelujah to our God.
    All God's faithful children
    sing hallelujah God.
    Sing hallelu, hallelu,
    sing hallelujah to our God.
    All God's faithful children
    sing hallelujah God.

2 Worship Him, worship Him,
bring worship to the Lord our God.
All God's faithful children
must learn to worship Him.
Worship Him, worship Him,
bring worship to the Lord our God.
All God's faithful children
must learn to worship Him.
    Sing hallelu . . .

447 Anon
Copyright control

Praise and thanksgiving
     let everyone bring,
unto our Father for every good thing!
All together, joyfully sing!

448 Paul Crouch and David Mudie
© 1991 Daybreak Music Ltd / CopyCare

Prayer is like a telephone
for us to talk to Jesus.
Prayer is like a telephone
for us to talk to God.
Prayer is like a telephone
for us to talk to Jesus.
Pick it up and use it every day.

We can shout out loud,
we can whisper softly,
we can make no noise at all;
but He'll always hear our call.

. . . . . . *is like a telephone*
for us to talk to Jesus.
. . . . . . *is like a telephone*
for us to talk to God.
. . . . . . *is like a telephone*
for us to talk to Jesus.
Pick it up and use it every day.

We can . . .

. . . . . . *is like a . . . .*
for us to talk to Jesus.
. . . . . . *is like a . . . .*
for us to talk to God.
. . . . . . *is like a . . . .*
for us to talk to Jesus.
Pick it up and use it every day.

We can . . .

. . . . . . *is like a . . . .*
for us to talk to . . . . .
. . . . . . *is like a . . . .*
for us to talk to . . .
. . . . . . *is like a . . . .*
for us to talk to . . . . .
Pick it up and use it every day.
Pick it up and use it every day.
Pick it up and use it every day.

449 Ian White
© Little Misty Music Ltd

Roll the stone, roll the stone,
roll the stone away.
Jesus died, but He's alive,
and this is Easter day.

1 We all like to paint our eggs,
sometimes blue and sometimes red.
First we roll them till they crunch,
then we eat them,
(*spoken*) munch, munch, munch!
Roll the stone . . .

2 We have chocolate eggs to eat,
and inside there's lots of sweets.
First they open with a crunch,
then we eat them,
(*spoken*) munch, munch, munch!
Roll the stone . . .

450 © 1992 Gill Robertson

1 **Saul had made himself
a number of enemies,**
who were busy plotting his death.
But his friends
had no desire to discover him
suffering from shortage of breath.
To avoid a tragedy,
they removed him secretly,
demonstrating brotherly love.
From enforced captivity,
carefully they set him free,
demonstrating brotherly love.

2 Following the Lord can sometimes
be difficult
if we try to do it alone.
We all need each other's help
and encouragement
as we learn to live as He's shown;
serving others joyfully,
showing generosity,
demonstrating brotherly love;
living in humility,
bearing burdens patiently,
demonstrating brotherly love.

3 All of us have different gifts and abilities,
which we need to learn how to share.
We can all take part in building
the fellowship,
showing the world we care.
Always speaking truthfully,
harbouring no enmity,
demonstrating brotherly love;
working for Him faithfully,
joined in perfect unity,
demonstrating brotherly love.

451 Ian White
© Little Misty Music Ltd

1 **See the man walking,**
      see the man walking,
  see the man walking on the water.
  BOYS   *This is a miracle,*
  GIRLS *His name is Jesus.*
  BOYS   *How does He do it?*
  GIRLS *He is the Son of God.*
  BOYS   *Can I believe Him?*
  GIRLS *You can believe Him.*
  BOYS   *Really believe Him?*
  GIRLS *Really believe Him.*

2 Hear the man talking,
      hear the man talking,
  hear the man talking words of wisdom.
      This is a miracle . . .

3 See the man healing,
      see the man healing,
  see the man healing people
      blind and lame.
      This is a miracle . . .

4 See the man dying, see the man dying,
  see the man dying and come back to life.
      This is a miracle . . .

5 Hear the man promise,
      hear the man promise,
  hear the man promise to be with me.
      This is a miracle . . .

452 © Timothy Dudley-Smith / OUP

1 **See, to us a Child is born –**
  glory breaks on Christmas morn!
  Now to us a Son is given –
  praise to God in highest heaven.

2 On His shoulder rule shall rest –
  in Him all the earth be blest!
  Wise and wonderful His name –
  heaven's Lord in human frame!

3 Mighty God, who mercy brings –
  Lord of lords and King of kings!
  Father of eternal days –
  every creature sing His praise!

4 Everlasting Prince of peace –
  truth and righteousness increase!
  He shall reign from shore to shore –
  Christ is King for evermore!

453 © 1992 Steve Kersys

Shine bright, dazzle, dazzle, shine bright,
    dazzle, dazzle.
The light of Jesus is shining bright;
shine bright, dazzle, dazzle, shine bright,
    dazzle, dazzle.
The light of Jesus is shining bright.
His life of love;
His life of light;
shines clear and bright in the darkest night.

454 From Psalm 98, Timothy Dudley-Smith
© Oxford University Press

1 **Sing a new song to the Lord,**
  He to whom wonders belong!
  Rejoice in His triumph
     and tell of His power –
  O sing to the Lord a new song!

2 Now to the ends of the earth
  see His salvation is shown;
  and still He remembers
     His mercy and truth,
  unchanging in love to His own.

3 Sing a new song and rejoice,
  publish His praises abroad!
  Let voices in chorus,
     with trumpet and horn,
  resound for the joy of the Lord!

4 Join with the hills and the sea
  thunders of praise to prolong!
  In judgement and justice
     He comes to the earth –
  O sing to the Lord a new song!

455
Derek Llewellyn
© 1991 Sandcastle Productions

1 **Sing praise to God the Father,**
God the Spirit, God the Son.
Sing praise to God who loves us.
Praise Him, everyone!

2 Sing praise to God the Father,
clap your hands and jump for joy.
He made the world around us
and He loves us all.

3 Sing praise to God's Son Jesus,
clap your hands and jump for joy.
Wave your arms and turn around.
He teaches us about the Father
and He loves us all.

4 Sing praise to the Holy Spirit,
clap your hands and jump for joy.
Wave your arms and turn around.
Stamp your feet and shout hooray.
He helps us to live like Jesus
and He loves us all.

5 Sing praise to God the Father,
God the Spirit, God the Son:
Sing praise to God who loves us.
Praise Him everyone!

456
© 1991 Greg Leavers

Sing and celebrate
(sing and celebrate);
God gave Jesus (God gave Jesus);
Light for all the world
(Light for all the world);
born at Christmas
(born at Christmas time).

1 Jesus, our light,
shines bright,
what delight;
came to reach us,
teach us,
lead us;
Sing and celebrate . . .

2 God so loved us,
gave us
Jesus;
Lord, we thank You,
love You,
serve You;
Sing and celebrate . . .

Jesus, Light of the world,
God's great gift of love.

457
© 1991 Greg Leavers

Sing and celebrate (sing and
celebrate);
Christ is risen (Christ is risen);
Champion of the world
(Champion of the world);
lives for ever (lives for evermore).

1 God so loved us,
gave us
Jesus;
died on Calvary,
set free
you and me;
Sing and celebrate . . .

2 Jesus our friend,
died, then
rose again;
Lord, we love You,
thank You,
praise You;
Sing and celebrate . . .

Jesus died for the world,
God's great gift of love.

458
Eddie Smith
© 1978 Pilot Point Music / CopyCare

1   **Six hundred years old
    was the preacher Noah**
    when the Lord said to build a boat;
    said a flood would come
        and cover the earth,
    and only Noah would stay afloat.
    Though the people laughed
        and called him names,
    he stayed right with his job.
    When he felt those drops,
        he knew his God
    had everything under control.
        *He's got everything under control,
        He's got everything under control.
        The stars and the planets
            are in His hand,
        the wind and the rain at His command.
        You and I, we're a part of His plan;
        He's got everything under control.*

2   Now Jonah had a whale of a problem
    when he turned that revival down.
    God tracked him down and boxed him in
    'cause he wouldn't go to that town.
    When He tells you to do
        what He wants you to do,
    don't think you can let it roll,
    'cause the God who made this universe
    has everything under control.
        He's got everything . . .

3   King Nebuchadnezzar lost his religion
    when the Hebrews wouldn't bow down.
    He lost his cool, fired up the furnace,
    called a holiday in the town.
    When he opened the door
        and threw them in,
    they smiled at the burning coals,
    'cause the God that allowed that fire
        to burn
    had everything under control.
        He's got everything . . .

4   Daniel was invited to be on the menu
    at the meeting of the lions' club,
    'cause he continued to pray
        three times a day
    to the Lord he had learned to love.
    When they threw him in he began to grin,
    'cause he knew what we all know;
    that the God who made those lions growl
    had everything under control.
        He's got everything . . .

459
Ian Smale
© 1978 Thankyou Music

So we're marching along, singing a song,
we're in the Lord's army.
We're fighting for right as we're learning
        what's wrong,
'cause – we're in the Lord's army.
He's got the victory, so let's really shout,
we're in the Lord's army.
We're in the Lord's (*yeah*),
        we're in the Lord's (*right*),
we're in the Lord's army.
So we're marching along . . .

460
© 1990 Greg Leavers

1   **Sometimes I'm naughty,**
    I know I've been bad;
    I say such unkind things
    and make people sad.
        *Father, I know I've done wrong;
        Lord, please forgive me I pray.
        I want to say,
        I want to say
        that I'm so sorry, Lord.*

2   I'm rude to my family,
    I want my own way.
    I don't show them kindness
    or do what they say.
        Father, I know . . .

3   In love You forgive me,
    I'm glad I'm Your child.
    Your Spirit lives in me
    to change me inside.

Father, help me today;
help me to please You, I pray.
I want to say,
I want to say
how much I love You, Lord.

3 Some people march and raise their
  hands
  and some are quiet but understand.
  There are many ways of worshipping
  the King of kings, the King of kings.

463

1 **Sorry, Lord, for all the things**
  that I've done wrong; please
  make me clean, forgive my sin –
  I want to follow You.

2 Thank You, Lord, for dying on
  the cross to save me;
  fill my heart for my new start –
  please come and live in me.

3 I love You, please help me Lord
  to follow closely;
  from today, in every way
  please make me more like You.

461

1 **Sometimes problems can be BIG,**
  sometimes problems can be *small*;
  but it doesn't really matter
  for whatever the size,
  Jesus wants to help us with them all –
  so we can tell Him all about it.
  Trust His word, don't doubt it.
  Don't be afraid;
  DON'T BE AFRAID,
  just (1, 2, 3, 4) believe.

2 Some days I wake up feeling GLAD,
  some days I wake up feeling *sad*;
  but it doesn't really matter
  for whatever the day
  Jesus wants to help us through them all.
  He's promised He will never leave us;
  He will not forsake us;
  don't be dismayed,
  DON'T BE AFRAID,
  just (1, 2, 3, 4) believe.

Words in Capitals spoken with a loud voice
Words in Italics spoken quietly

464

1 **Spies were sent out to**
  view the promised land.
  Ten said, 'There are giants there:
  we can't do as we planned.'
  Joshua and Caleb said,
  'We must make a stand.'
  The Lord said, 'Follow Me,
  I'll place them in your hand.'
    We've got to hear, believe and obey,
    whatever the Father might say;
    for He is a good God and He only wants
    the best for us.

2 When Joshua saw the size of
  Jericho's great wall –
  towering high above him,
  many metres tall –
  though it looked impossible
  to take the town at all,
  the Lord said, 'Obey Me
  and down the walls will fall.'
    We've got to . . .

462

1 **Some people laugh, some people sing,**
  some people clap; and so they bring
  their worship to the King of kings.
  What do you do? What do you do?

2 Some people dance, some bring a word,
  some people cry before the Lord;
  and so they bring their worship to
  the King of kings, the King of kings.

3 So when you're feeling scared or
 things are looking blue –
 you've a job that seems so
 difficult to do –
 don't forget His promises
 He's made to help you through:
 the Lord says, 'Don't be afraid,
 I'll always be with you.'
   We've got to . . .

465 Ian Smale
© 1984 Thankyou Music

**Spirit of God, please fill me
   now to overflowing.**
Spirit of God, give me the words
   You want me to say.
Spirit of God, release my tongue to
   praise the Holy Son;
Spirit of God, free this spirit of mine.

466 © 1992 Gill Robertson

   ***Standing in Your presence, Lord,
   we are here to praise Your name.
   Standing in Your presence, Lord,
   Your great goodness we proclaim.***

1 You alone are God the Lord,
 Master of the earth and sky.
 All the stars in heaven worship, and yet,
 when we call You Lord, You hear our cry.
   *Standing in Your presence, Lord,
   we will lift our hands to You.
   Standing in Your presence, Lord,
   giving thanks for all You do.*

2 You have brought us here today,
 kept and guided for so long.
 There's no need for tears or sadness,
 the joy that You give us, Lord,
   will make us strong.
   *Standing in Your presence, Lord,
   listening to Your holy law.
   Standing in Your presence, Lord,
   we will praise You evermore.*

467 © 1989 Andy Silver

**Thank You for the love
   that our mums give to us each day;**
thank You for the help
   and the care that they bring our way.
Lord, we thank You for everything they do,
show us how to help them too.
Show us how to live,
   teaching us to appreciate;
show us how to live so that we don't infuriate.
Lord, we ask that in everything they do,
may our mums be blessed by You.

468 Valerie Collison
© 1970 Campbell Connelly & Co Ltd

1 **The journey of life may be easy,
   may be hard,**
 there'll be dangers on the way;
 with Christ at my side I'll do battle
   as I ride
 'gainst the foe that would lead me astray.
   *Will you ride, ride, ride
   with the King of kings,
   will you follow my Leader true;
   will you shout 'Hosanna!'
   to the holy Son of God,
   who died for me and you?*

2 My burden is light and a song
   is in my heart,
 as I travel on life's way;
 for Christ is my Lord and
   He's given me His word,
 that by my side He'll stay.
   Will you ride . . .

3 When doubts arise and when tears
   are in my eyes,
 when all seems lost to me;
 with Christ as my guide I can smile
   whate'er betide,
 for He my strength will be.
   Will you ride . . .

4 I'll follow my Leader wherever he may go,
for Jesus is my friend;
He'll lead me on to the place
    where He has gone,
when I come to my journey's end.
Will you ride . . .

469 Paul Kenchington
© 1984 Kevin Mayhew Ltd

1 **The Lord is risen today!**
The Lord is risen today!
The Lord is risen today!
The Lord is risen today!
Alleluia! Alleluia! Alleluia!
The Lord is risen today!

2 And we will sing His praise,
and we will sing His praise,
and we will sing His praise;
the Lord is risen today!
Alleluia! Alleluia! Alleluia!
The Lord is risen today!

3 O, Jesus died for me!
Yes, Jesus died for me!
Yes, Jesus died for me,
but the Lord is risen indeed!
Alleluia! Alleluia! Alleluia!
The Lord is risen today!

All sing 1 in unison, followed by 2 in unison.
One group begins 1 again and as they reach 2,
the other group begins at 1.
The accompaniment is common in both 1 and 2.

470 Ian Smale
© 1985 Thankyou Music

**The most important thing
    for us as Christians**
is not what we eat or drink,
but stirring up goodness, peace and joy
from the Holy Spirit.

471 Hilda Rostron
© Christian Education

1 **The shepherds found the stable**
and saw the Baby there;
they quietly knelt beside Him
and said a 'thank you' prayer.

2 The wise men found the Baby
and gave gifts, one, two, three;
today it is His birthday:
My gift is – LOVE from me.

472 Damien Lundy
© Kevin Mayhew Ltd

1 **The Spirit lives to set us free,**
walk, walk in the light;
He binds us all in unity,
walk, walk in the light.
*Walk in the light,
walk in the light,
walk in the light,
walk in the light of the Lord.*

2 Jesus promised life to all,
walk, walk in the light;
the dead were wakened by His call,
walk, walk in the light.
Walk in the light . . .

3 He died in pain on Calvary,
walk, walk in the light;
to save the lost like you and me,
walk, walk in the light.
Walk in the light . . .

4 We know His death was not the end,
walk, walk in the light;
He gave His Spirit to be our friend,
walk, walk in the light.
Walk in the light . . .

5 By Jesus' life our wounds are healed,
walk, walk in the light;
the Father's kindness is revealed,
walk, walk in the light.
Walk in the light . . .

6 The Spirit lives in you and me,
    walk, walk in the light;
    His light will shine for all to see,
    walk, walk in the light.
        Walk in the light . . .

473 Alan J Price
© 1990 Daybreak Music Ltd / CopyCare

**The word of the Lord is
    planted in my heart**
and I want to see it grow.
The word of the Lord is planted in my heart
and I want you to know.
I won't let the enemy take it,
or let bad times shake it;
I won't let other things choke it out,
        (*choke choke choke choke*)
'cause I want to let it grow, grow, grow,
'cause I want to let it grow! (*last time*) (*Yeah!*)

474 Mick Gisbey
© 1985 Thankyou Music

The word of God is living and active,
sharper than any double-edged sword.
The word of God is living and active,
sharper than any double-edged sword.

475 © 1992 Gill Robertson

1 **There he stood – Goliath –
    mighty man in armour bright;**
    compared to him you'd not say David
        was prepared to fight.
    When Goliath saw him,
        he could not believe his eyes:
    before him stood a boy he did despise.
    'Do you think I am a dog,
        to fight me with a stick?
    I'll throw your flesh to animals,
        your bones for birds to pick!'
    Shouting murderous curses, he cried out,
        'Prepare to die!'
    But David spoke up boldly in reply.

*'Not with spear, not with sword
but in the name of the Lord;
in the name of the One you have defied.
He's victorious in battle,
He will save us by His power;
strength and deliverance He'll provide;
I'm fighting on the Lord almighty's side!'*

2 Moving closer in, Goliath
        started his attack
    but David ran to meet him –
        he did not turn and run back.
    With his sling he threw a stone
        which to Goliath sped;
    it broke his skull and sank into his head!
    The giant had been conquered –
        he fell down upon the floor –
    then David chopped his head off
        and Goliath was no more!
    All of Israel's army knew
        the mighty deed was done
    and in whose name the victory
        had been won.
        'Not with spear . . .

3 Life is filled with problems
        which may give us cause to fear.
    But though they seem like giants,
        just remember God is near.
    He will always help us
        when we put our trust in Him.
    In the name of Jesus we shall win.
        'Not with spear . . .

476 Paul Field
© 1991 Daybreak Music Ltd / CopyCare

There is no-one else like you,
there's no-one else like me.
Each of us is special to God,
that's the way it's meant to be.
I'm special, you're special,
we're special, don't you see?
there is no-one else like you,
there's no-one else like me.

Black or white, short or tall,
good or bad, God loves us all.
Loud or quiet, fat or thin,
each of us is special to Him.

There is no-one . . .

477 Anon
Copyright control

There once was a man called Daniel
(*good old Daniel*).
And Daniel prayed three times a day
(*good old Daniel*).
But the King's decree said, 'Worship me!'
(*poor old Daniel*).
But Daniel would not bend the knee!
(*good old Daniel*).
So the gates went 'crash' (*crash*),
and the locks went 'click' (*click*),
and the lions began to roar,
and the lions began to roar.
But they couldn't eat Daniel if they tried
(*good old Daniel*),
because the Lord was on his side
(*good old Daniel*).

478 Albert Midlane (1825–1909)
© in this version The Jubilate Group

1   **There's a song for all the children**
    that makes the heavens ring,
    a song that even angels
    can never, never sing;
    they praise Him as their maker
    and see Him glorified,
    but we can call Him Saviour
    because for us He died.

2   There's a place for all the children
    where Jesus reigns in love,
    a place of joy and freedom
    that nothing can remove;
    a home that is more friendly
    than any home we know,
    where Jesus makes us welcome
    because He loves us so.

3   There's a friend for all the children
    to guide us every day,
    whose care is always faithful
    and never fades away;
    there's no-one else so loyal –
    His friendship stays the same;
    He knows us and He loves us,
    and Jesus is His name.

479 Susan Sayers
© 1984 Kevin Mayhew Ltd

1   **Think big: an elephant.**
    Think bigger: a submarine.
    Think bigger: the highest mountain that
        anyone has ever seen.
    Yet big, big, bigger is God!
    And He loves us all.

2   Think old: a vintage car.
    Think older: a full-grown tree.
    Think older: a million grains of the sand
        beside the surging sea.
    Yet old, old, older is God!
    And He loves us all.

3   Think strong: a tiger's jaw.
    Think stronger: a castle wall.
    Think stronger: a hurricane that leaves
        little standing there at all.
    Yet strong, strong, stronger is God!
    And He loves us all.

480 Graham Kendrick
© 1988 Make Way Music

1   **This Child secretly comes in the night;**
    oh, this Child, hiding a heavenly light;
    oh, this Child, coming to us like a
        stranger;
    this heavenly Child.
        *This Child, heaven come down
            now to be with us here;
        heavenly love and mercy appear;
        softly in awe and wonder come near
        to this heavenly Child.*

2 This Child, rising on us like the sun;
  oh, this Child, given to light everyone;
  oh, this Child, guiding our feet
      on the pathway
  to peace on earth.
      This Child, heaven come down . . .

3 This Child, raising the humble and poor;
  oh, this Child, making the proud ones to
      fall;
  this Child, filling the hungry
      with good things;
  this heavenly Child.
      This Child, heaven come down . . .
      This Child, heaven come down . . .

482 © 1985 Andy Silver

Wandering like lost sheep,
    we were going our own way,
when Jesus the good shepherd
    found us, led us home,
laid down His life before us
    that we might all be saved.
We now belong to Jesus,
    we now belong to Him.
We are His sheep, we are His sheep,
we hear His voice, and follow Him.
We are His sheep, we are His sheep,
we hear His voice, and follow Him.

481 Alan J Price
© 1990 Daybreak Music Ltd / CopyCare

This is a catchy songa,
we sing it to the Conga,
we dance and sing
to Christ the King.
Why don't you sing alonga,
while we dance the Conga?
Praise God above for all His love!

1 King David danced before the Lord,
  worship filled his heart;
  we can dance before Him, too,
  this is how we start.
      This is a catchy songa . . .

2 Jesus is the greatest friend,
  alive for us today,
  He said, 'I'm with you till the end,
  I'm with you all the way.'
      This is a catchy songa . . .

Verses spoken, not sung

483 © 1990 Greg Leavers

We are soldiers of the King,
of His victory we will sing;
living every hour by the Spirit's power,
marching in the name of Jesus.
Enemies are all around,
as we praise they're losing ground;
trusting in God's word – it's a mighty sword –
forever friendly, faithful followers fighting
        for the King.

484 Alan J Price
© 1990 Daybreak Music Ltd / CopyCare

We need to grow, grow, grow, grow,
grow in the grace of the Saviour.
We need to grow, grow, grow, grow,
grow in the knowledge
*   of Jesus our Lord.*
We need to grow, grow, grow, grow,
grow in the grace of the Saviour.
We need to grow, grow, grow, grow,
grow in the knowledge
*   of Jesus our Lord.*

1 We'll grow as we pray to Him,
  spend some time each day.
  We'll grow as we worship Him,
  give Him our love and praise!

We need to grow, grow, grow, grow,
grow in the grace of the Saviour.
We need to grow, grow, grow, grow,
grow in the knowledge
of Jesus our Lord.

2 We grow as we read of Him
   and the way for us to live;
   we'll grow as we work for Him,
   as our lives to Him we give.
   We need to grow . . .

3 We grow as we learn and share
   with others that we know;
   these are the things to do
   if we really want to grow.
   We need to grow . . .
   grow in the knowledge of,
   grow in the knowledge
   of Jesus our Lord.

485 Ian Smale
© 1984 Thankyou Music

We will praise, we will praise,
   we will praise the Lord;
we will praise the Lord because He is good.
We will praise, we will praise,
   we will praise the Lord,
because His love is everlasting.
We will praise, we will praise,
   we will praise the Lord;
we will praise the Lord because He is good.
We will praise, we will praise,
   we will praise the Lord,
because His love is everlasting.

Bring on the trumpets and harps,
let's hear the cymbals ring;
then in harmony
lift our voices and sing, sing.

We will praise, we will praise,
   we will praise the Lord;
we will praise the Lord because He is good.
We will praise, we will praise,
   we will praise the Lord,
because His love is everlasting.

486 Ian Smale
© 1984 Thankyou Music

1 **We'll praise Him on the trumpet**
      and we'll praise Him on guitar,
   we'll praise Him with a drum
      and with a harp and a lyre.
   We'll praise Him with our voices
      'cause we want to lift Him higher;
   and all God's people shout, 'Hallelujah!'
      Hallelujah, hallelujah, hallelujah,
      hallelujah.
      Hallelujah, hallelujah,
      and all God's people shout,
      'Hallelujah!'

2 We'll praise Him for His favour
      and we'll praise Him for His deeds;
   we'll praise Him – though the road is
      rough, He's still the one who leads.
   We'll praise Him for provision
      as He cares for all our needs,
   and all God's people shout, 'Hallelujah!'
      Hallelujah, hallelujah . . .

3 We'll praise Him that upon a cross
      the Lamb of God was slain;
   we'll praise Him that He conquered death
      and now He lives again.
   We'll praise Him – He's the King of kings
      who will forever reign,
   and all God's people shout, 'Hallelujah!'
      Hallelujah, hallelujah . . .

4 We'll praise Him that He's making us
      the people we should be;
   we'll praise Him that our chains are gone,
      we're now completely free.
   We'll praise Him – we don't know defeat,
      we live in victory,
   and all God's people shout, 'Hallelujah!'
      Hallelujah, hallelujah . . .

487

We're following Jesus,
just like Matthew, Peter and John.
We're following Jesus,
just like Thaddeus, Philip and Tom.
We're following Jesus,
just like Simon, James and Andrew.
Like them, the Lord is calling
me and you.

1 They all loved Him (*I want to love Him*),
they all served Him (*I want to serve Him*).
They all knew Him (*I want to know Him*),
they all followed. (*I want to follow*).
We're following . . .

2 Jesus taught them (*Teach me, Lord*),
Jesus led them (*Lead me, Lord*),
Jesus fed them (*Feed me, Lord*),
Jesus used them (*Use me, Lord*).
We're following . . .

488 © Timothy Dudley-Smith / OUP

1 **What colours God has made**
in flower and field and tree!
From springing green of leaf and blade
I learn His love for me.

2 The summer's yellow sand,
the blue of sky and sea,
they tell of God their maker's hand,
and all His love for me.

3 The turning autumn leaves,
the fruit so full and free,
the golden glow of harvest sheaves,
declare His love for me.

4 He frames the winter's skies,
His silver stars I see;
He makes the sun in splendour rise,
the God who cares for me.

5 So sing my Father's praise,
the living God is He,
whose colours brighten all our days,
who loves and cares for me.

489

1 **What do you give a God**
      who has everything?
What do you give a God who has it all?
He is the One who flung the
      shining galaxies in space!
He is the One who hung the
      stars in place!

2 What do you give a God
      who has everything?
What do you give the maker of the earth?
Give Him your life and let Him guide you;
trust Him in all your ways!
Give Him your heart;
      He'll fill it up with praise!
Give Him your heart;
      He'll fill it up with praise!

490

1 **What drives the stars**
      without making a sound?
Why don't they crash
      when they're spinning around?
What holds me up when
      the world's upside down?
I know it's a miracle!
Who tells the ocean
      where to stop on the sand?
What keeps the water
      back from drowning the land?
Who makes the rules I don't understand?
I know it's a miracle!
   It's a miracle just to know
   God is with me wherever I go.
   It's a miracle as big as can be,
   that He can make a miracle of me!

2 Who shows the birds
    how to make a good nest?
How can the geese fly so far without rest?
Why do the ducks go south
    and not west?
I know it's a miracle!
What makes a brown seed
    so tiny and dry
burst into green and grow up so high?
And shoot out blossoms
    of red by and by?
I know it's a miracle!
  It's a miracle . . .

3 When a spring makes a brook
    and a brook makes a stream,
the stream makes the river water
    fresh as can be.
Who puts the salt in
    when it gets to the sea?
I know it's a miracle!
There are thousands of people
    in cities I see,
the world must be crowded
    as crowded can be;
but God knows my name
    and He cares about me.
I know it's a miracle!

491 Anon
Copyright control

1 **What a mighty God we serve . . .**
  (*4 times*)

2 He created you and me . . .

3 He has all the power to save . . .

4 Let us praise the living God . . .

5 What a mighty God we serve . . .

492 © 1992 Gill Robertson

1 **What made a difference
    in the life of Saul,**
to change him from a sinner
    to Apostle Paul?
He met Jesus and suddenly knew
that all he'd hated turned out to be true.
Instead of persecuting those
    who followed His name,
he started in the synagogue His love
    to proclaim.
Yes, who'd have thought that Saul
    could be
transformed into the greatest missionary.

2 On several journeys the apostle was sent,
and suffered many difficulties as he went.
Beaten, shipwrecked, imprisoned was he
but learnt to glory in adversity.
The churches grew and flourished
    and the Gospel was spread,
and many found salvation
    through the things that he said.
Yes, who'd have thought that Saul
    could be
transformed into the greatest missionary.

3 He wrote some letters to the churches
    he knew,
to Ephesus, Colossi and Galatia too.
To Philippi and Corinth he wrote,
to Rome and Thessalonica,
    epistles of note.
Timothy and Titus and Philemon all heard
and what he wrote has now become
    a part of God's Word.
Yes, who'd have thought that Saul
    could be
transformed into the greatest missionary.

4   If you've decided that your life
         must change,
    then give it to the Lord for Him
         to rearrange.
    He will be your Saviour and friend,
    and on His presence you can depend.
    You may not be a missionary
         or travel around,
    but all of us can witness to the joy
         that we've found.
    Yes, what the Lord could do for Saul,
    He's ready now to do for one and all!

493 © 1991 Greg Leavers

When I'm feeling lonely,
      when I'm feeling blue,
when I'm feeling so fed up,
      I can always talk to You.
Lord, You hear me when I pray;
Lord, You're near me every day.
Thank You, Lord,
      You always see me through;
I'll never, ever, find a friend as good as You.
I'll never, ever, find a friend as good as You.

494 Paul Field and Ralph Chambers
© 1991 Daybreak Music Ltd / CopyCare

When the dark clouds are above you,
there's no sunshine anywhere;
when you feel that no-one loves you,
when you feel that no-one cares;
talk to the Saviour,
He knows how you feel.
His love lasts forever,
His love for you is real.
Talk to the Saviour,
no matter what you do.
You've got a friend in Jesus,
He always loves you.

When the dark . . .

495 © 1988 Andy Silver

When we look up to the sky
and we see the sparrows fly,
let's remember that Jesus knows them all.
When we see the lovely trees
and the flowers and the leaves,
let's remember that Jesus made them all.
J.E.S.U.S. C.A.R.E.S.
Jesus cares for all the things He made:
that means you and me,
our friends and family.
Thank You, Jesus, for caring for me.

496 Paul Field and Ralph Chambers
© 1991 Daybreak Music Ltd / CopyCare

When you're feeling good
      put your thumbs up.
When you're feeling bad put them down.
When you're feeling happy
      you can smile all day.
When you're feeling low wear a frown.
But don't just follow your feelings.
Trust in God and His word.
No matter what you feel put your thumbs up,
put your faith in the Lord.

497 © 1991 Joan Robinson

When God breathes His Spirit in my life;
when God breathes His Spirit in my life;
when God breathes His Spirit in my life,
then I will shine, shine for Him.

498 P M Verrall
© Herald Music Service

1   **Would you walk by on the other side**
    when someone called for aid?
    Would you walk by on the other side,
    and would you be afraid?
      Cross over the road, my friend;
      ask the Lord His strength to lend;
      His compassion has no end.
      Cross over the road.

2 Would you walk by on the other side
   when you saw a loved one stray?
   Would you walk by on the other side,
   or would you watch and pray?
       Cross over the road . . .

3 Would you walk by on the other side
   when starving children cried?
   Would you walk by on the other side,
   and would you not provide?
       Cross over the road, my friend,
       ask the Lord His strength to lend,
       His compassion has no end.
       Cross over the road.
       Cross over the road,
       cross over the road.

499 Ian Smale
© 1987 Thankyou Music

Yet to all who received Him,
to those who believed in His name,
He gave the right to become
        the children of God.
Yet to all who received Him,
to those who believed in His name,
He gave the right to become
        the children of God.

500 © 1991 Greg Leavers

You are holy, so You hate all we do wrong.
You are loving, for our sin
        You gave Your Son.
You are Father, the great protector;
You are mighty, the great Creator;
You are faithful, You are wonderful,
You are King and You are God.

501 Chris Brown
© 1988 Oxford University Press

1 **You can weigh an elephant's auntie,**
   you can weigh a pedigree flea;
   but you can't weigh up all the love
   that Jesus has for me, me, me,
   that Jesus has for me.

2 You can measure the length
        of a wiggly worm,
   or the height of a nanny goat's knee;
   but you can't measure all the love
   that Jesus has for me, me, me,
   that Jesus has for me.

3 You can add up two and two, make four,
   it's as easy as A, B, C;
   but you can't add up all the love
   that Jesus has for me, me, me,
   that Jesus has for me.

4 You can amaze me by subtraction,
   you can even take three from three;
   but you can't take away the love
   that Jesus has for me, me, me,
   that Jesus has for me.

502 Ralph Chambers
© 1991 Daybreak Music Ltd / CopyCare

**You can't catch a plane
        to take you to heaven.**
Not even a spaceship can get that far.
You can't take a hovercraft
        or helicopter journey
or drive in the fastest racing car.
Only Jesus, only Jesus,
        only Jesus is the way.
Only Jesus, only Jesus,
        only Jesus is the way.

503 © 1991 Joan Robinson

You're my maker, You're my music,
You're the Master of my life.
You're my maker, You're my music,
You're the Master of my life.
You're my maker, You're my music,
You're the Master of my life,
and I love You, Jesus my Lord.

504 Steve Morgan-Gurr
© 2001 Thankyou Music

And our voices will sing
and our praise we'll bring,
as we worship the King, hallelujah!
And when heaven hears the noise
of us girls and boys,
they will add to our voices and sing.

1 The sound of children praising God
   is such a mighty thing,
   it helps defeat His enemies,
   so let's join in and sing.
   And our voices will sing . . .

2 There will be days when we don't praise
   and music can't be heard,
   but God enjoys His children
   as they live life by His word.
   And our voices will sing . . .
   They will add to our voices and sing.

505 Jim Bailey
© 1997 Thankyou Music

As for me and my house,
as for me and my family,
as for me and my children,
we will serve the Lord.

As for me . . .

In this family,
we're gonna do things properly,
read God's word every day
and then we'll try to pray;
although we get it wrong,
we will still carry on,
make Jesus number one in this place.
In this place we're gonna say grace.

As for me . . .

506 Estelle White
© 1969 Stainer & Bell Ltd

1 **Autumn days when the grass is**
   jewelled,
   and the silk inside a chestnut shell,
   jet planes meeting in the air
      to get refuelled,
   all these things I love so well.
   So I mustn't forget,
   no, I mustn't forget,
   to say a great big thank you,
   I mustn't forget.

2 Clouds that look like familiar faces,
   and a winter's moon with frosted rings,
   smell of bacon as I fasten up my laces,
   and the song the milkman sings.
   So I mustn't forget . . .

3 Whipped-up spray that is
      rainbow-scattered,
   and a swallow curving in the sky,
   shoes so comfy though they're worn-out
      and they're battered,
   and the taste of apple pie.
   So I mustn't forget . . .

4 Scent of gardens
      when the rain's been falling,
   and a minnow darting down a stream,
   picked-up engine
      that's been stuttering and stalling,
   and a win for my home team.
   So I mustn't forget . . .

507 David J Evans
© 1986 Thankyou Music

1 **Be still,**
   for the presence of the Lord,
      the Holy One, is here;
   come bow before Him now
   with reverence and fear:
   in Him no sin is found –
   we stand on holy ground.
   Be still,
   for the presence of the Lord,
      the Holy One, is here.

2 Be still,
    for the glory of the Lord
      is shining all around;
    He burns with holy fire,
    with splendour He is crowned:
    how awesome is the sight –
    our radiant King of light!
    Be still,
    for the glory of the Lord
      is shining all around.

3 Be still,
    for the power of the Lord
      is moving in this place:
    He comes to cleanse and heal,
    to minister His grace –
    no work too hard for Him.
    In faith receive from Him.
    Be still,
    for the power of the Lord
      is moving in this place.

508   Mark and Helen Johnson
            © 1995 Out of the Ark Music

1 **Before You made the skies and sea,**
    Your heart was full of love for me.
    You knew the person I would be,
    thank You for loving me.

2 You came to earth to live like us,
    with words of life and arms of love.
    You showed the way to heaven above,
    thank You for loving us.
    Thank You, Jesus,
    thank You, my Lord.
    Your love came down from heaven,
    come fill up my heart evermore.

3 Because God loved the world so much
    You paid the price for all of us.
    You gave your life upon a cross,
    thank You for loving us.
    Thank You, Jesus . . .

4 So thank You, Lord, for loving me
    today and all eternity.
    And may my song forever be,
    thank You for loving me.
    Thank You, Jesus . . .
    Thank You, Jesus . . .

509   Don Moen
            © 1986 Integrity's Hosanna! Music

Blessèd be the name of the Lord,
He is worthy to be praised and adored;
so we lift up holy hands
    in one accord, singing,
'Blessèd be the name, blessèd be the name,
blessèd be the name of the Lord!'

510   From Proverbs 18, Clinton Utterbach
            © 1989 Utterbach Music Incorporated /
            Polygram International Publishing Corporation

1 **Blessèd be the name of the Lord,**
    blessèd be the name of the Lord,
    blessèd be the name of the Lord
      most high!
    Blessèd be the name of the Lord,
    blessèd be the name of the Lord,
    blessèd be the name of the Lord
      most high!
    The name of the Lord
      is a strong tower –
    the righteous run into it,
    and they are saved;
    the name of the Lord is a strong tower –
    the righteous run into it,
    and they are saved.

2 Glory to the name of the Lord,
    glory to the name of the Lord,
    glory to the name of the Lord most high!
    Glory to the name of the Lord,
    glory to the name of the Lord,
    glory to the name of the Lord most high!
    The name of the Lord . . .

3 Holy is the name of the Lord,
    holy is the name of the Lord,
    holy is the name of the Lord most high!
    Holy is the name of the Lord,
    holy is the name of the Lord,
    holy is the name of the Lord most high!
    The name of the Lord . . .

511 Mark and Helen Johnson
© 2002 Out of the Ark Music

1 **Cabbages and greens,**
   broccoli and beans,
   cauliflower and roasted potatoes,
   taste so good to me!

2 Apricots and plums,
   ripened in the sun,
   oranges and yellow bananas,
   good for everyone!
      It's another Harvest Festival
      when we bring our fruit and vegetables,
      'cause we want to share the best of all
      the good things that we've been given.
      It's another opportunity,
      to be grateful for the food we eat,
      with a samba celebration to say
      'Thank You' to God the Father.

3 Golden corn and wheat,
   oats and sugar beet,
   fluffy rice and tasty spaghetti,
   wonderful to eat!

4 Coffee, cocoa, tea,
   growing naturally,
   herbal plants and all kinds of spices,
   very nice indeed!
      It's another Harvest Festival . . .

   Thank You for the harvest,
   thank You for Your goodness,
   for all of the fruit and vegetables
   and the wonderful things that grow.
   Thank You for the harvest,
   thank You for Your goodness,
   for all of the fruit and vegetables
   and the wonderful things that grow.

   VOICE 1 REPEAT VERSES 1 & 2
   VOICE 2
   Thank You for the harvest,
   thank You for Your goodness.
   For all of the fruit and vegetables
   and the wonderful things that grow.
      It's another Harvest Festival . . .

512 Mark and Helen Johnson
© 1994 Out of the Ark Music

1 **Child in a manger born,**
   lies in a cattle stall.
   Safely He's sleeping,
   Mary is keeping
   close beside her baby so small.

2 Angels watch over Him,
   softly their praises sing.
   Voices ascending,
   joy never ending,
   glory be to Jesus the King,
      and God in the heavens above,
      looks down with a heart full of love.

3 Leaving their flocks behind,
   shepherds have come to find
   Jesus the Saviour,
   Lord of the Ages,
   here within the stable tonight,
      and God in the heavens . . .

4 Wise men from far and wide,
   kneel at the baby's side,
   gazing in wonder,
   praising the Son who
   came to earth to lay down His life,
      and God in the heavens . . .

5 Child in a manger born,
   I want to know You more,
   know You are near me,
   love You more dearly
   Jesus, my Lord.

513 © Greg Leavers

Do be, do be, do be, do be strong.
Do what, do what, do what God wants done.
Don't be afraid, don't be dismayed,
for the Lord your God is with you.

Take a look in His book,
make a note of what He wrote
then do what God says is best,
   and trust in Him to do the rest.

Do be, do be, do be, do be strong.
Do what, do what, do what God wants done.
Don't be afraid, don't be dismayed,
for the Lord your God is with you.

514 Sam Horner
© Daybreak Music Ltd / CopyCare

Don't be afraid or put off,
*just trust with all your might,
stand up, speak out
    and live for the things of God.
So if you're scared, or let down,
just learn from what's gone on,
stand up, speak out
    and live for the things of God.*

1 Doesn't matter if you're young or old,
or if you're rich or poor;
there's no easy way to live for God,
of that you can be sure.
    Don't be afraid . . .

2 Doesn't matter if you're big or small,
strong or insecure;
there's no easy way to live for God,
of that you can be sure.
    Don't be afraid . . .

515 Mark and Helen Johnson
© Out of the Ark Music

1 **Easter jubilation
    fills the streets and towns,**
celebrations have begun.
Hear the music and the dancing now,
join the laughter and the fun!
    *Oh, raise a joyful shout!
    Clap your hands and dance,
    let your feelings out.
    Oh, hear what it's about:
    Christ, the Lord,
        has come to set us free.*

2 Put aside your sorrows,
    wipe your tears away,
for a better time will come.
There's a promise of a better day,
join the laughter and the fun!
    Oh, raise a joyful shout! . . .

3 La, la, la, la, la, *etc.*
    Oh, raise a joyful shout! . . .

4 Easter jubilation
    fills the streets and towns,
celebrations have begun.
Hear the music and the dancing now,
join the laughter and the fun!
    *Oh, raise a joyful shout! . . .
    Hoy!*

516 Judy Mackenzie-Dunn
© 2004 Daybreak Music Ltd / CopyCare

Even if you're lost in space,
Jesus can find you.
He's bigger than the universe,
He's all around you.
It doesn't matter where you are,
even on the farthest star,
there isn't anywhere too far from Him.

Even if I'm lost in space,
Jesus can find me.
He's bigger than the universe,
He's all around me.
It doesn't matter where we are,
even on the farthest star,
there isn't anywhere too far from Him.

517 Judy Mackenzie-Dunn
© 2004 Daybreak Music Ltd / CopyCare

1 **Every blade of grass,**
    (every blade of grass,)
every sunset sky,
    (every sunset sky,)
every starry night,
    (every starry night,)
every mountain high,
    (every mountain high,)
every single thing
    (every single thing)
that Your hands have made,
    (that Your hands have made,)
gives You glory,
    (gives You glory,)
gives You praise
    (gives You praise).

And I want to praise You too,
for no-one is as wonderful as You.
And I want the world to see
that the God of all creation
*   is a friend to me.*

2 Every bird that sings,
   (every bird that sings,)
   every shining sea,
   (every shining sea,)
   every blooming flower,
   (every blooming flower,)
   every towering tree,
   (every towering tree,)
   every single thing
   (every single thing)
   that Your hands have made
   (that Your hands have made)
   gives You glory,
   (gives You glory,)
   gives You praise
   (gives You praise).
   And I want to praise . . .

518 Trevor Ranger
         © 2005 Daybreak Music Ltd / CopyCare

1 **Every second, every minute,**
   every hour and every day,
   You're the ever present God
      throughout the year.
   Every village, every city,
   every road along the way,
   You're the God of everywhere
   and always here.
      You are the Lord God Almighty,
      You are the Lord God Almighty,
      You are the Lord God Almighty,
      Ruler of all the earth.

2 Every wording, every sentence,
   every thought in every mind,
   You're the God for whom there is
      no mystery.
   Every secret, every longing,
   every deed of every kind,
   oh, Your knowledge is too
   wonderful for me.
      You are the Lord . . .

3 Every ocean, every island,
   every hill and every stream,
   You're the God whose power and works
      are on display.
   Every creature, every planet,
   everything that's ever been,
   You're the God of awesome power
   in every way.
      You are the Lord . . .

519 Doug Horley
         © 1999 Thankyou Music

Faith as small as a mustard seed
   will move mountains, move mountains.
Faith as small as a mustard seed
   will move mountains
      by the power of God.

Faith as small . . .

Believe what Jesus said was true,
believe He meant it just for you.
Wait and see what God will do,
as you pray, pray, as you pray.

Faith as small . . .

Faith as small . . .

Do da do da do da do do da,
do da do da mountains.
Do da do da do da do do da,
do da do da mustard.

Do da do da . . .

520 Dave Godfrey
         © 2007 Daybreak Music Ltd / CopyCare

Father, may Your name be honoured,
Father, may Your kingdom come,
and Father, please give us today
   all our daily bread.
Father, will You please forgive us,
Father, as we forgive others,
Father, will You lead us safely
   from all temptation.

For Yours is the Kingdom,
the power and the glory,
for ever and ever, amen.
For Yours is the Kingdom,
the power and the glory,
for ever and ever, amen.

Father, may Your name be honoured,
Father, may Your kingdom come,
and Father, please give us today
all our daily bread.
Father, will You please forgive us,
Father, as we forgive others,
Father, will You lead us safely
from all temptation.

521 Simon Parry
© 2001 Vineyard Songs

Father God, (Father God,)
Father God, (Father God,)
Father God, I want to know You.
Father God, (Father God,)
Father God, (Father God,)
Father God, I want to know You.
*I want to know You like a friend,
feel You beside me every day.
I want to know You deep within,
Father God.*

Father God, (Father God,)
Father God, (Father God,)
Father God, I want to know You.
Father God, (Father God,)
Father God, (Father God,)
Father God, I want to know You.
I want to know You . . .

I want to know You, Lord.
I want to know You more and more.
Take all I am and make it Yours,
Father God.
I want to know You . . .

522 Paul Crouch and David Mudie
© 1994 Daybreak Music Ltd / CopyCare

1 **Father God, You love me
and You know me inside out.**
You know the words that I will say
before I speak them out.
You are all around me,
You hold me in Your hand,
Your love for me is more
than I can ever understand.

2 Father God, from Your love
there is nowhere I can hide.
If I go down into the depths
or cross the ocean wide,
there Your love would find me,
You'd take me in Your hand.
Your love for me is more
than I can ever understand.

523 Danny Daniels
© 1989 Vineyard Songs

1 **Father, I can call You Father,**
for I am Your child
today, tomorrow and always,
You are my Father.

2 Father, how I love You,
Father, I will sing Your praise,
today, tomorrow and always,
for You're my Father.
*Father, Father, Father, to me.
Father, holy Father, Father to me.*

3 Father, I will serve You,
Father, I will seek Your face,
today, tomorrow and always,
You are my Father.
Father, Father . . .

524 © Greg Leavers

**Father, when I think
    of how naughty I can be,**
I'm so very glad to know
    that Jesus died for me.
Your love, I don't deserve it,
    but I'd be lost without it,
Jesus, Friend of sinners, be a friend to me.

525 © Geoffrey Gardner

1   **From the tiny ant,**
        from the tiny ant,
    to the elephant,
        to the elephant,
    from the snake to the kangaroo,
        from the snake to the kangaroo,
    from the great white shark,
        from the great white shark,
    to the singing lark,
        to the singing lark –
        care for them, it's up to you,
        care for them, it's up to you,
        care for them, it's up to you,
        care for them, it's up to you.
        No one else will care for them.
        It's up, it's up, it's up to you.

2   From the tabby cat,
        from the tabby cat,
    to the desert rat,
        to the desert rat,
    from the hamster to the chimpanzee,
        from the hamster to the chimpanzee,
    from the common tern,
        from the common tern,
    to the crawling worm,
        to the crawling worm –
        care for them . . .
        It's up, it's up, it's up to me.

3   From the mongrel dog,
        from the mongrel dog,
    to the snorting hog,
        to the snorting hog,
    from the badger to the platypus,
        from the badger to the platypus,
    from the small minnow,
        from the small minnow,
    to the white rhino,
        to the white rhino –
        care for them . . .
        It's up, it's up, it's up to us.

526   Nick Harding
          © 1995 Daybreak Music Ltd / CopyCare

For ever I will live my life by faith;
I'm always gonna live my life by faith.
For ever I will live my life by faith;
I'm always gonna live my life by faith.

1   By faith I can obey,
    by faith I praise and pray,
    by faith I am made new,
    by faith I know it's true.
        For ever I will live . . .

2   By faith I take God's hand,
    by faith I understand,
    by faith I am made pure,
    by faith I can be sure.
        For ever I will live . . .

527   John Hardwick
          © 1994 Daybreak Music Ltd / CopyCare

For God so loved the world
He gave His only Son,
and whoever believes in Him shall not die,
but have eternal life.

L is for the love that He has for me,
I am the reason He died on the tree,
F is for forgiveness and now I am free,
E is to enjoy being in His company.

For God so loved . . .

528 Doug Horley and Jamie Horley
© Thankyou Music

For the measure of the treasure
   that you store in heaven,
is the measure that'll last forever.
But the measure of the treasure
   that you store on earth
might be carried away by a thief one day,
or rot when the moths get hungry.

For the measure . . .

For where your treasure is,
that's where your heart is.
For where your treasure is
there'll be your heart.

For where your . . .

529 Andy Gilmore
© 2004 Thankyou Music

Genesis, Exodus, Leviticus,
   Numbers, Deuteronomy.
Genesis, Exodus, Leviticus,
   Numbers, Deuteronomy.
Joshua and Judges, Ruth the leading lady.
1 and 2 Samuel, 1 and 2 Kings,
   1 and 2 Chronicles.
Ezra and Nehemiah, Esther the second lady.
This concludes the history
   of the Israelites and Jews.

Job, Psalms, Proverbs, Ecclesiastes,
   Song of Songs.
Job, Psalms, Proverbs, Ecclesiastes,
   Song of Songs.
Isaiah and Jeremiah
   who also wrote Lamentations.
Ezekiel, Daniel, Hosea, Joel,
   Amos and Obadiah.
Jonah and Micah, Nahum
   and the book of Habakkuk.
Zephaniah, Haggai, Zechariah, Malachi:
   the prophets of these books.

530 Mike Burn
© 2004 Daybreak Music Ltd / CopyCare

Get into the word,
get reading the word,
get living the word of God.
I said:
Get into the word,
get reading the word,
get living the word of God.

1   Sharper than a two-edged sword,
    power-packed and full of life.
    Shining brightly on our feet,
    lighting up the road ahead,
    showing us the way we should go.
       Get into the word . . .

2   The Bible is the greatest book,
    the one that everyone should read.
    Every chapter, every verse
    shows us just what God is like,
    as Jesus' face comes shining through.
       Get into the word,
       get reading the word,
       get living the word of God.
       I said word of God.

531 Doug Horley
© 2005 Thankyou Music

Glory and honour to You we bring.
Beautiful Saviour Your praise we sing.
Heaven bows down
       and worships Your name.
God of creation we praise.

Glory and honour to You we bring
Beautiful Saviour Your praise we sing.
Heaven bows down
       and worships Your name.
God of creation we praise.
God of creation we praise.

And so to You, we'll give You praise,
we'll give You glory to You always.
And so to You, we'll give You praise,
we'll give You glory to You always.

Glory and honour . . .
And so to You . . .
God of creation we praise.
God of creation we praise.

Honour the King, honour the King.
We will honour the King of kings.
We will honour the King, honour the King.
We will honour the King of kings.

We will honour the King, honour the King.
We will honour the King of kings.
We will honour the King, honour the King.
We will honour the King of kings.

And so to You, we'll give Your praise,
we'll give You glory to You always.
And so to You, we'll give Your praise,
we'll give You glory to You always.

Glory and honour to You we bring.
Beautiful Saviour Your praise we sing.
Heaven bows down,
          and worships Your name,
God of creation we praise.
God of creation we praise.

532 Mike Burn
© 2004 Daybreak Music Ltd / CopyCare

God is as good as His word,
God is as good as His word,
and His word is good.
God is as good as His word,
God is as good as His word,
and His word is good.
    His word is good,
    His word is true,
    His word is strength and hope
      and light to see us through.
    But most of all
    His word reveals
    the One He loves,
    His precious Son,
    Jesus Christ the living Word.

God is as good as His word,
God is as good as His word,
and His word is good.
    His word is good . . .
    His word is good . . .

533 Henry Smith
© 1978 Integrity's Hosanna! Music /
Integrity Praise! / Sovereign Music UK

Give thanks with a grateful heart,
give thanks to the Holy One;
give thanks because He's given
Jesus Christ, His Son.
Give thanks . . .

And now let the weak say, 'I am strong',
let the poor say, 'I am rich',
because of what the Lord has done for us;
and now let the weak say, 'I am strong',
let the poor say, 'I am rich',
because of what the Lord has done for us.
    Give thanks . . .

And now . . .

534 Jim Bailey
© 1997 Thankyou Music

God is raising up an army
made of those who are still young.
God is lifting up their voices,
through the weak He'll shame the strong.
It's been prophesied they will prophesy,
God's salvation they will show;
for the promise is to the children,
to our daughters and our sons.

Children of the cross, a shining example,
children of the cross are singing His praise.
Children of the cross
          are silencing the enemy,
children of the cross
          are saying the Lord saves.

535 Doug Horley
© 1999 Thankyou Music

God loves me, whoopah, wahey!
God loves you, whoopah, wahey!
God loves us, whoopah, wahey!
God loves you.
God loves me . . .

I'm gonna shout, gonna make some noise,
I'm gonna sing, gonna raise my voice,
I'm gonna dance, gonna go a little crazy,
    will you?
Will you go, will you go?
I'm gonna jump, gonna jump up high,
I'm gonna raise my hands to the sky,
I'm gonna dance, gonna go completely
    loopy, will you?

God loves me . . .
God loves me . . .

I'm gonna shout . . .

Whoo, whoopah, wayehheyeh!
Whoo, whoopah, wayehheyeh!
Whoo, whoopah, wayehheyeh!
God loves you and nothing you can do will
    ever change that.
Whoo, whoopah . . .

God loves me . . .
God loves me . . .
God loves me . . .
God loves me . . .
God loves us, whoopah, wahey!
God loves you.

1 Your legs may be long or short,
    it doesn't matter one bit –
    God looks at you and announces
      to the world:
    'What a star! What a picture!
      What a hit!'
      God made the chickens . . .

2 Your nose may be big or little,
    it doesn't matter one bit –
    God looks at you and announces
      to the world:
    'What a star! What a picture!
      What a hit!'
      God made the chickens . . .

3 You hair may be straight or curly,
    it doesn't matter one bit –
    God looks at you and announces
      to the world:
    'What a star! What a picture!
      What a hit!'
      God made the chickens . . .

4 Your face may be black or white,
    it doesn't matter one bit –
    God looks at you and announces
      to the world:
    'What a star! What a picture!
      What a hit!'
      God made the chickens . . .

536 Bob Hartman

    **God made the chickens and the
      cows and the bees,**
    *God made the shrubs and the flowers
      and the trees,*
    *God made the tops and the bottoms
      and the knees
      and God made me!*
    *God made the alligator
      and the kangaroo,*
    *God made the elephant
      and the pygmy shrew,*
    *God made the mountains
      and the valleys in Peru
      and God made you!*

537 Gill Robertson

1 **God of the earth and sky and sea,**
    great is His love for you and me.
    He is the God with a loving heart.
    He is the God whose word is true,
    He knows the things we say and do.
    He is the God with a loving heart.

    He wants us all to trust Him,
    our maker and our friend.
    He's always there beside us,
    His love will never end.

2 He is the God who shows He cares,
   He is the one who's always there,
   He is the God with a loving heart.
   He is the God whose praise we sing,
   He is the Lord of everything,
   He is the God with a loving heart.
   He is the God with a loving heart.

538 Simon Parry
© 2005 Vineyard Songs

1 **God who made the universe,
     the earth the sun,**
   the moon and stars
     has a place in His heart for me.
   From the beginning to the end,
     God will always be my friend,
   so I can jump and shout
   God's love is big, God's love is great,
   God's love is fab and He's my mate.
   God's love surrounds me every day,
   and I love to sing and say:
   God's love is big, God's love is strong,
   God's love goes on and on and on,
   God's love surrounds me every day,
   and I love to sing and say:
   'God loves me, Wahey!'

2 Since before the world began
     God knew me and had a plan
     for my life and How I'm gonna be.
   He sent Jesus to be my friend,
     to show His love will never end,
   so I can jump and shout
   God's love is big . . .

   God's love is big! Big!
   God's love is great! Great!
   God's love is fab! Fab!
   God's love is strong! Strong!
   God's love is big! Great! Fab! Strong!
   Big! Great! Fab! Strong!
   Big! Great! Fab! Strong!
   Big! Great! Fab! Strong!
   Big! Great! Fab! Strong! Yaee!
   God's love is big . . .

539 Cindy Rethmeier
© 1995 Mercy / Vineyard Publishing

Good news!
Jesus was born.
Good news!
He died on the cross.
Good news!
He rose again.
Good news!
He's coming back soon.

Good news! . . .

God sent Jesus,
His only son,
to save me from my sin.
He's the only one
who can change my heart
and make me His own.
He saved me,
He loves me,
my heart is His home.

Good news!
Jesus was born.
Good news!
He died on the cross.
Good news!
He rose again.
Good news!
He's coming back soon.
Good news!
He's coming back soon.
Good news!
He's coming back soon!

540 Paul Crouch and David Mudie
© 1989 Daybreak Music Ltd / CopyCare

1 **Grace is when God gives us**
     the things we don't deserve.
   Grace is when God gives us
     the things we don't deserve.
   He does it because He loves us;
   He does it because He loves us.
   Grace is when God gives us
     the things we don't deserve.

2 Mercy is when God does not
       give us what we deserve.
   Mercy is when God does not
       give us what we deserve.
   He does it because He loves us;
   He does it because He loves us.
   Mercy is when God does not
       give us what we deserve.

541 Tim Cullen
        © 1975 Thankyou Music

Hallelujah, my Father,
for giving us Your Son;
sending Him into the world
to be given up for men,
knowing we would bruise Him
and smite Him from the earth.
Hallelujah, my Father,
in His death is my birth;
Hallelujah, my Father,
in His life is my life.

542 Steve and Kay Morgan-Gurr
        © 1999 Daybreak Music Ltd / CopyCare

He changed water into wine,
healed the sick and cured the blind;
told His friends where they would find
    the best fish in the sea.
Miracles His power show,
though it happened long ago;
the greatest miracle I know is
what He's done for me,
what He's done for me.

1 Miracles are there
       to show us all who Jesus was,
   and to make us listen to what He said.
   And they make it clear
       that He's the Son of God
   because no one else
       could give life to the dead.
   He changed water . . .

2 If we turn to Jesus
       and are sorry for our sin,
   God's word makes it plain for all to see:
   from that brand new start,
       the greatest miracle begins,
   the miracle of life eternally.
       He changed water . . .

543 Ian Smale
        © 2005 Daybreak Music Ltd / CopyCare

1 **How great is the love of God.**
   How great is the love of God.
   How great, (how great,)
   how great (how great).
   It's as great as great could ever be.

2 How deep is the love of God.
   How deep is the love of God.
   How deep, (how deep,)
   how deep (how deep).
   It's as deep as deep could ever be.

3 How strong is the love of God.
   How strong is the love of God.
   How strong, (how strong,)
   how strong (how strong).
   It's as strong as strong could ever be.

4 How great is the love of God.
   How great is the love of God.
   How great, (how great,)
   how great (how great).
   It's as great as great could ever be.

544 Isaac Balinda
        © 1990 Integrity's Hosanna! Music /
        Integrity Praise! / Sovereign Music UK

Higher, higher, higher, higher,
higher, higher, higher,
lift up Jesus higher.
Higher, higher . . .

Lower, lower, lower, lower,
lower, lower, lower,
lower Satan lower.
Lower, lower . . .

Cast your burdens onto Jesus,
He cares for you.
Cast your burdens onto Jesus,
He cares for you.
Higher, higher, higher, higher,
higher, higher, higher,
lift up Jesus higher.
Higher, higher . . .

545 Ian Smale
© 2004 Daybreak Music Ltd / CopyCare

1 **Holy, Lord, make us more holy,**
make us more like Jesus
than we've ever been before.

2 Loving, Lord, make us more loving,
make us more like Jesus
than we've ever been before.

3 Powerful, Lord, make us more powerful,
make us more like Jesus
than we've ever been before,
make us more like Jesus
than we've ever been before.

546 Jim Bailey
© 1990 Thankyou Music

I can do all, (all!) all, (all!)
all things through Christ
who strengthens me.
I can do all, (all!) all, (all!)
all things through Christ
who strengthens me.

1 Go to school: all things.
Obey the rules: all things.
Keep my cool: all things,
through Christ who strengthens me.
I can do all . . .

2 Make new friends: all things.
Give and lend: all things.
Make amends: all things,
through Christ who strengthens me.
I can do all . . .

3 Pray and sing: all things.
Love our King: all things.
Everything: all things,
through Christ who strengthens me.
I can do all . . .

547 Brian Duane and Kathryn Scott
© 2001 Vineyard Songs

1 **I can see your loveliness.**
And I can see your love for Me.
As I look upon your face,
My child of grace.

2 I have called you 'chosen one'.
And I have formed you in my hands.
Felt the warmth of your embrace,
My child of grace.
For you are My beloved one.
I have called you by your name.
I am yours and you are Mine,
My child of grace.
So come to Me with all your cares.
I see no guilt nor fear or shame.
As I look into your face,
My child of grace.
For I am your Father
and My love will never change.
I am yours and you are Mine,
My child of grace.
I am yours and you are Mine,
My child of grace.

548 Judy Mackenzie-Dunn
© 2004 Daybreak Music Ltd / CopyCare

1 **I don't know how You made the world**
or how You keep it turning,
I'll never really understand
the laws of time or space.
I don't know why the sky is blue,
or how the sun keeps burning,
or why You love the human race.
All I know is that You died for me
so that I could be forgiven.
And all I know is that You lived on earth
so that I could live in heaven.

2 I don't know how You stay the same
   when all around is changing,
   or why You always care for me,
   no matter what I do.
   I don't know how You hear my prayer
   when half the world is praying,
   but You have promised me it's true.
   All I know is . . .

549 Gwen F Smith
         Copyright control

1 **I love the sun,**
      it shines on me,
   God made the sun,
      and God made me.

2 I love the stars,
      they twinkle on me,
   God made the stars,
      and God made me.

3 I love the rain,
      it splashes on me,
   God made the rain,
      and God made me.

4 I love the wind,
      it blows round me,
   God made the wind,
      and God made me.

5 I love the birds,
      they sing to me,
   God made the birds,
      and God made me.

550 John Hardwick
         © 2005 Daybreak Music Ltd / CopyCare

I may not have good looks,
I may not have fame,
but 'Praise the Lord,'
I don't mind,
God knows my name.
I may not have big muscles,
I may not be too smart,
but 'Praise the Lord,'
I don't mind,
God knows my heart.

God knows my heart,
He knows me inside out,
yet He still loves me,
that's why I love to shout:
Hallelujah!
Thank You for loving me.
I have been accepted
into God's family.

I may not have . . .

Isn't it good to be part of God's family,
isn't it good to belong to someone,
isn't it good to be part of what's
      close to His heart?
He will finish the work He has begun.

Isn't it good . . .

Isn't it good . . .
He will finish the work He has begun.

551 Ian Smale
         © 1998 Thankyou Music

I may live in a great big city,
I may live in a village small,
I may live in a tiny house,
I may live in a tower tall,
I may live in the countryside,
I may live by the sea,
but wherever I live,
I know that Jesus also lives with me,
but wherever I live,
I know Jesus lives with me.

I may live in a great big city,
I may live in a village small,
I may live in a tiny house,
I may live in a tower tall,
I may live in the countryside,
I may live by the sea,
but wherever I live,
I know that Jesus also lives with me,
but wherever I live,
I know Jesus lives with me,
but wherever I live,
I know Jesus lives with me.

552
Chris Christensen
© 1990 Integrity's Hosanna! Music /
Integrity Praise! / Sovereign Music UK

1 **I was made to praise You,**
   I was made to glorify Your name,
   in every circumstance
   to find a chance to thank You.
   I was made to love You,
   I was made to worship at Your feet,
   and to obey You, Lord,
   I was made for You.

2 I will always praise You,
   I will always glorify Your name,
   in every circumstance
   I'll find a chance to thank You.
   I will always love You,
   I will always worship at Your feet,
   and I'll obey You, Lord,
   I was made for You.

553   © Tom McGuinness

   I will bring to You the best gift
   I can offer;
   I will sing to You the best things
   in my mind.

1 Paper pictures, bits of string,
      I'll bring You almost anything.
   I'll bring a song that only I can sing:
   the rainbow colours in the sky,
      the misty moon that caught my eye,
   the magic of a newborn butterfly.
      I will bring to You . . .

2 I'll bring a song of winter trees,
      the skidding ice, the frozen leaves,
   the battles in our snowball-shouting
      streets.
   I'll bring You summers I have known,
      adventure trips and journeys home,
   the summer evenings
      playing down our road.
      I will bring to You . . .

3 I'll share my secrets and my dreams,
      I'll show You wonders I have seen,
   and I will listen
      when You speak Your name;
   and if You really want me to,
      I will share my friends with You,
   everyone at home and in my school.
      I will bring to You . . .

554
Judy Bailey
© 1993 Daybreak Music Ltd / CopyCare

   I reach up high, I touch the ground,
   I stomp my feet and turn around.
   I've got to (woo woo) praise the Lord.
   I jump and dance with all my might,
   I might look funny but that's all right.
   I've got to (woo woo) praise the Lord.

1 I'll do anything just for my God,
   'cause He's done everything for me.
   It doesn't matter who is looking on,
   Jesus is the person that I want to please.
      I reach up high . . .

2 May my whole life be a song of praise,
   to worship God in every way.
   In this song the actions praise His name,
   I want my actions every day
      to do the same.
      I reach up high . . .

555
Mark Depledge
© 2001 Vineyard Songs

   I'm gonna clap my hands
   to show I love You.
   Gonna shout out loud,
   gonna sing Your praise,
   'Cause You are everything to me.
   Jesus I love Your name.
   I'm gonna stamp my feet
   to show I love You.
   Gonna jump around,
   gonna sing Your praise,
   'Cause You are everything to me.
   Jesus I love Your name.

You are the best friend
     that I could ever know.
I lift my hands to You
'cause You died for me upon the cross.
You took away my sin and shame.
   I'm gonna clap my hands . . .

556

adpt. Capt. Alan Price CA
© 1991 Daybreak Music Ltd / CopyCare

1 **I'm gonna click, click, click,**
I'm gonna clap, clap, clap,
I'm gonna click, I'm gonna clap
   and praise the Lord!
Because of all He's done,
   I'm gonna make Him 'number one',
I'm gonna click, I'm gonna clap
   and praise the Lord!

2 I'm gonna zoom, zoom, zoom,
around the room, room, room,
I'm gonna zoom around the room
   and praise the Lord!
Because of all He's done,
   I'm gonna make Him 'number one',
I'm gonna zoom around the room
   and praise the Lord!

3 I'm gonna sing, sing, sing,
I'm gonna shout, shout, shout,
I'm gonna sing, I'm gonna shout
   and praise the Lord!
Because of all He's done,
   I'm gonna make Him 'number one',
I'm gonna sing, I'm gonna shout
   and praise the Lord!

4 I'm gonna click, click, click,
I'm gonna clap, clap, clap,
I'm gonna zoom around the room
   and praise the Lord!
Because of all He's done,
   I'm gonna make Him 'number one',
I'm gonna sing, I'm gonna shout
   and praise the Lord!

557

Piers Land and Ruth Wills
© 1995 Scripture Union

*I'm gonna worship my God
  (He's so cool!),
I'm gonna worship my God.
I'm gonna worship my God
  (He's so cool!),
I'm gonna worship my God.*

1 Every day I'll sing His praises,
I'm gonna shout out loud.
Every day I'll follow Jesus,
I'm not gonna follow the crowd.
Every day I'll sing His praises,
I'm gonna shout out loud.
Every day I'll follow Jesus,
I'm not gonna follow the crowd.
   I'm gonna worship . . .

2 Every day I'll sing His praises,
Whether I'm up or down.
Every day I'll follow Jesus,
His love is all around.
Every day I'll sing His praises,
Whether I'm up or down.
Every day I'll follow Jesus,
His love is all around.
   I'm gonna worship . . .

3 RAP
Worship Jesus, worship the King,
He is the Lord of everything.
He is the one who hears me every day,
He never ever leaves me and so I will say,
Jesus! He's the King of kings,
Jesus! He's the King of kings,
Jesus! He's the King of kings.
Let's get ready to sing 2, 3, 4 . . .
   I'm gonna worship . . .

558

Ian White
© 1996 Thankyou Music

1 **I'm just a shepherd, David is my name,**
I live in a village called Bethlehem.
My brothers are soldiers
   and they're fighting in the war,
but I don't understand
   what the fighting is for!
I don't understand what the fighting is for!

2 I go to see my brothers
        and I bring them cheese and bread,
   I see Goliath
        and I hear the things he says.
   He's big and mean and ugly,
        he's a very wicked man,
   but I'm gonna get him if I can!
   I'm gonna get him if I can!
        Well, who's gonna win, tell me,
        how's it gonna be?
        Is it gonna be him,
          or is it gonna be me?
        I'm not very tall and I'm not very wide,
        but I've got the fire of the Lord inside!
        I've got the fire of the Lord inside!

3 Well, I don't need spears,
        I don't need armour plate,
   if the Lord will deliver me,
        He'll do it anyway.
   I'd rather use something that I know,
   I take a little stone and here I go!
   I take a little stone and here I go!
        Well, who's gonna win, . . .

4 Well, Goliath, you can fight me with your
        spear and with your sword,
   but I come against you
        in the name of the Lord!
   And everyone who gathers here
        will understand
   the battle is the Lord's
        and it's in our hands,
   the battle is the Lord's
        and it's in our hands!
        Well, who's gonna win, . . .

559 Doug Horley
         © 2001 Thankyou Music

I'm gonna jump up and down,
        gonna spin right around,
gonna praise Your name forever.
I'm gonna shout out loud,
        gonna deafen the crowd,
gonna send my praise to heaven.

I'm gonna jump . . .

I will run this race and I will never stop.
I'll follow Jesus till the day I drop.
I can do all things through Christ
        who strengthens me.
When you've got such a lot,
        when you've got not a lot, what?
Be happy!

I'm gonna jump . . .

I'm gonna jump . . .

560 Mark and Helen Johnson
         © 1998 Out of the Ark Music

1 **If I go to the furthest place**
        that I could go,
   He'll be there, He'll be there,
   to the East or the West,
        to the sun or snow,
   He will always be there!
        Oh yeah!
        Oh yeah!
        He will never leave me,
        I know!
        He cares,
        He's the only one I know
          who's always there!

2 In the dark of the night
        or in the light of the day,
   He'll be there, He'll be there,
   when I'm all on my own,
        or I've lost my way,
   He will always be there!
        Oh yeah! Oh yeah! . . .

3 When I'm down in the dumps
        and things are looking bad,
   He'll be there, He'll be there,
   when I'm over the moon,
        (when I'm really glad),
   He will always be there!
        Oh yeah! Oh yeah! . . .

        Oh yeah! (He'll be there)
        Oh yeah! (He'll be there)
        He will never leave me,
        I know! (Oh I know)
        He cares, (how He cares)
        He's the only one I know
          who's always there!

561 Mark and Helen Johnson
© 1998 Out of the Ark Music

PART 1
If you're feeling sad and weary
  and you're down in the dumps,
down in the dumps, down in the dumps,
if you're feeling sad and weary
  and you're down in the dumps,
there's something you can do:

PART 2
Don't be grumpy,
don't go on and on,
don't be grumpy,
don't you spoil the fun!

PART 3
Count your blessings,
name then one by one,
count your blessings,
see what God has done!

562 Ian Smale
© 1985 Thankyou Music

**In the beginning, God created the heavens
  and the earth.**
On day one, God made light.
Light, and God was pleased with all He
  made.

On day two, sea and sky.
Sea and sky, light, and God was pleased with
  all He made.

On day three, land, plants, seeds,
land, plants, seeds sea and sky, light,
  and God was pleased with all He made.

On day four, sun, moon, stars.
Sun, moon, stars, land, plants, seeds, sea
  and sky, light,
  and God was pleased with all He made.

On day five, fish and birds.
Fish and birds, sun, moon, stars, land,
  plants, seeds,
  sea and sky, light,
  and God was pleased
  with all He made.

On day six, animals, humans.
Animals, humans, fish and birds, sun, moon,
  stars, land,
  plants, seeds, sea and sky, light,
  and God was pleased
  with all He made.

On day seven, God took a rest,
after making animals, humans, fish and
  birds, sun, moon,
  stars, land, plants, seeds, sea and sky,
  light,
  and God was pleased
  with all He made.

563 Gerrit Gustafson and Steve Israel
© 1988 Integrity's Hosanna! Music /
Integrity Praise! / Sovereign Music UK

**Jesus Christ is the Lord of all,
  Lord of all the earth,**
Jesus Christ is the Lord of all,
  Lord of all the earth.
Jesus Christ is the Lord of all . . .

Only one God over the nations,
  only one Lord of all;
in no other name is there salvation,
  Jesus is Lord of all.
  Jesus Christ is Lord of all,
  Jesus Christ is Lord of all;
  Jesus Christ is Lord of all,
  Jesus Christ is Lord of all.

Jesus Christ is the Lord of all . . .

Only one God . . .

564 John Hardwick
© 1999 Daybreak Music Ltd / CopyCare

**Jesus never, never, never
turned anyone away.**
No! No! No!
Jesus never, never, never
    turned anyone away.
He welcomed the young,
    He welcomed the old,
He never left anyone out in the cold.
He welcomed the hungry,
    He welcomed the lame:
Jesus welcomes everyone the same.

Jesus never, never, never
    turned anyone away.
No! No! No!
Jesus never, never, never
    turned anyone away.
He never, never, never, never,
never, never, never, never,
never, never, never, never, never
turned anyone away.
No, He never, never, never, never,
never, never, never, never,
never, never, never, never, never
turned anyone away.

565 Capt. Alan Price, CA
© 1991 Daybreak Music Ltd / CopyCare

1   **Jesus is the lighthouse,
        shining all around,**
    shining in the darkness,
        where evil things abound.
    Jesus is the lighthouse,
        showing us the way,
    we can leave the darkness,
        live the Jesus way.

2   Jesus is the foghorn
        when trouble's very near,
    when hidden dangers threaten,
        His warning sound you hear.
    Jesus is the lighthouse,
        showing us the way,
    we can miss the dangers,
        live the Jesus way.

3   Shine your light in me, Lord,
        I want to live for You,
    help me shine for You, Lord,
        in all I say and do.
    I want to be a lighthouse
        for Jesus every day,
    help me make a difference
        in Your world, I pray!

566 Gill Robertson
© Sea Dream Music

Jesus is greater than the greatest heroes,
Jesus is closer than the closest friends.
He came from heaven
    and He died to save us,
to show us love that never ends.

Jesus is greater . . .

Son of God, and the Lord of glory,
He's the light, follow in His way.
He's the truth, that we can believe in,
and He's the life, He's living today.

Son of God . . .

567 Paul Crunch and David Mudie
© 2005 Daybreak Music Ltd / CopyCare

**Jesus, we're amazed
        at just how wonderful You are,**
nothing in the universe is a patch on You,
        by far.
All the world's great treasures
        and its wealth and power and fame
are nothing to the glory,
        and the wonder of Your name.

Jesus, we're amazed . . .

Jesus, Jesus, Jesus, Jesus.
Jesus, Jesus, Jesus, Jesus.

Jesus, we're amazed . . .

Jesus, we're amazed . . .

Jesus, Jesus, Jesus, Jesus.
Jesus, Jesus, Jesus, Jesus.

568 Nancy Gordon and Jamie Harvill
© 1994 Integrity's Hosanna! Music /
Integrity Praise! / Sovereign Music UK

Jesus, You're my firm foundation,
I know I can stand secure;
Jesus, You're my firm foundation,
I put my hope in Your holy word,
I put my hope in Your holy word.

1   I have a living hope, (I have a living hope,)
I have a future; (I have a future;)
God has a plan for me,
      (God has a plan for me,)
of this I'm sure,
of this I'm sure.
      Jesus, You're my firm foundation . . .

2   Your word is faithful,
      (Your word is faithful,)
mighty in power, (mighty in power,)
God will deliver me, (God will deliver me,)
of this I'm sure,
of this I'm sure.
      Jesus, You're my firm foundation . . .

569 Andrew and Pauline Pearson
© 1999 Daybreak Music Ltd / CopyCare

Jesus, Your name is wonderful,
Jesus, Your name is truth,
Jesus, Your name is powerful,
Jesus, we love You.

Jesus, Your name . . .

In Your name the blind will see.
In Your name the lame will dance.
In Your name we are set free to follow You.
In Your name, Your powerful name.

570 © 1955 Sy Miller and Jill Jackson
Jan-Lee Music

Let there be peace on earth
and let it begin with me;
let there be peace on earth,
the peace that was meant to be.
With God as our Father,
brothers all are we.
Let me walk with my brother
in perfect harmony.
Let peace begin with me,
let this be the moment now.
With every step I take,
let this be my solemn vow:
to take each moment and live each moment
in peace eternally.
Let there be peace on earth
and let it begin with me.

Let there be peace . . .

571 John Hardwick
© 2004 Daybreak Music Ltd / CopyCare

Let's sing praises to the King of kings,
let's raise our voices, everybody, sing!
It's time for a celebration (for a celebration).
It's time for a celebration (for a celebration).

Let's sing praises . . .

Lift your arms, clap those hands,
      wave them in the air,
Lord Jesus, we love You,
      no-one can compare.
Turn around with delight,
      when will we realise?
Jesus is victorious, we're on the victory side!
Triumphant, (triumphant,)
      glorious, (glorious,)
Jesus rules eternally.
Risen, (risen,) Saviour, (Saviour,)
Jesus, You have set us free.
It's time for a celebration (for a celebration).
It's time for a celebration (for a celebration).

Let's sing praises . . .

Let's sing praises . . .

Lift your arms . . .

572 Ian Smale
© 1988 Thankyou Music

Lord, I need to know You love me,
Lord, I need to know You care;
in the times I feel rejected,
I need to know You're there.
God says, 'Listen, my little child,
I'm a father who'll never leave you,
and though all your friends may fail you,
you can always trust in me.
For you're priceless and you're precious
and your value cannot be measured,
you're an heir to my kingdom,
you're in my chosen family.'

Lord, I need to know . . .

573 © Jancis Harvey

Lord of the harvest, Lord of the field,
give thanks now to God
in nature revealed.

1 Give thanks for the sun,
        the wind and the rain,
    and thanks for the crops
        that feed us again.
    The corn safely cut is gathered inside.
    We thank You, O Lord,
        that You can provide.
    Lord of the harvest . . .

2 The trees ripe with fruit
        stand proud in the sun,
    we gather them
        now that summer is gone.
    For Yours is the wonder,
        Yours is the power.
    Yours is the glory of fruit and of flower.
    Lord of the harvest . . .

3 So in all our plenty, help us to see,
    the needs all around whatever they be.
    With food for the body,
        strength for the soul,
    it's healing and caring,
        making them whole.
    Lord of the harvest . . .

574 Iain Craig
© 1994 Daybreak Music Ltd / CopyCare

1 **Lord of the future,**
    Lord of the past,
    Lord of our lives,
    we adore You.
    Lord of for ever,
    Lord of our hearts,
    we give all praise to You.

2 Lord of tomorrow,
    Lord of today,
    Lord over all,
    You are worthy.
    Lord of creation,
    Lord of all truth,
    we give all praise to You.

575 Graham Kendrick
© 1987 Make Way Music

1 **Lord, the light of Your love is shining,**
    in the midst of the darkness, shining:
    Jesus, Light of the world, shine upon us;
    set us free by the truth You now bring us –
    shine on me, shine on me.
        Shine, Jesus, shine,
        fill this land with the Father's glory;
        blaze, Spirit, blaze,
        set our hearts on fire.
        Flow, river, flow,
        flood the nations with grace and mercy;
        send forth Your word, Lord,
        and let there be light!

2 Lord, I come to Your awesome presence,
    from the shadows into Your radiance;
    by Your blood
        I may enter Your brightness:
    search me, try me,
        consume all my darkness –
    shine on me, shine on me.
        Shine, Jesus, shine . . .

3 As we gaze on Your kingly brightness
    so our faces display Your likeness,
    ever changing from glory to glory:
    mirrored here,
        may our lives tell Your story –
    shine on me, shine on me.
        Shine, Jesus, shine . . .

576 Chris Jackson
© 1988 Powerpack / Learning Curve Music

**Love the Lord your God
with all your heart,**
with all your mind.
Love the Lord your God
with all your strength.
Love the Lord with all your heart,
love the Lord with all your strength.

577 Philip and Stephanie Chapman
© 2002 Kevin Mayhew Ltd

Make a joyful noise to the Lord,
make a joyful noise and sing out loud,
make a joyful noise to the Lord,
sing, sing to the Lord.
Hallelujah, hallelujah,
hallelujah, sing out loud.
Hallelujah, sing, sing to the Lord.

578 Mark and Helen Johnson
© 1998 Out of the Ark Music

Matthew twenty-two,
verses thirty-four to forty.
Matthew twenty-two,
verses thirty-four to forty.

One day a Pharisee came to Jesus Christ
and he said, 'Tell me –
    what's the greatest commandment?'
One day a Pharisee came to Jesus Christ
and he said, 'Tell me –
    what's the greatest commandment?'

This is what He said:

1 Love the Lord your God
        with all your heart
    with all your soul, with all your mind,
    with all your strength.
    Love the Lord your God
        with all your heart,
    with all your soul, with all your mind,
    with all your strength.

2 Love your neighbour as yourself,
    and do to others as you'd have them
        do to you.
    Love your neighbour as yourself,
    and do to others as you'd have them
        do to you.

3 One day a Pharisee came to Jesus Christ
    and he said 'Tell me –
        what's the greatest commandment?'
    One day a Pharisee came to Jesus Christ
    and he said 'Tell me –
        what's the greatest commandment?'

4 Matthew twenty-two,
    verses thirty-four to forty.
    Matthew twenty-two,
    verses thirty-four to forty.

579 Mark and Helen Johnson
© 1998 Out of the Ark Music

May God bless our teachers,
and all our helpers,
may God show His goodness
    in all that they do.
We ask for the children,
that God's hand be on them,
and may we find His love in this school.

May God bless our teachers,
and all our helpers,
may God show His goodness
    in all that they do.
We ask for the children,
that God's hand be on them,
and may we find His joy in this school.

May God bless our teachers,
and all our helpers,
may God show His goodness
    in all that they do.
We ask for the children,
that God's hand be on them,
and may we find His peace in this school.

580 Doug Horley
© 2001 Thankyou Music

**May the God of hope fill you
   with all joy and peace,**
as you trust in Him, as you trust in Him.
May the God of hope fill you
   with all joy and peace,
as you trust in Him, as you trust in Him.
So that you might overflow with hope,
by the power of the Holy Spirit.
So that you might overflow
   with hope, with hope,
by the power of the Holy Spirit.

May the God of hope . . .

Father God, I love You,
   Father God, I trust You,
Father God, I need You every day.
Fill me with Your hope, Lord,
   fill me with Your joy, Lord,
fill me with Your peace, let Your love flow.

Father God, I love You . . .

581 Darlene Zschech
© 1993 Hillsong Publishing / Kingsway Music

My Jesus, my Saviour,
Lord, there is none like You.
All of my days I want to praise
the wonders of Your mighty love.
My comfort, my shelter,
tower of refuge and strength,
let every breath, all that I am,
never cease to worship You.
   Shout to the Lord all the earth, let us sing,
   power and majesty, praise to the King.
   Mountains bow down
   and the seas will roar
   at the sound of Your name.
   I sing for joy at the work of Your hands,
   for ever I'll love You, for ever I'll stand.
   Nothing compares to the promise
   I have in You.

582 Ian Smale
© 2001 Thankyou Music

No matter how big I am,
no matter how big I am.
I could never look odd.
The Lord wants me to know,
that the Bible says it's so,
I'm made in the image of God.

No matter how small I am,
no matter how small I am.
I could never look odd.
The Lord wants me to know,
that the Bible says it's so,
I'm made in the image of God.

Sometimes I look in the mirror
and don't like what I see.
I want to look like someone else,
but Jesus loves me looking just like me.

No matter how big I am,
no matter how small I am.
I could never look odd.
The Lord wants me to know,
that the Bible says it's so,
I'm made in the image of God.

583 John Hardwick
© 1993 Daybreak Music Ltd / CopyCare

**Nobody's a nobody, believe me
   'cause it's true,**
nobody's a nobody, especially not you.
Nobody's a nobody
   and God wants us to see
that everybody's somebody
   and that means even me.

I'm no cartoon, I'm human,
   I have feelings, treat me right.
I'm not a superhero
   with super strength and might.
I'm not a mega pop star or super a-the-lete,
but did you know I'm special –
In fact I'm quite unique!

Nobody's a nobody . . .

584
Trevor Ranger
© 2004 Daybreak Music Ltd / CopyCare

1 **Nothing good I do,**
   nothing good I say,
   could ever make You love me more
   than You do today.
   I don't deserve Your love,
   I cannot pay my way.
   Lord, You pour Your love
        upon my life anyway.
   Anyway, anyway,
   Lord, You pour Your love
        upon my life anyway.

2 Nothing bad I do,
   nothing bad I say,
   would ever make You leave my side,
   turn the other way.
   I don't deserve Your love,
   I cannot pay my way,
   Lord, You pour Your love
        upon my life anyway.
   Anyway, anyway,
   Lord, You pour Your love
        upon my life anyway.

3 Everything I do,
   everything I say,
   in every moment, every hour,
   teach me, Lord, Your way.
   I don't deserve Your love,
   I cannot pay my way,
   Lord, I want to live my life for You anyway.
   Anyway, anyway,
   Lord, I want to live my life for You anyway.

585
Doug Horley
© 2005 Thankyou Music

Nothing's too big, big, big for His power,
nothing's too little, little for His care.
Nothing's too big, big, big for His power,
nothing's too iddly, widdly for His care.
Nothing's too big, big, big for His power,
nothing's too incy, wincy for His care.
Nothing's too big, big, big for His power,
nothing's too teeny weeny for His care.

He is God of the big, God of the little,
God of the stuff somewhere in the middle,
the King of moving mountains loves you
more than you will ever know, oh, oh, oh!

Nothing's too big . . .

He is God of the big . . .

Nothing's too big, nothing's too small,
nothing's too much, He cares for it all.

Nothing's too big . . .

He is God of the big . . .

586
Lincoln Brewley
© 2002 Integrity's Hosanna! Music /
Integrity Praise! / Sovereign Music UK

1 **O Lord, my God, in You I put my trust;**
   O Lord, my God, in You I put my hope;
   O Lord, my God, in You I put my trust;
   O Lord, my God, in You I put my hope.
   In You, in You I find my peace;
   in You, in You I find my strength;
   in You, in You I find my peace;
   in You, in You I find my strength
   let everything I say and do
   be founded by my faith in You;
   I lift up holy hands and sing,
   let the praises ring.

2 O Lord, my God, to You I give my hands;
   O Lord, my God, to You I give my feet;
   O Lord, my God, to You I give my
        everything;
   O Lord, my God, to You I give my life.
   In You . . .
   Let the praises ring.

587
Doug Horley
© 1997 Thankyou Music

Oi, oi, we are gonna praise the Lord.
Oi, oi, we are gonna praise the Lord.
Oi, oi, we are gonna praise the Lord.
He's an exciting, powerising,
        c-colossal, humungousmungous God!

But it's sometimes hard to understand
that the God who made the earth and man
would point a finger down from heaven
and shout: 'Hey you! I love you.
Hey you! I love you.
Hey you, you! I love you' –
but it's true!

Oi, oi, we are gonna praise the Lord.
Oi, oi, we are gonna praise the Lord.
Oi, oi, we are gonna praise the Lord.
He's an exciting, powerising,
    c-colossal, humungousmungous God!

He's higher than a skyscraper
and He's deeper than a submarine.
He's wider than the universe
and beyond my wildest dreams.
And He's known me and He's loved me
since before the world began.
How wonderful to be a part
of God's amazing plan.
    Our God is a great big God . . .
    And He holds us in His hands.

588 Paul Baloche
© 1997 Integrity's Hosanna! Music /
Integrity Praise! / Sovereign Music UK

Open the eyes of my heart, Lord,
open the eyes of my heart.
I want to see You,
I want to see You.
Open the eyes of my heart, Lord,
open the eyes of my heart.
I want to see You,
I want to see You.
    To see You high and lifted up,
    shining in the light of Your glory.
    Pour out Your power and love,
    as we sing, 'Holy, holy, holy.'

Open the eyes of my heart, Lord . . .
To see You high and lifted up . . .

Holy, holy, holy,
holy, holy, holy,
holy, holy, holy,
I want to see You.

Holy, holy, holy . . .

589 Jo and Nigel Hemming
© 2001 Vineyard Songs

Our God is a great big God,
our God is a great big God,
our God is a great big God
and He holds us in His hands.
Our God is a great big God . . .

590 Kevin Mayhew
© 1976 Kevin Mayhew Ltd

1 **Peace, perfect peace,**
    is the gift of Christ our Lord.
  Peace, perfect peace,
    is the gift of Christ our Lord.
  Thus, says the Lord,
    will the world know My friends.
  Peace, perfect peace,
    is the gift of Christ our Lord.

2 Love, perfect love,
    is the gift of Christ our Lord.
  Love, perfect love,
    is the gift of Christ our Lord.
  Thus, says the Lord,
    will the world know My friends.
  Love, perfect love,
    is the gift of Christ our Lord.

3 Faith, perfect faith,
    is the gift of Christ our Lord.
  Faith, perfect faith,
    is the gift of Christ our Lord.
  Thus, says the Lord,
    will the world know My friends.
  Faith, perfect faith,
    is the gift of Christ our Lord.

4 Hope, perfect hope,
    is the gift of Christ our Lord.
  Hope, perfect hope,
    is the gift of Christ our Lord.
  Thus, says the Lord,
    will the world know My friends.
  Hope, perfect hope,
    is the gift of Christ our Lord.

5 Joy, perfect joy,
    is the gift of Christ our Lord.
Joy, perfect joy,
    is the gift of Christ our Lord.
Thus, says the Lord,
    will the world know My friends.
Joy, perfect joy,
    is the gift of Christ our Lord.

591 Peggy Blakeley
© A & C Black Publishers Ltd

Rat-a-tat-tat, rat-a-tat-tat,
No! No! No!
There isn't any room
and you can't stay here,
there isn't any room for strangers.
The wind may be chill
and the night may be cold,
and be full of nasty noises in the dark
    and dangers.
But there isn't any room,
there isn't any room,
there isn't any room for strangers.

Rat-a-tat-tat, rat-a-tat-tat,
Yes! Yes! Yes!
There is a little room
and you may stay here,
we have a little place for strangers.
Come in from the night
to the stable so bare
which is full of warmth and friendliness
    and safe from dangers.
Yes, there is a little room,
there is a little room,
there is a little room for strangers.

592 Paul Field
© 1995 Windswept Pacific Music Ltd

Safe in the Father's hands,
we are safe in the Father's hands.
There may be things we don't
    understand,
we're safe in the Father's hands.

1 So many things we'll never learn,
no matter how hard we try.
Though we may feel small
    the maker of all
watches with loving eyes.
    Safe in the . . .

2 Trusting in God, we can be sure
no matter where life may lead,
His promises told, He's in control,
He's everything we need.
    Safe in the . . .

593 Nick Harding
© 1995 Daybreak Music Ltd / CopyCare

So I'll trust (so I'll trust)
   in God (in God),
wherever I am, I know I can,
so I'll trust (so I'll trust) in God (in God),
'cause God has got a plan,
    God has got a plan.

1 God was, God is and always will be.
He knows what I hear and do and see.
He made me, loves me, leads me too.
He's got a plan for me and you.
    So I'll trust . . .

2 God was, and God is with me here,
He sent His Son, He takes my fear,
His Spirit lives deep in my heart –
I'm in His plan right from the start.
    So I'll trust . . .

594 Ian Smale
© 1985 Thankyou Music

So I've made up my mind
that I'm gonna follow Him,
wherever Jesus leads me I will go.
So I've made up my mind
that I'm gonna follow Him,
wherever Jesus leads me I will go.

1 I may be scared
by the things I see,
but Jesus won't
let them destroy me.
    So I've made up . . .

2 I may be scared
   by the things I hear,
   but Jesus won't
   let me live in fear.
       So I've made up . . .

3 I may be scared
   by the things I know,
   but Jesus won't
   ever let me go.
       So I've made up . . .

595 Jo and Nigel Hemming
© 2001 Vineyard Songs

**Sometimes I feel afraid
       of getting things all wrong;**
of people who will tease me
       when they see the things I've done.
And then I remember there's no need
       to be afraid.

Because my God, He is big,
He's gigantic, He's enormous,
He is powerful and strong.
He is amazing and He's awesome,
and there's nothing in this world
that He couldn't pulverize.
So I know I've got nothing to fear. No! No!
So I know I've got nothing to fear.

Sometimes I feel afraid of being on my own,
with no one here to play with me,
       I'll always be alone.
And then I remember there's no need
       to be afraid.

Because my God . . .

Sometimes I feel afraid of things I cannot see
of monsters in the dark
       who might be chasing after me
And then I remember
       there's no need to be afraid.

Because my God . . .

Because my God . . .
So I know I've got nothing to fear. No! No!
So I know I've got nothing to fear.

596 Mark and Helen Johnson
© 1998 Out of the Ark Music

1 **Sometimes I wonder**
   why people suffer –
   why all the pain and sorrow?
   So much injustice,
   weeping and sadness,
   here in our world today.
       *Pain won't be here forever,
       sadness will turn to laughter,
       mourning will turn to dancing
       and our tears will be wiped away.*

2 Looking around me
   I see such anger –
   why must we hurt each other?
   So many people,
   living in sadness,
   here in our world today.
       Pain won't be . . .

3 INSTRUMENTAL
       Pain won't be . . .

4 Where there is heartache,
   where there is grieving,
   I want to feel compassion.
   May I give comfort,
   where there is hurting,
   may I bring love again.

597 Paul Crouch and David Mudie
© 2004 Daybreak Music Ltd / CopyCare

   Stop, look and listen;
   there's a voice that must be heard.
   Stop, look and listen;
   take some time out with God's word.

1 Let's stop what we are doing
   as we give time to God.
   And focus our attention
   on the message of His word.
       Stop, look and listen . . .

2 Let's look into the Bible
   as we give time to God.
   And let our lives be open
   to the message of His word.
       Stop, look and listen . . .

3   Let's listen to the Spirit
    as we give time to God;
    the quiet voice agreeing
    with the message of His word.
        Stop, look and listen . . .

598 Traditional, adpt. Geoffrey Gardner

Shalom, shalom,
may peace be with you
throughout your days;
in all that you do,
may peace be with you
shalom, shalom.

599 Mark and Helen Johnson
© 1998 Out of the Ark Music

1   **Tell me who made all of creation,**
    who designed the wonders of nature?
    Whose idea was pattern and colour,
    wonderful to see?
        Everywhere around me,
        I can see the hand of God,
        the evidence surrounds me,
        in the greatness of His world.

        Everywhere . . .

2   Tell me who made music and laughter,
    who designed our bodies to start with?
    Whose idea was thinking and feeling,
    who gave life to me?
        Everywhere . . .

3   Don't stop looking, don't stop believing,
    God is to be found when you seek Him.
    All creation tells of His glory,
    for eternity.
        Everywhere . . .

        Everywhere . . .
        Everywhere around me!

600 Judy Mackenzie-Dunn
© 2004 Daybreak Music Ltd / CopyCare

The Lord bless you, the Lord keep you,
the light of His face shine on you.
The Lord bless you, the Lord keep you,
the light of His face shine on you.
The Lord be gracious to you,
the Lord be gracious to you.
May He turn His face to you
and give you peace.
May He turn His face to you
and give you peace.

The Lord bless you . . .

601 Earl Robinson
© 1956, 1970 & 1971 Templeton Music Publishing

1   **The ink is black,**
    the page is white,
    together we learn to read and write,
    to read and write.
    And now a child can understand
    this is the law of all the land,
    all the land:
    the ink is black,
    the page is white,
    together we learn to read and write,
    to read and write.

2   The slate is black,
    the chalk is white,
    the words stand out so clear and bright,
    so clear and bright.
    And now at last we plainly see
    the alphabet of liberty,
    liberty:
    the slate is black,
    the chalk is white,
    the words stand out so clear and bright,
    so clear and bright.

3 A child is black,
a child is white,
the whole world looks upon the sight,
a beautiful sight.
For very well the whole world knows
this is the way that freedom grows,
freedom grows:
a child is black,
a child is white,
the whole world looks upon the sight,
a beautiful sight.

4 The world is black,
the world is white,
it turns by day and then by night,
it turns by night.
It turns so each and every one
can take his station in the sun,
in the sun:
the world is black,
the world is white,
it turns by day and then by night,
it turns by night.

602 Paul Field
© 1997 Daybreak Music Ltd / CopyCare

1 **The Lord is my Shepherd,**
He'll watch over me;
whatever I go through
He's all that I need.
Wherever He leads me,
I know sure enough,
I will live my life
surrounded by His love.

2 The Lord is my Shepherd,
He'll stay by my side
when I feel afraid
in the darkest of nights.
I'm safe in the hands
of the Father above.
I will live my life
surrounded by His love.
And I will sing His praise.
Surely goodness and mercy
are following me
all of the days of my life.
Now and forever my home will be
here in the house of the Lord,
surrounded by His love.

3 The Lord is my Shepherd,
He's gentle and strong.
I know in His presence
I'll always belong.
The peace that He gives me
is more than enough.
I will live my life
surrounded by His love.
And I will sing . . .
Surely . . .

603 Ian Smale
© 1999 Thankyou Music

The Lord loves me,
He really, really loves me.
The Lord loves me,
I want you all to know.
Hey! The Lord loves me,
He really, really loves me:
I am His and He is mine,
the Bible tells me so.

The Lord loves me . . .

604 © Greg Leavers

The Lord's my Shepherd,
He's everything I need,
The Lord's my Shepherd,
He lets me rest in safety,
the Lord's my Shepherd,
He leads me to find peace,
to Him be all the glory, all the praise!
Surely His love and unfailing mercy
will follow me all of my life,
and I will live in God's house forever,
in God's house for evermore.

He's close beside me,
guides me on right paths,
He's close beside me
walking through dark valleys,
He's close beside me,
I'll not be afraid,
to Him be all the glory, all the praise!
Surely His love . . .

The Lord invites me,
He's prepared a feast,
The Lord invites me
in the presence of my enemies,
the Lord invites me,
His anointed guest,
to Him be all the glory, all the praise!
Surely His love . . .

605
Steve Morgan-Gurr
© 1999 Daybreak Music Ltd / CopyCare

1 **There's nothing,
      nothing I can do or say**
   to make God love me more.
   He fathers me in such a way
   it lasts for evermore.
   The Bible says that it's called grace,
   I see it there in Jesus' face,
   there's nothing, nothing I can do or say
   to make God love me more,
   to make God love me more.

2 There's nothing, nothing I can do or say
   to make God love me less.
   I need forgiveness every day,
   and Jesus' righteousness.
   But when I turn to Him and pray
   He gives His mercy right away,
   there's nothing, nothing I can do or say
   to make God love me less,
   to make God love me less.
   To make God love me more,
   to make God love me more.

606
John Hardwick
© 2005 Daybreak Music Ltd / CopyCare

Turn Your frown upside down,
turn Your frown upside down,
turn Your frown upside down
and smile for a while.

Turn Your frown . . .

Smile for a while,
smile for a while,
for Jesus will be with You
mile after mile.
Put a smile on Your face,
make the world a friendlier place;
smile for a while,
yes, smile for a while.
Turn Your frown . . .

Smile for a while . . .

Thank You, Jesus,
for all You do for me.
Thank You, Jesus,
for all You've given me.
Thank You, Jesus,
thank You for loving me.
You've put the smile on my face!

Smile for a while . . .

We want to see mile after mile of smiles,
we want to see mile after mile of smiles.

607
Ruth Wills
© 2004 Scripture Union

Ah! Ah! Ah! Ah!
Twisting, everybody we're twisting,
*everybody we're twisting back in time
   to find
what God had in His mind.
To hear the things He had to say,
back in time and for today.
Twisting . . .*

1 God had a plan worked out,
   for ordinary people there was no doubt.
   He'd do great things and He can today!
   He'd do great things, and He will today!
   So everybody, let's all twist and shout!
   Twisting . . .

2 God has a plan for us,
   we're ordinary people, but there's no
      fuss.
   He'll do great things, and He can today!
   He'll do great things, and He will today!
   So everybody, let's all twist and shout!
   Twisting . . .

Ah! Ah! Ah! Ah! Yeah!

608 Doug Horley
© 1993 Thankyou Music

We want to see Jesus lifted high,
a banner that flies across this land,
that all men might see the truth and know
He is the way to Heaven.
We want to see Jesus lifted high . . .

We want to see,
we want to see,
we want to see Jesus lifted high,
we want to see,
we want to see,
we want to see Jesus lifted high.

Step by step we're moving forward,
little by little taking ground,
every prayer a powerful weapon,
strongholds come tumbling down
    and down and down and down.

We want to see Jesus lifted high . . .

We're gonna see,
we're gonna see,
we're gonna see Jesus lifted high,
we're gonna see,
we're gonna see
we're gonna see Jesus lifted high.

609 © Geoffrey Marshall-Taylor

1 **We are climbing Jesus' ladder, ladder,**
   we are climbing Jesus' ladder, ladder,
   we are climbing Jesus' ladder, ladder,
   children of the Lord.
       So let's all rise and shine
           and give God the glory, glory,
       rise and shine
           and give God the glory, glory,
       rise and shine
           and give God the glory, glory,
       children of the Lord.

2 We are following where he leads us,
       leads us,
   we are following where he leads us,
       leads us,
   we are following where he leads us,
       leads us,
   children of the Lord.
       So let's all rise . . .

3 We are reaching out to others, others,
   we are reaching out to others, others,
   we are reaching out to others, others,
   children of the Lord.
       So let's all rise . . .

4. We are one with all who serve Him,
       serve Him,
   We are one with all who serve Him,
       serve Him,
   We are one with all who serve Him,
       serve Him,
   children of the Lord.
       So let's all rise . . .

610 Chris Tomlin and Louie Giglio
© 2003 Thankyou Music

We stand and lift up our hands,
for the joy of the Lord is our strength.
We bow down and worship Him now;
how great, how awesome is He.
And together we sing, everyone sing:
    Holy is the Lord God Almighty;
    the earth is filled with His glory.
    Holy is the Lord God Almighty;
    the earth is filled with His glory,
    the earth is filled with His glory.

We stand and lift up our hands,
for the joy of the Lord is our strength.
We bow down and worship Him now;
how great, how awesome is He.
And together we sing, everyone sing:
    Holy is the Lord . . .

It's rising up all around;
it's the anthem of the Lord's renown.
It's rising up all around;
it's the anthem of the Lord's renown.
And together we sing, everyone sing:
    Holy is the Lord . . .

611
Ali Croxford
© 2006 Thankyou Music

We're following the star to the stable,
we're following the star in the sky.
We're following the star to the stable,
we're gonna see the baby Jesus Christ.
We're following the star . . .

1 First there were the shepherds
       sitting in the field,
   working day and night,
       looking after sheep.
   Then a group of angels came to them
       and said,
   'Go and see the King, born in Bethlehem.'
       We're following the star . . .

2 Then there were three wise men
       living far away,
   wanted to see Jesus, sleeping in the hay.
   They began their journey
       and when they arrived
   they gave special presents.
       What a nice surprise!
       We're following the star . . .
       We're gonna see the baby Jesus Christ,
       we're gonna see the baby Jesus Christ!

612
Nigel Hemming
© 2005 Vineyard Songs

1 **We're gonna celebrate, celebrate the**
   goodness of our Lord,
   we're gonna lift our hands
       and wave our branches high.
   We're gonna shout and praise
       and sing His name for now and
       evermore,
   see His promises fulfilled,
       He has come to change our lives.
       Hosanna, hosanna!
       Blessed is the King,
       the King who comes to reign.
       Hosanna, hosanna!
       Blessed is the King
       who comes in the name of the Lord.

2 We're gonna celebrate, celebrate
       the goodness of our Lord,
   we're gonna tell the world
       of all that He has done.
   We're gonna shout and praise
       and sing His name for now and
       evermore,
   He gives joy to every heart,
       He gives hope to all who come.
       Hosanna, hosanna . . .

613
Debby Kerner
© 1982 Rettino Kerner Publishing /
Word Music / CopyCare

Welcome to the family,
we're glad that you have come
    to share your life with us,
as we grow in love;
and may we always be to you
    what God would have us be,
a family always there,
to be strong and to lean on.

May we learn to love each other
    more with each new day,
may words of love be on our lips
    in everything we say.
May the Spirit melt our hearts
    and teach us how to pray,
that we might be a true family.

Welcome to the family,
we're glad that you have come
    to share your life with us,
as we grow in love;
and may we always be to you
    what God would have us be,
a family always there,
to be strong and to lean on.

614
Doug Horley
© 2004 Thankyou Music

1 **What greater gift has ever been**
   known?
   What greater love has ever been shown?
   That God himself would leave His throne.
   Swap heaven's crown for this dark earth.

How precious must we be to You?
How special in Your eyes we are?
Though we have sinned Your love is
*   true.*
Almighty God we worship You.

2 But it's so sad that every day,
   outrageous love is turned away.
   And men choose death instead of life,
   rejecting You for an earthly prize.
       How precious . . .

3 But one day soon, across the skies,
   You will return before our eyes.
   And to their knees all men will fall,
   before their King, our Christ, our Lord.
       How precious . . .

615 Paul Booth
        © Stainer & Bell Ltd

1 **When God made the garden of**
   creation,
   He filled it full of His love;
   when God made the garden of creation,
   He saw that it was good.
   There's room for you,
   and room for me,
   and room for everyone,
   for God is a father who loves His children,
   and gives them a place in the sun.
   When God made the garden of creation,
   He filled it full of His love.

2 When God made the hamper of creation,
   He filled it full of His love;
   when God made the hamper of creation,
   He saw that it was good.
   There's food for you,
   and food for me,
   and food enough for all,
   but man is so greedy,
       so wastes God's bounty,
   that some won't get any at all.
   When God made the garden of creation,
   He filled it full of His love.

3 When God made the family of creation,
   He filled it full of His love;
   when God made the family of creation,
   He saw that it was good.
   There's love for you,
   and love for me,
   and love for everyone;
   but man is so greedy,
       forgetting his neighbour;
   He seeks his own place in the sun.
   When God made the family of creation,
   He filled it full of His love.

4 When God made us stewards of creation,
   He made us His vision to share,
   when God made us stewards of creation,
   our burdens He wanted to bear.
   He cares for you,
   He cares for me,
   He cares for all in need;
   For God is a father
       who loves His children,
   no matter what colour or creed.
   When God made us stewards of creation,
   He gave us His vision to share.

616 Mark and Helen Johnson
        © Out of the Ark Music

When I think about the cross,
when I think of Jesus,
I'm reminded of His love,
love that never leaves me.
Who am I that He should die,
giving life so freely?

When I think about the cross,
when I think of Jesus,
I'm reminded of His love,
love that never leaves me.
Who am I that He should die,
giving life so freely?
When I think about the cross,
help me to believe it.

617

Jan Struther
© Oxford University Press

1 **When a knight won his spurs,
      in the stories of old,**
   he was gentle and brave,
      he was gallant and bold;
   with a shield on his arm
      and a lance in his hand,
   for God and for valour
      he rode through the land.

2 No charger have I,
      and no sword by my side,
   yet still to adventure and battle I ride,
   though back into storyland
      giants have fled,
   and the knights are no more
      and the dragons are dead.

3 Let faith be my shield
      and let joy be my steed
   'gainst the dragons of anger,
      the ogres of greed;
   and let me set free,
      with the sword of my youth,
   from the castle of darkness,
      the power of the truth.

618

Jodie Frye
© 2005 Vineyard Songs

1 **When the sun is bright,**
   when the sky is blue,
   when it's all alright,
   I will praise You.
   When life seems to go
   like I want it to,
   things are as I'd hoped,
   I will praise You.
      *Through the sun, through the rain,
      You never change, You are so worthy.
      I'll lift Your name
      and no matter what I'm going through,
      I will praise You.*

2 When it's raining hard,
   when it's all gone wrong,
   I'll still sing this song,
   I will praise You.
   When I've been promised things
   that aren't happening,
   and I'm still waiting,
   I will praise You.
      Through the sun . . .

   I will, I will, I will praise You,
   I will, I will, I will praise You.
      Through the sun . . .

619

Unknown
Copyright control

1 **Who made the twinkling stars,**
   the twinkling stars, the twinkling stars?
   Who made the twinkling stars?
   Our Father God.

2 Who made the birds that fly,
   the birds that fly, the birds that fly?
   Who made the birds that fly?
   Our Father God.

3 Who made the rolling seas,
   the rolling seas, the rolling seas?
   Who made the rolling seas?
   Our Father God.

4 Who made you and me,
   you and me, you and me?
   Who made you and me?
   Our Father God.

620

Doug Horley
© 2004 Thankyou Music

Wonderful Lord, wonderful God,
You are my shield, my protector.
I can lie down, go off to sleep,
knowing You're watching over me.
Wonderful Lord, wonderful God,
help me to trust You forever.
I need not fear
'cause You are near,
I can lie down and sleep in peace.

621
Tim Hughes
© 2002 Thankyou Music

1 **Wonderful, so wonderful**
is Your unfailing love;
Your cross has spoken mercy over me.
No eye has seen, no ear has heard,
no heart could fully know
how glorious, how beautiful You are.
Beautiful One, I love You,
beautiful One, I adore,
beautiful One, my soul must sing.

2 Powerful, so powerful,
Your glory fills the skies,
Your mighty works displayed
for all to see.
The beauty of Your majesty
awakes my heart to sing
how marvellous, how wonderful You are.
Beautiful One . . .
Beautiful One . . .

You opened my eyes
to Your wonders anew,
You captured my heart with this love,
'cause nothing on earth
is as beautiful as You.
You opened my eyes
to Your wonders anew,
You captured my heart with this love,
'cause nothing on earth
is as beautiful as You.
Beautiful One . . .

My soul, my soul must sing,
my soul, my soul must sing,
my soul, my soul must sing,
beautiful One.
Beautiful One . . .

622
Jim Bailey
© 2006 Daybreak Music Ltd / CopyCare

1 **You put diamonds in the sky,**
sunshine in my eyes,
treasure in a jar of clay.
From the lips of little babes,
You have ordained praise,
angels look and wonder why.
And it is a mystery
why You should love me.

This is love, wider than the ocean.
This is love, deeper than the sea.
This is love, higher than a mountain.
This is love, amazing love for me.

2 You became a human boy,
started it by choice,
finished it at Calvary,
kissed a guilty world in love,
the power of Your blood
echoes in eternity.
You died forgiving
so we could start living.
This is love . . .

Higher, deeper, wider, stronger;
this is love.
Higher, deeper, wider, stronger;
this is love.
This is love . . .

623
Stuart Dauermann and Steffi Geiser Rubin
© 1975 Lillenas Publishing / CopyCare

You shall go out with joy
and be led forth with peace,
and the mountains and the hills
shall break forth before you.
There'll be shouts of joy
and the trees of the field
shall clap, shall clap their hands,
and the trees of the field
shall clap their hands,
and the trees of the field
shall clap their hands,
and the trees of the field
shall clap their hands,
and you'll go out with joy.

624
Ian White
© 1991 Little Misty Music Ltd / Kingsway

Your name is Jesus, Your love is true;
You ask Your children to come to You,
to learn to follow Your Spirit's ways,
and with our whole lives bring You praise.

Your name is Jesus . . .

And with our whole lives bring You praise.

INDEX OF FIRST LINES

Titles which differ from first lines are shown in italics.

The King of love – 241
The Lord bless you – 600
The Lord has need of me – 242
The Lord is my shepherd – 244
The Lord is my shepherd – 602
The Lord is risen today – 469
The Lord loves me – 603
The Lord's my shepherd – 243
The Lord's my shepherd – 604
The most important thing – 470
The Old Testament Song (Genesis, Exodus) – 529
The Servant King (From heaven You came) – 341
The shepherds found – 471
The sower song (The word of the Lord is planted) – 473
The Spirit lives – 472
The steadfast love – 250
The virgin Mary had a baby boy – 251
The wise man built his house upon the rock – 252
The wise may bring – 253
The word of God – 474
The word of the Lord is planted – 473
There are hundreds of sparrows – 246
There he stood – Goliath – 475
There is a green hill – 245
There is no-one else – 476
There isn't any room (Rat-a-tat-tat) – 591
There once was a man – 477
There's a song for all the children – 478
There's a song of exaltation – 247
There's a way back – 248
There's new life in Jesus – 249
There's nothing, nothing – 605
They are watching you (Though the world has forsaken God) – 257
Think big: an elephant – 479
Think of a world without any flowers – 254
This Child – 480
This is a catchy songa – 481
This is a miracle (See the man walking) – 451
This is God's world (Don't know much) – 328
This is love (You put diamonds in the sky) – 622
This is my prayer (I want to love You, Lord) – 374
This is the day – 255
This joyful Eastertide – 256
This little light of mine – 258
Though the world has forsaken God – 257
Thumbs up (When you're feeling good) – 496
To God be the glory! – 259
Turn your eyes upon Jesus – 260
Turn Your frown upside down – 606
Twelve men went to spy – 261
Twisting back in time (Twisting, everybody we're twisting) – 607
Twisting, everybody we're twisting – 607
Two little eyes – 262

Unto us a boy is born! – 263

Wandering like lost sheep – 482
We are climbing – 609
We are soldiers of the King – 483
We are the Church (I am the Church) – 367
We have a king who rides a donkey – 264
We have heard a joyful sound – 266
We love to praise You – 265
We need to grow – 484
We plough the fields – 267
We really want to thank You, Lord – 268
We stand and lift up our hands – 610
We three kings of Orient are – 271
We want to see Jesus lifted high – 608
We will praise – 485
We'll praise Him on the trumpet – 486
We're following Jesus – 487
We're following the star – 611
We're gonna celebrate – 612
We've a story to tell – 272
Welcome to the family – 613
Were you there? – 269
What a friend we have in Jesus – 273
What a mighty God we serve – 491
What a wonderful Saviour – 274
What colours God has made – 488
What do you do (Some people laugh) – 462
What do you give – 489
What drives the stars – 490
What greater gift has ever been known – 614
What made a difference – 492
When a knight won his spurs – 617
When God breathes – 497
When God made the garden of creation – 615
When I needed a neighbour – 275
When I survey – 277
When I think about the cross – 616
When I'm feeling lonely – 493
When Israel was in Egypt's land – 276
When morning gilds the skies – 278
When the dark clouds – 494
When the Lord in glory comes – 280
When the road is rough and steep – 279
When the sun is bright – 618
When the trumpet of the Lord – 281
When we look up – 495
Wherever I am – 282
Wherever I am I will praise You – 283
Whether you're one – 284
While shepherds watched – 285
Who is on the Lord's side? – 287
Who made the twinkling stars – 619
Who put the colours in the rainbow? – 288
Who took fish and bread? – 286
Whoopah, wahey! (God loves me) – 535